NATIONAL MINORITIES
AN INTERNATIONAL PROBLEM

NATIONAL MINORITIES

AN INTERNATIONAL PROBLEM

by INIS L. CLAUDE, Jᴿ.
Assistant Professor of Government
Harvard University

GREENWOOD PRESS, PUBLISHERS
WESTPORT, CONNECTICUT

The Library of Congress cataloged this book as follows:

Claude, Inis L
    National minorities; an international problem, by Inis
L. Claude, Jr. New York, Greenwood Press ₁1969, ᶜ1955₁

    xii, 248 p. 23 cm.

    Includes bibliographical references.

1. Minorities.   ɪ. Title.

JC311.C47 1969   301.45   78–90486
SBN 8371–2283–X   MARC

Library of Congress   70 ₍7₎

To
Marie

PREFACE

Of making many books there is no end, according to the ancient Preacher. Of making many problems there is no end, the student of international politics may reply. The excuse for this book is that a problem exists: the problem of national minorities.

There is not only a problem, but a question: why has the problem commanded so little official attention in the years since the Second World War, as compared with the period after the first great war of this century? This study is the result of an effort to find answers to that question which go deeper than such facile observations as that the minority problem is overshadowed today by others of greater moment, or that it has been neglected because the political possibilities of solving it are negligible. I have tried to avoid the specialist's professional disease of obsession with the importance of his topic, and to withstand the temptation to produce a neat solution which would handily dispose of the problem, if only international politics were not international politics, and men were not men. The problem of national minorities persists, as a significant though not the crucial factor in the disharmony of international life, and it demands not a bookish solution but practical management, within the confines of the political and ideological setting from which it cannot realistically be divorced.

I am deeply indebted to my colleagues in the Department of Government at Harvard University for their specific assistance and encouragement, as well as for their immeasurable contributions to my general preparation for undertaking this study. Special gratitude must be reserved for Professor Rupert Emerson, who provided the stimulus for my interest in the subject, introduced me to the complexities of the fields of nationalism and international organization, and guided my early efforts to deal with this topic.

I have profited from the advice of Alan Burr Overstreet, Associate Professor of Political Science at Smith College, and Lawrence S. Finkelstein, of the Carnegie Endowment for International Peace, who read an earlier version of the manuscript. Nehemiah Robinson, of the World Jewish Congress, supplied helpful assistance. My work was greatly facilitated by the courteous coöperation of members of the library staffs at Harvard University and the World Peace Foundation, and by the editorial advice of Miss Ann Staffeld of the Harvard University Press.

Grateful acknowledgment is due to G. Bernard Noble, Chief of the Historical Division, Department of State, for making available for publication excerpts from an unpublished study by the Post-War Programs Committee, dated 22 November 1944, and to MacAlister Brown, who brought the existence of that document to my attention. John P. Humphrey, Director, Division of Human Rights, United Nations Secretariat, was most coöperative in providing essential documents.

My greatest debt is to my wife, Marie Stapleton Claude, who typed the manuscript and viewed its stylistic vagaries with a skeptical eye. I alone bear the responsibility for the final product, but she bore with me during the process of production.

I. L. C., Jr.

Cambridge, Massachusetts
25 November 1954

CONTENTS

INTRODUCTION

INTRODUCTION

The relationship between majorities and minorities is a perennial problem of politics. Whenever a political society comprises a group of persons who exhibit characteristics which differentiate them from the bulk of the members of that society in any respect which is felt to be politically relevant, a minority problem arises. Concepts of political relevance are subject to variations in time and space; hence, the fundamental nature of minority problems is not always and everywhere the same. Generally speaking, human beings have seldom been able to accommodate themselves to the fact of human diversity; in most socio-political settings, differences of one sort or another — religious, racial, or ethnic — have been so seriously regarded as to give rise to politically significant minority problems.

The characteristic minority problem of the Western world for the last century and a half has been that of *national* minorities. The rise of this problem was the logical consequence of the doctrinal ascendancy of nationalism in Western Europe, which was produced largely by the upheavals associated with the French Revolution. Nationalism, while consolidating its dominant position in Western Europe and beginning its global sweep, injected into politics a profoundly significant idea: the principle that national and state boundaries should coincide — i.e., that the state should be nationally homogeneous, and the nation should be politically united.

The problem of national minorities arises out of the conflict between the ideal of the homogeneous national state and the reality of ethnic heterogeneity. The intermingling of nations has produced a situation to which the formula, "one nation, one state," is not applicable. The existence of national minorities is indicative of the incomplete realization of the ideal; such minorities are a problem in the modern state because they consti-

tute a standing reminder of the failure to establish an identification of political and national divisions. The majority nationality
tends to resent the presence of an unassimilated mass in its body
politic. The minority group may react to the violation of the
national state principle involved in its being included in the
state of another nationality. A neighboring national state may
feel aggrieved because a fragment of its nation has been severed
by a political boundary. Whether such situations are the results
of human policy or of stubborn ethnographic facts, they will
continue to present a troublesome problem so long as the concept
of the national state is dominant in the minds and hearts of men.

The complexity of the problem is enhanced by the difficulty
of defining the terms. Efforts to establish a set of objective
criteria for the identification of a nation or a national minority
are condemned to futility by the fact that nationality is in essence a subjective phenomenon. A group of people constitute
a nation when they feel that they do — when they have an active
sense of belonging together and of being distinct from other
groups, a sense of solidarity and of differentiation. While these
feelings may be related, as cause or effect, to observable characteristics of the group, there is no uniform or necessary pattern
of objective factors whence national feeling is derived or in
which it manifests itself.

The fundamentally subjective nature of the concept of the
nation prevents a precise statement of the scope of our problem.
Racial, religious, or linguistic differentiations may be treated as
useful clues to the existence of national minorities, but not as in-
fallible indices. We can only say that a national minority exists
when a group of people within a state exhibits the conviction
that it constitutes a nation, or a part of a nation, which is distinct
from the national body to which the majority of the population
of that state belongs, or when the majority element of the population of a state feels that it possesses a national character in which
minority groups do not, and perhaps cannot, share. The *problem*
of national minorities arises when such a situation exists within
the conceptual framework of the national state. If either the
majority or the minority is devoted to the ideal of fashioning
a political entity which includes all members of a given nation
and excludes all others, and which serves as the political embodi-

ment of that nation, then difficulties are likely to stem from the national heterogeneity of the state.

The problem of national minorities has appeared in virtually every country which has been affected by the process of Europeanization. As Western influences have penetrated every region of the globe, the idea of the national state has been widely diffused, bringing in its wake the problem of national minorities. This problem is not everywhere equally acute, nor does it take the same form in every situation, but it is today a general problem, not one confined to any particular region.

The ramifications of the problem extend to the basic issues of social and political philosophy. Viewed in its general theoretical setting, it is seen as one aspect of the broader problems of democracy, constitutionalism, and political cohesion and adjustment. It is related to such problems as the nature of the state, the legitimacy and the limits of political authority, and the adjustment of relationships between individuals, groups, and the state. It has a bearing on fundamental problems of rights and values; it introduces the question of a dichotomy between culture and politics, and thus leads to an examination of the role of sub-state associations and an evaluation of the moral function of government. It raises the question of the degree of uniformity which is essential to political society and the relevance of compulsion to its attainment, thereby presenting itself as a phase of the moral problem of human freedom and toleration.

The relationship between majority and minority national groups is a constitutional problem of prime importance, profoundly affecting the political, cultural, and economic life of states. The minority problem is first of all an issue of domestic policy, a matter of internal adjustment.

The conflict of national groups within the state is also a matter of serious international concern. If the national aspirations of minorities take on political implications, involving demands for secession or for union with ethnically related states, the stability of the international structure may be threatened. If another state displays an active interest in the treatment of its co-nationals by their host state, a bilateral dispute may develop, endangering the peace. If a state persecutes its minority national groups, the moral indignation of other peoples may lead to international action against the offending government. External efforts to control the treatment of national minorities introduce controversies relating to such basic international questions as the nature of international law, the subordination of sovereign states to the authority of the international community, the definition of the boundaries of domestic and international jurisdiction, and the legal propriety of intervention.

It is with the international aspects of the problem of national minorities that we are primarily concerned in the present study. The scope of the problem in the modern world is such that the fundamentals of the solution must be worked out on the international level, even though their detailed and continuous application may be largely an administrative function of domestic authorities. While its international implications cannot be absolutely divorced from the problem as a whole, the emphasis of this study has been placed upon the examination of those implications and the treatment of the minority problem as a facet of the general problem of international order.

In particular, we are concerned with the question of the extent to which, and the manner in which, international organization has undertaken to deal with this problem. It is only since the First World War that the rudimentary international community has been equipped with a general political organization capable of assuming, in some degree, the responsibility for attempting to solve the complex and interrelated problems of international life. Consequently, the story of the international treatment of the problem of national minorities effectively begins with the creation of the League of Nations, extends through the era of planning for a "brave new world" which accompanied the Second World War, and continues into the postwar period of the formal establishment and pragmatic development of the new institutional structure of international relations. The story is unfinished, for the postwar settlement remains in fundamental respects incomplete, and final decisions have not been reached as to the role which the United Nations will play — or attempt to play — in connection with the minority problem. Nevertheless, the period with which we are concerned is one rich in developments in international attitudes toward the minority problem; if the time has not arrived for stating definitive conclusions, the search for trends which may be useful in determining the prospects for an international solution of the problem is clearly in order.

A NOTE ON TERMINOLOGY

In the interest of succinctness and clarity, we have found it desirable to adopt, rather arbitrarily, a specialized vocabulary for dealing with our subject.

A state which regards itself as standing in a special relationship to a national minority in another state, by reason of ethnic affinity, is designated as a "kin-state," or a "co-national state." Conversely, a state which contains within its population an ethnically alien group, whose members are nonetheless nationals of that state, is referred to as a "host state," or a "minority state."

We use the concept of "positive minority rights" to refer to special rights for national minorities, which go beyond the literal equality of nondiscrimination and provide the essential basis for preservation and development of the characteristics or cultural manifestations which national minorities may value as their distinguishing marks.

Finally, wherever the unqualified term, "Sub-Commission," occurs, reference is intended to the Sub-Commission on the Prevention of Discrimination and the Protection of Minorities, a subordinate agency of the United Nations whose cumbrous title represents one of the most grievous sins ever committed by international organization against the writers and readers of books.

1

INTERNATIONAL TREATMENT OF THE MINORITY PROBLEM BEFORE THE SECOND WORLD WAR

CHAPTER I: *BACKGROUND OF THE LEAGUE MINORITY SYSTEM*

The international protection of minorities originated in the attempt to safeguard the position of dissident religious groups. Beginning as early as the thirteenth century, and becoming increasingly important with the disintegration of Catholic Christendom in the sixteenth century, international efforts to protect religious minorities against persecution took the highly unsystematic form of intervention by states on behalf of their fellow-religionists in other countries.

In the seventeenth century, the practice arose of making territorial cessions conditional upon the acceptance of treaty obligations to respect the religious freedom of the inhabitants. This principle was frequently applied in the nineteenth century, especially in connection with the rise of new states and the shifting of boundaries in the Balkans.[1] The protection of minorities became, at least in theory, an act of European public policy, rather than an arbitrary act of interested states, when plenipotentiaries of the great powers at the Congress of Berlin in 1878 declared that prospective members of the European family of states should affirm the principle of religious liberty as one indication of their general acceptance of "the principles which are the basis of social organization in all States of Europe."[2]

Religious divisions may or may not be identical with national divisions. To a certain extent, the early international arrangements for the protection of religious groups had the effect of affording protection to national minorities in the states which were bound by those undertakings; this was particularly true in the Balkans, where the religious label continued to serve as an accepted badge of nationality as late as 1923.[3]

The first explicit recognition and international guarantee of the rights of *national* minorities, as such, is to be found in the Final Act of the Congress of Vienna, in which Russia, Prussia, and Austria committed themselves to respect the nationality of their Polish subjects.[4] During the nineteenth century, such international arrangements as were developed in Europe were substantively concerned with religious liberties, but were increasingly recognized as being relevant to a solution of the national question. As the spirit of nationalism took hold, the guaranteed *rights* continued to be primarily religious ones, but the protected *groups* tended to assume the character of national minorities.

The rudimentary system of international protection of minorities, as it had evolved up to the end of the nineteenth century, was by no means universal in scope. Religious toleration had been declared a fundamental principle of European social organization, but the domestic application of that principle had not been recognized as a matter of international concern except in those states, usually newly recognized or newly enlarged states, upon which special obligations had been imposed by treaty. Commitments regarding treatment of minorities were a price exacted by the great powers for their acquiescence in the revision of political frontiers. For the most part, minority obligations had been imposed only upon states which were small and weak, and which were considered somewhat backward and illiberal; thus, Balkan states figured prominently in the system, while no guarantees were required of the relatively strong and presumably enlightened new German and Italian national states. Though there were exceptional instances, the general picture was that of a powerful, stable, liberal Western Europe imposing restrictions upon a weak, turbulent, illiberal Eastern Europe.

So far as the administration of the system was concerned, the shift from unilateral "humanitarian intervention" by self-appointed protectors of particular groups to control by the body of great powers who constituted themselves the custodians of Europe during the era of the "Concert of Europe," marked a formal advance. However, the change was not fundamental. Even though minority obligations came to be incorporated in a network of multilateral treaties, in which the great powers figured as joint signatories, claiming the right of joint enforcement, the right of intervention was still that of individual powers, not of a genuine collective organization;[5] the sanction remained indefinite and unsystematized, leaving to the powers the arbitrary and unregulated exercise of self-help.

The nineteenth century Concert system was patently defective and inadequate to secure the protection of even the restricted number of minority groups to which it purported to apply. There was a fatal lack of machinery for the supervision of the treatment of minorities, and of means whereby members of oppressed groups could articulate their grievances. The imprecision of the treaty provisions and the lack of an impartial tribunal authorized to construe them made it feasible for the restricted states to nullify their obligations by resorting to evasive unilateral interpretations.[6] Even when a clear violation occurred, there was little likelihood of redress, since political rivalry among the great powers prevented common action in most cases. The system could have worked satisfactorily only if the great powers had acted together; in practice, each power concerned itself primarily with its own material or political interests, and the Concert of Europe seldom functioned as an instrument for the collective protection of minorities.[7]

The imperfection of the system lay not only in the uncertainty that it would operate effectively when legitimate occasions arose, but also in the possibility that it might afford a pretext for arbitrary and politically motivated intervention by great powers in the affairs of the treaty-bound states, even when the latter were carrying out their obligations in good faith. This sort of abuse was restricted by the mutual jealousy of the great powers, but it remained a danger to which the treaty-bound states were acutely sensitive.

The system of minority protection based upon special treaties guaranteed by the great powers was condemned to failure by the inadequacy of its scope, the vagueness of its substantive provisions, the rudimentary nature of its machinery and organization, and the uncertainty, ineffectiveness, and susceptibility to abuse of its sanctions.

THE NATIONAL QUESTION AT THE OUTBREAK OF THE FIRST WORLD WAR

It was clear in 1914 that the national question remained on the agenda of international relations as a major unsolved problem. The century preceding the outbreak of the First World War had been an era of the spreading and intensification of national consciousness and of determined, ruthless campaigns for the suppression of the national movement.

The great polyglot empires of Eastern and Central Europe had generally responded to the challenge of disintegrative nationalism by attempting to obliterate the national characteristics of subject peoples, apply forcible restraints to particularistic tendencies, and impose a common pattern of nationality upon their heterogeneous populations, or in some cases, by undertaking to segregate, expel, or exterminate groups of people whose national consciousness seemed ineradicable.[8] Liberal nationalism had tended to give way to the spirit expressed by Prince von Bülow, German Chancellor from 1900 to 1909, who rationalized his efforts to make Prussia a specifically German state in these terms:

> In the struggle between nationalities one nation is the hammer and the other the anvil; one is the victor and the other the vanquished. . . . If it were possible henceforward for members of different nationalities, with different languages and customs, and an intellectual life of a different kind, to live side by side in one and the same State, without succumbing to the temptation of each trying to force his own nationality on the other, things on earth would look a good deal more peaceful. But it is a law of life and development in history, that where two national civilizations meet they fight for ascendancy.[9]

The attempt to impose an artificial uniformity upon self-conscious national groups was in no case successful. The effort of the state to become a nation aroused the determination of the nation to become a state. Oppression of minorities intensified their sense of national identity. Assimilative policies strengthened the determination of minorities to perpetuate the linguistic, cultural, and religious characteristics which they regarded as symbolic of their solidarity and exclusiveness. The evidence of experience pointed clearly to the conclusion "that a unitary national state is impossible, where even a relatively small but fully conscious national minority is determined to preserve its individuality." [10]

The abortive attempt to force national minorities into an alien mold had disastrous consequences. In 1914, "the whole area of mixed population in Europe was occupied, to the exclusion of almost any other subject, with an unremitting and unrelenting national strife. . . ." [11] The nationality issue had become a major factor in European politics, contributing significantly to the deterioration of international order which culminated in the First World War. [12]

The outbreak of hostilities in 1914 demonstrated conclusively that the treatment of national minorities was an international problem of the greatest importance, that neither the calculated oppression of national minorities nor the halfhearted and unsystematic efforts of the past to afford them international protection had disposed of the problem, and that the creators of a new world order would build in vain unless they were able to devise some means of dealing effectively with this source of domestic and international antagonism and instability.

EFFECTS OF THE FIRST WORLD WAR ON THE NATIONAL PROBLEM

The First World War was not merely in large measure the *product* of conflicts engendered by the national question; it was also a *cause* of the accelerated growth and extension of the ideology of nationalism. The wartime experiences of peoples and policies of governments sharpened the sense of national solidarity in existing national states, strengthened nationalism where it was nascent, helped to implant the idea of the national state in regions previously unaffected by it, and, most significantly, heightened the national hopes and aspirations of the submerged peoples of Eastern and Central Europe.

The Allies and the Central Powers competed, during the early stages of the war, in exploiting and in violating the principle of nationality, guided by considerations of political expediency.

Nationality propaganda was a weapon to be handled cautiously, since both sides were vulnerable to its explosive potentialities. The situation changed in 1917, when the collapse of Czarist Russia left the Allies free to use this weapon with relatively little danger that it would prove a boomerang, and the entry of the United States into the war enabled President Wilson to make his influence decisive.

The idea of national self-determination, which had originated in the French Revolution and reached its peak of influence during the period from 1848 to 1870,[13] was now brought to the fore. Wilson declared an idealistic concern for the rights and liberties of small nations, and proclaimed national self-determination as a moral principle essential to the achievement of justice and world peace.[14]

Wilson's preachments concerning national self-determination were characterized by more evangelical fire than clarity of definition or analysis. Not only was the concept vague, but its consistent application as the absolute criterion for the settlement of all boundary questions would have involved more drastic consequences for the map of Europe than Wilson realized when he began to function as its prophet or was willing to support when he was confronted with political realities.[15] Nevertheless, the wartime President fervently championed the principle, which he regarded as an essential corollary of democracy.[16] His conception that popular consent was as necessary for the moral validity of international arrangements as for the legitimacy of domestic regimes made him the central figure in the ideological development of the national question during the war.

The strains placed upon the tenuous bonds of unity in the empires of Central and Eastern Europe by wartime exigencies, the spontaneous discontent of increasingly self-conscious minorities, and the ferment resulting from the Wilsonian gospel of liberation, produced a movement to carve new national states out of those empires. "Well treated or no, the submerged nationalities had come, with hardly an exception, to entertain as their true and ultimate ambition the ideal of complete independence." [17] The leaders of national minorities in the multinational empires seized upon the concept of self-determination with an alacrity which was disconcerting to its Western proponents; they convened a "Congress of Oppressed Nationalities" at Rome in April 1918, and forced the hands of the Allied statesmen — who were in doubt about the wisdom of disrupting the unity of the Danubian basin — by presenting them with the *fait accompli* of the Balkanization of Eastern and Central Europe.[18]

THE PEACE CONFERENCE AND THE NATIONAL PROBLEM

The concept of national self-determination entered significantly into the deliberations of the statesmen assembled at the Peace Conference to determine the European settlement. The Conference allowed and sponsored the operation of that principle in a number of cases, chiefly where it worked to the disadvantage of the defeated powers, but admitted other factors as coördinate and, in some cases, overriding elements in the determination of frontiers. The principle of "one nation, one state" was not realized to the full extent permitted by the ethnographic configuration of Europe, but it was approximated more closely than ever before.

Some of the minority problems of Europe were eliminated or alleviated by the action of the Péace Conference. Many former minority groups were incorporated in states where they constituted parts of the majority nationality, as a result of the creation of new states and the shifting of boundaries. The principle of the physical transfer of population also played a limited role in the efforts of the Conference to solve the national problem. The Committee on New States and Minorities supported a Greek proposal that the Balkan states should arrange for voluntary migration by members of national minorities to the countries where, according to the theory of the national state, they "belonged." [19] In accordance with this plan, Greece and Bulgaria signed a convention for reciprocal emigration on 27 November 1919.[20] The Conference gave further evidence of its approval of the principle of voluntary transfer by writing provisions for the individual exercise of the right of option into the various peace treaties.

However, the revision of frontiers and the reshuffling of populations did not by any means remove the problem of national minorities. While some minorities were eliminated by these means, others, including the Jews, the Poles of German Upper

Silesia, and the Macedonians, continued to hold minority status in states dominated by other nationalities. Still other masses of people, among them large numbers of Germans, Hungarians, Albanians, and Bulgarians, were converted by the settlement into new national minorities.[21] The most thoroughgoing application of the principle of national self-determination could not have eliminated all the national minorities of the old European order, or avoided the creation of new ones. The limited application of that principle which was effected at Paris reduced the scope of the European minority problem by half, but it left or made national minorities including in their ranks an estimated 25 to 30 millions, roughly one-fifth to one-fourth of the population of the states in which they lived.[22]

The problem of national minorities not only persisted, but it was to a certain extent exacerbated by the preaching and the partial application of national self-determination. False hopes had been aroused in many cases, and the discontent of minorities at being denied the "right" of national self-determination was not easily allayed by assurances that their sacrifice was essential to the stability and economic welfare of Europe, or that stern ethnographic facts militated against their liberation. The prospect of trouble was also raised by the psychology of the new host states. Peoples who had long suffered as minorities now found large numbers of their former oppressors handed over to them, and the temptation to act vengefully was strong. The new political entities of Eastern and Central Europe looked upon themselves as national states,[23] and were eager to inaugurate policies of consolidation. It was not unreasonable to expect that newly emancipated and inexperienced ruling peoples might make drastic demands for uniformity.

For a variety of reasons, the victorious powers were disposed to make a new effort to solve the minority problem. Effective pressure was exerted by numerous private groups, including particularly Jewish organizations, which had been active during the war in formulating proposals for international minority protection,[24] and whose demands were supported in 1919 by the government of defeated Germany.[25] The powers were influenced by a sense of moral responsibility for the welfare of national minorities, since they had claimed to fight for the liberties of oppressed peoples, and had stirred up national aspirations which were in many cases, necessarily or not, denied fulfillment. In violation of proclaimed Wilsonian principles, they were handing over masses of people to alien sovereignties, and, as Clemenceau pointed out to Paderewski in his oft-quoted letter justifying the imposition of restrictions upon Poland's minority policy,[26] they felt a solemn obligation to protect those peoples whose future minority status was determined by their decision. They were equally motivated by dutiful concern for the stability and viability of the new states which they were helping to create. They believed that only an international guarantee of minority rights could reconcile national minorities to their position in the new states and thus produce the essential domestic tranquillity.[27] Finally, the major allies regarded action concerning the minority problem as a means of fulfilling their responsibility for maintaining world peace; Wilson made this motivation explicit when he suggested that "Nothing . . . is more likely to disturb the peace of the world than the treatment which might in certain circumstances be meted out to minorities." [28]

The leaders of the Peace Conference not only saw the need for minority protection and recognized their responsibility, but they also realized that they possessed an unparalleled opportunity to take a major step forward in this respect. A great war had dissolved the old order in Europe; the political situation was extraordinarily fluid. New states were clamoring for recognition, and others were looking to the great powers for approval of territorial accessions. Plans were afoot for the creation of an unprecedented set of international machinery. Thus, it was now possible to secure the acceptance of legal obligations concerning minority treatment by a number of states in the area where the problem assumed its largest proportions, and to utilize the machinery of the new League of Nations for the enforcement of those obligations.

Wilson was the most active of the official delegates to the Peace Conference in pressing for the international protection of national minorities.[29] He first attempted to write the principle of minority protection into the League Covenant.[30] He dropped that project when its political impracticability became apparent, but he continued to insist that the Conference should deal effectively with the problem, and his influence was of decisive importance in determining the nature of the minority system which was adopted.

The negative attitudes of certain of the delegations at the Peace Conference were no less important in determining the shape and scope of the League minority system. The small states which faced the prospect of having their national minorities placed under international guarantees were generally opposed to the very principle of minority protection.[31] Paderewski, representing Poland, and Bratianu, representing Rumania, were among the most articulate opponents of the system.[32]

The influence of the major powers was not exclusively favorable to the creation of an ambitious system of minority protection. Being extremely reluctant to do violence to the sacred principle of sovereignty, they endeavored to restrict the interference of international organs in the domestic affairs of states to those cases where it appeared absolutely necessary. France insisted, for political and strategic reasons, that the obligations imposed upon the small states of Eastern and Central Europe should not be so drastic as to compromise their integrity and reduce their value as bulwarks of the new *status quo*.[33] Italy indicated that it regarded the international guarantee of the rights of national minorities as a derogation of sovereignty too humiliating to be endured by a great power, and thereby threw its influence on the side of limiting the application of the protective system;[34] this attitude of superiority offended the pride of the small states which were being asked to accept treaty obligations, and strengthened their case against the plan.

In summary: The victorious powers at Paris recognized the necessity, the obligation, and the opportunity to deal effectively with the problem of national minorities. The shifting of frontiers and transfer of populations by no means eliminated the problem. A plan for the international protection of national minorities seemed the only solution, and such a plan was evolved out of a welter of conflicting interests and points of view.

CHAPTER 2

THE PROTECTION OF MINORITIES BY THE LEAGUE OF NATIONS

The formal basis of the League system for the international protection of national minorities consisted of a collection of instruments whereby particular states accepted provisions relating to the treatment of minority groups and the recognition of the League of Nations as guarantor.[1]

These instruments took various forms. Austria, Hungary, Bulgaria, and Turkey, as defeated states, were bound by minority provisions inserted in the various peace treaties. Poland, Czechoslovakia, Yugoslavia, Rumania, and Greece, as new or enlarged states, concluded special minority treaties with the Principal Allied and Associated Powers, in accordance with an obligation stated in the peace treaties. As a result of pressure brought to bear upon them when they applied for membership, ·Albania, Lithuania, Latvia, Estonia, and Iraq made declarations, analogous to the minority treaties, to the Council of the League of Nations.[2] Finland made a similar declaration, applicable only to the Aaland Islands. Germany came under the system to a limited extent, on the basis of the Geneva Convention of 15 May 1922, a bilateral treaty in which Poland and Germany created an elaborate special minority regime for Upper Silesia and assigned an important role to the League.[3]

Except for the Upper Silesian arrangement, the League minority system rested upon multilateral engagements, in which the concept of the kin-state was not recognized. A number of bilateral minority agreements were concluded during the years immediately following the Peace Conference, but they were external to the League minority system.[4]

The exceptional nature of the League system is worthy of particular emphasis. It purported not to establish "a general jurisprudence applicable wherever racial, linguistic or religious minorities existed," but to facilitate the solution of minority problems in countries where "owing to special circumstances, these problems might present particular difficulties." [5] In fact, its scope was more limited than the criteria of "special circumstances" or "particular difficulties" would suggest. Italy was exempted, even though it had acquired national minorities in the peace settlement and seemed likely to be confronted with an acute minority problem.[6] Germany remained outside the system, except for the reciprocal obligations contracted with Poland, ostensibly because it was not a new or enlarged state or one containing minorities whose welfare could be assumed to require international intervention. Actually, both these cases reflected a general policy of exempting all great powers and all "Western" states from the system, and confining international supervision to Eastern and Central European states which had important minority problems and were too weak to offer effective resistance.

The acceptance of minority obligations was in no case purely voluntary and gratuitous. Some of the instruments were virtual impositions; the others were in the nature of bargains, with recognition of a state's independence, guaranteed extension of territory, or admission to the League compensating for the acceptance of obligations which were regarded as onerous by most of the states concerned.[7]

RIGHTS GUARANTEED TO MINORITIES

The basic instruments of the League minority system purported to safeguard certain rights of "racial, religious or linguistic minorities," but the framers of the system made it clear that they regarded this terminology as synonymous with "national minorities." [8] The general provisions of the treaties and declarations followed, with minor variations, the pattern of the Polish Minority Treaty.

The acquisition of legal nationality, or citizenship, was regulated in considerable detail.[9] The importance of this matter lay in the facts that, historically, revocation or denial of legal nationality had often been a tactical preliminary to deprivation of rights, and that the operative provisions of the instruments applied only to those members of minorities who were nationals of the states in which they lived.

Arrangements for the exercise of the right of option[10] implied at least a limited recognition of the concept of national self-determination and the subjective criterion for determination of membership in a national group; persons newly assigned to one of the treaty-bound states were set at liberty to follow the dictates of their national consciousness by choosing to become members of another national state, provided that they were prepared to migrate to that state. It was hoped that the most irreconcilable nationalists would take advantage of this right, thereby helping to reduce the problems of majority-minority relations to manageable proportions.

The substantive rights guaranteed to national minorities in the treaty-bound states fell into two major categories: (1) the rights of individuals as such, rights unimpaired by membership in national minorities; (2) the rights of individuals as members of distinct minority groups, rights arising out of such membership and facilitating the maintenance and development of group life.

The safeguarding of the first class of rights demanded a regime of negative equality, of nondiscrimination. Thus, the minority states committed themselves to assure to members of national minorities full protection of life and liberty, freedom of religion, and complete equality with members of national majorities with respect to civil and political rights.[11]

These provisions represented an attempt to secure the general establishment in the minority states of the fundamental Western conceptions of freedom, justice, and good government. Even though the international guarantee applied to these articles only in so far as they affected members of minorities,[12] the enjoyment of basic human rights by all inhabitants was stipulated.[13] However ineffective this gesture of comprehensiveness may have been, it reflected the conviction that the rights of minorities could be genuinely secure only in a setting of generalized political liberalism.

The requirement that members of minorities be granted the elementary rights of freedom and equality, which was fully compatible with the individualistic orientation of constitutional democracy, was the essential foundation of the system.[14] It was rightly conceived that no structure of minority rights, however elaborate, would be meaningful unless it rested upon such a basis of respect for individuals.

The safeguarding of the second category of rights required

that the system of negative equality — protection against discriminatory treatment — be supplemented by a regime of "positive equality" — provisions for the equal opportunity of minorities to "preserve and develop their national culture and consciousness."[15]

Positive minority rights related primarily to language, education, and cultural activity in its various forms. The treaty-bound states were required to permit the free use of minority languages in a wide variety of specified relationships, and to grant members of minorities "an equal right to establish, manage and control at their own expense charitable, religious and social institutions, schools and other educational establishments, with the right to use their own language and to exercise their religion freely therein." They agreed to provide instruction to minority children in their own languages in the public primary schools, wherever the minorities constituted "a considerable proportion" of the population, and to allot to minorities "an equitable share" of public subventions for educational, religious, and charitable purposes.[16]

These positive privileges constituted the *raison d'être* of the system, so far as national minorities were concerned. If the foundation was the free and equal citizenship of individuals, the edifice for which a foundation was wanted was the effective opportunity for maintaining distinctive national characteristics and traditions. Linguistic and institutional rights were the principal components of such an edifice.

The general pattern of rights established by the treaties and declarations[17] provided no definite answer to the question whether minority groups, as collective entities, possessed rights which it was the function of the League system to safeguard. Wilson and his fellow-architects of the League were saturated with the individualist traditions of liberalism, and consequently found the concept of group rights somewhat alien to their way of thinking. In general, the documents reflected this atomistic bias; the drafters deliberately avoided terminology from which it might have been inferred that minorities as corporate units were the intended beneficiaries of the system.[18] It was generally held that to recognize minorities *per se* would have been inconsistent with the concept of sovereignty,[19] as such a step conjured up ideas of "a state within a state." The principles of individualism, on the one hand, and of state sovereignty, on the other hand, left little room between them for the concept of the group.

The repudiation of the concept of collectivity was not absolute. Exceptionally, the treaties and declarations contained references to agencies of minority communities and stipulations concerning political or cultural autonomy for particular minorities which could be interpreted as granting indirect or implicit recognition to groups *per se*.[20] However, these concessions to the principle of collective rights were exceedingly meager and cautious; the League system was fundamentally a product of the individualistic point of view.

THE NATURE OF THE INTERNATIONAL GUARANTEE

The heart of the minority treaties and declarations, the feature which bound them together into a system and made them an integral part of the postwar settlement, was the guarantee clause, which in each case followed closely the lines laid down in Article 12 of the Polish Treaty. The stipulations of the various instruments, so far as they affected persons belonging to racial, religious, or linguistic minorities, were held to constitute obligations of international concern and were placed under the guarantee of the League of Nations. The parties invited the Council of the League to assume the right and duty of supervising the execution of the treaties; the Council accepted this offer; thus, a group of multilateral conventions, along with the unilateral declarations subsequently made and placed under League guarantee, became the constituent elements of the first regularized and institutionalized international system for the protection of national minorities.

The League guarantee was *external* in its fundamental nature. It remained true that the first bulwark of minority rights was the constitutional guarantee of the state concerned. The operation of the treaties and declarations depended heavily upon the compliance of the minority states with the obligation to treat the stipulations as fundamental laws and to implement them by internal legislation.[21] However, it was deemed essential to supplement internal provisions by an external guarantee, based on the premise that the treatment of minorities in the treaty-bound states was a problem of international concern.

The intervention of an external agency in the relationship between a state and its own nationals was clearly incompatible with the concept of absolute sovereignty. But all international law, and the whole of the elaborate international structure of which the minority system was a part, rested upon the invalidity of that concept. The League of Nations could be conceived only on the fundamental assumption of the relativity and divisibility of sovereignty, with the state ranking as a component part of a larger community and exercising authority within a sphere limited by norms of an international character. The international guarantee was legally justified by the fact that the states concerned had formally consented to it, and had thereby transferred their minority problems, to the extent stipulated, from the sphere of exclusively domestic jurisdiction to the sphere of international jurisdiction. From a conceptual point of view, the erection of this external guarantee was an important step in the process of breaking down the principle of absolute sovereignty.

The League guarantee was *collective*; the task of enforcing the obligations of the minority states was assigned to the League of Nations, or, more specifically, to its Council, not to individual states or to the great powers in combination.[22] The attempt was made to ensure that the position of national minorities should be safeguarded by an impartial agency of the international community. It was intended that "action taken in defence of the rights of minorities should, both in fact and in public opinion, be taken without reference to the special interests of any individual Powers." [23] The guarantee was designed to obviate the cardinal defects of the nineteenth century system — the uncertainty and ineffectiveness of the protection which it afforded to minorities, and the liability of minority states to suffer arbitrary and politically motivated intervention by the great powers.[24]

It was significant that the guarantee was entrusted to the highest *political* agency of the new international system, the Council of the League, with the proviso that it should "take such action and give such direction as it may deem proper and effective in the circumstances." [25] The minority system was merely one part of a larger system designed to facilitate the peaceful adjustment of political relations; hence, the guarantee of minority rights was envisaged as a political function.[26]

A *judicial* element was injected into the guarantee by providing for the binding decision of the Permanent Court of International Justice in any case submitted to it by a member of the Council. Moreover, the Council had authority to request advisory opinions on minority questions, as on other matters. The creators of the system evidently believed that the League should and would enforce the minority commitments primarily by judicial means,[27] despite the fact that their motivations in erecting the system were fundamentally political.

The guarantee article was a compromise between the political and the judicial conceptions of the problem of protecting minorities, with the former conception clearly predominant. Judicial procedures were available for optional use, but the guarantee, as established, was basically political in nature.

THE OPERATING PROCEDURE

The minority treaties and declarations did not prescribe a rigid and detailed method of procedure to be followed in the execution of the League guarantee. They stipulated that the Council should act only after having had its attention directed by one of its members to an infraction, or a danger of infraction, and that a member of the Council might invoke the jurisdiction of the Permanent Court of International Justice. Otherwise, the Council of the League was left free to develop the necessary mechanism for the discharge of its supervisory function. This was a task of more than technical importance, since it involved determining the definitive nature of the League system, as well as its operative effectiveness.

Under the second paragraph of Article 11 of the Covenant, each member of the League had the right "to bring to the attention of the Assembly or of the Council any circumstance whatever affecting international relations which threatens to disturb international peace or the good understanding between nations upon which peace depends." There seemed to be no inherent reason why disputes growing out of the minority instruments could not be thus brought before the Council. Article 11 was in fact invoked on several occasions by states interested in the protection of particular minorities.[28]

This procedure was, however, unacceptable as the normal mode of dealing with minority problems. It conflicted with the agreed principle that the Assembly should be excluded from sharing in the supervisory function and that states not members of the Council should be debarred from seizing that body of cases arising out of the treaties and declarations.[29] Moreover, it tended to give minority cases the form of bilateral disputes, with the Council serving as a mediator between two contesting states, in violation of the ideal that the protection of minorities, by becoming the recognized function of an international agency, might cease to embitter the bilateral relations of interested states.

The Council decided, on 9 June 1928, that minority cases should be brought under Article 11 only in exceptional circumstances, when peace was jeopardized by the gravity of the situation; to allow the routine treatment of minority questions as bilateral disputes under Article 11 "would create the very dangers which the Minorities Treaties were intended to avert." [30]

The same objection applied to the exercise by members of the Council of their right to submit disputes relating to the minority treaties to the Permanent Court of International Justice. It was the premise of the League system that the welfare of national minorities was the concern of the international community, not a matter for either dispute or litigation between states to which minorities owed political allegiance and states serving as self-appointed champions of particular minority groups.

The Council assumed from the beginning the necessity of devising a special procedure for the discharge of its function as guarantor. It developed this procedure empirically, on the basis of reports and resolutions which reflected the inherent necessities of the problem and the limits of feasibility set by the attitudes of the various parties whose coöperation was essential. The evolution of procedural methods began with the Tittoni Report of 1920, and was virtually concluded in 1929, with the adoption of alterations recommended by a special committee headed by Adatci, the Japanese representative who served as Rapporteur on minority questions.[31]

In its final form, the League minority procedure operated as follows: The Minorities Section of the Secretariat stood ready to receive, from any source, petitions alleging the mistreatment of minorities in violation of the treaties and declarations. If a

petition was adjudged by the Secretary-General to meet prescribed standards as to form and content (and if that decision
was not successfully challenged by the accused state), it was
submitted to the state against which the complaint was directed,
for possible comment or rebuttal. The petition, together with
the answering comments, if any, was then communicated
simultaneously to each member of the Council for purely in-
formational purposes, and to a special committee, composed
normally of the President of the Council and two other members
chosen by himself. This "Committee of Three" studied the
problem with the assistance of the Minorities Section of the
Secretariat, and disposed of it by either dropping it as an un-
founded complaint, securing remedial action through informal
negotiation with the accused state, or deciding that the evidence
warranted examination of the case by the Council itself. In the
latter case, the Council was seized of the matter by one or more
of its members,[32] and it dealt with the complaint in conjunction
with a representative of the accused state, who took a seat at
the Council in accordance with Article 4, paragraph 5, of the
League Covenant.

Since the Council could not reach a decision without the con-
curring vote of the accused state, it accepted the necessity of
achieving settlement by means of an agreed solution. In some
cases, legal questions were submitted to special committees of
jurists or to the Permanent Court of International Justice for
advisory opinions.[33] The Council relied upon the pressure of
public discussion, the prestige of the League and the Court, and
the power of diplomacy, to induce the governmental leaders of
the accused state to adopt a conciliatory attitude.

The procedure of the Council was the subject of continuous
controversy which reflected profound differences of opinion
among the interested parties as to the essential nature and purpose
of the League system.

The minorities were profoundly discontented with the minor
procedural role which was assigned to them. They understood
that the system had been devised for their benefit, as a partial
compensation for the failure to allow them the "right" of national
self-determination, and they professed amazement at finding
themselves treated by the League as if the functioning of the

system were none of their business. They deplored the secrecy which characterized the operations of the system — the withholding from petitioners of information concerning the disposition of their complaints, and the failure to publicize negotiations with accused states. The minorities wished to be recognized as collective entities, competent to argue their cases through chosen representatives and to participate in the negotiations sponsored by the Committees of Three, if not to assume a role comparable to that of states in proceedings before the Council and the Permanent Court.[34] They criticized the treatment of minority cases as matters to be settled by political techniques, and urged the Council to base its decision in every case upon an advisory opinion of the Court.[35]

The demands of minority groups for procedural changes were generally supported by such states as Germany, Austria, Hungary, and Bulgaria, which were motivated by concern for their ethnic relatives in minority status. These states clamored for recognition as interested parties in cases involving their co-nationals. They objected to the rule adopted by the Council on 10 June 1925, which excluded from membership on the Committee of Three dealing with any case, "the representative of a State the majority of whose population belong from the ethnical point of view to the same people as the persons belonging to the minority in question." [36] They criticized the provision of the guarantee articles which prevented an interested state which was not a member of the Council from seizing that body of alleged violations of the minority instruments. Champions of the point of view of the minorities pointed out that the League procedure did not measure up to judicial standards, since the minorities and the states most concerned with their protection were limited to the submission of petitions, which had a purely informatory nature, and were not treated as parties equally with the states against which complaints were lodged; moreover, the Council's technique was not even valid as a process of political adjustment, inasmuch as spokesmen for minorities and interested states were not admitted to the negotiations for the settlement of minority questions. The kin-states, denying that the protection of national minorities should be left entirely to an international agency, continually sought to bilateralize the League procedure and thus to

gain for themselves the right to lead the fight for the protection
of their co-nationals.

In general, the position of the minority states on procedural
questions was diametrically opposite to that of the minorities
and their sympathizers. They resisted all efforts of the Council
to adopt interpretations of the system which would result in
the direct or indirect expansion of their responsibilities or
liability to external control.[37] They opposed the erection of any
League machinery which would subject their minority policy
to continuous observation and supervision. They favored very
strict standards of receivability [38] and the most stringent restrictions on the circulation and publication of petitions, on the
ground that complaints were likely to be utilized as instruments
of hostile propaganda. They were unalterably opposed to the
recognition of minorities or other petitioners as parties to the
League procedure; hence, they sought to minimize the correspondence of the Secretariat with petitioners and to exclude
minority organizations from any sort of contact with Committees of Three or the Council. Being extremely anxious to
prevent intervention in their internal affairs by kin-states, they
resisted every effort of such states to inject elements of bilateralism into ·the proceedings. The attitude of the minority states
toward procedural problems was largely determined by their
concern for *sovereignty* — that is, for the right to manage their
own affairs, with a minimum of supervision by the League, and
without accountability to domestic or international organizations of minority groups or to other states.

The focal issues in the bitter controversy relating to procedure
were of fundamental importance for the determination of the
nature of the system. What formal *locus standi* and actual role
in the operation of the system should be assigned to individual
petitioners, organized minority groups, and kin-states? In what
degree should the technique of settlement be political and in
what degree judicial? What should be the balance between
publicity designed to force the hands of minority states, and
secrecy designed to facilitate conciliation by negotiation? Should
the League's responsibility be discharged by continuous supervision of the treatment of minorities, or merely by sporadic
action called forth by well-substantiated complaints?

The Council did not take an absolutely firm and immutable position in regard to these issues. It made some concessions to the demands of minorities and their supporters, relating to the effective development of the right of petition, communication between the League and complainants, and the use of publicity to influence recalcitrant minority states.[39] Its adoption of the Committee of Three technique could be construed as a device for circumventing the restrictive rules of the treaties and declarations concerning the initiation of formal Council action, since the Committees in effect took preliminary action of an investigatory and conciliatory nature on the basis of petitions, without waiting for formal seizin by a member of the Council.[40]

Nevertheless, the overwhelming tendency of the Council was to accept the point of view of the treaty-bound states concerning the basic procedural issues. In general, the Council maintained a restrictive attitude toward the right of petition. It adamantly refused to concede to minorities any *locus standi* except that of informers who could be ignored at will; the League was too thoroughly devoted to the principle of sovereignty to approve the pluralistic principle that a group within the state might haul its government before a tribunal and engage as a party on equal terms with the state in litigious proceedings. The Council established a regime of secrecy in the disposition of petitions and the conduct of negotiations which was never effectively broken down. In adopting this policy, it implicitly gave priority to the values of the minority states — immunity from propagandistic activity, avoidance of indignities embarrassing to sovereign states, and emphasis upon political adjustment — over the values stressed by spokesmen for minorities — general confidence in the efficacy of the protection offered by the League, use of moral sanctions to prevent oppression of minorities, and the dispensing of justice by means of a straightforward judicial technique. When national minorities and national states competed for status before the League of Nations, the issue was never in doubt.

The procedural devices adopted by the League reflected the determination to internationalize the protection of minorities. The Council not only denied formal recognition to the claims of kin-states to serve as special guardians of their co-nationals, but it also attempted to use the institution of the Committee of Three as a means of imparting a multilateral flavor to the act of seizin, hoping thereby to spare the "neutral" members of the Council the onerous necessity of appearing as the initiators of Council action and thus as the unilateral "accusers" of minority states.[41]

In so far as the League sought to exclude bilateral elements from its minority procedure, it was attempting to achieve the political purposes for which the system had been created. In so far as it undertook to make international protection effective, it was responding to the demands of minorities and their supporters. In so far as it opted for secrecy, for political rather than judicial techniques of settlement, and for the exclusion of minorities from formal status as interested parties in the operation of the system, it was catering to the demands of the treaty-bound states and expressing its own inherent respect for the concept of sovereignty.[42]

THE RESULTS OF THE MINORITY SYSTEM

One of the difficulties in evaluating the work of the League minority system is the problem of deciding upon the criterion to be applied. The minorities and their champions insisted that the system should be judged in terms of its humanitarian achievement in affording protection to national minorities. There was another school of thought, however, which emphasized the political purpose of maintaining international peace, and defined the criterion of success as the avoidance of bilateral conflicts over minority questions, not the enjoyment by minorities of just and liberal treatment.

The truth seems to be that the League system was based upon the premise that the two aims of peace and justice were correlative and interdependent. The political aim was given greater prominence at the Peace Conference because the legitimacy of humanitarianism, as such, in the programs of governments, was not then (nor is it today) fully and universally accepted. However, there can be no doubt that the liberal statesmanship of such men as Wilson, Smuts, and Lord Robert Cecil, was based on the assumption that peace and justice, international harmony and governmental rectitude in dealing with minorities, must inexorably go hand in hand. To the extent that this faith is valid, there is no necessity for choosing between the two standards. Difficulties' arise from the fact that the twin aims of protecting minorities and promoting amicable relations among states frequently came, or were thought to come, into conflict with each other. A general evaluation of the system must take into account its successes and failures in respect of both purposes.

The useful results of the League system were not negligible. It is generally credited with the prevention of a great deal of oppression which might otherwise have been meted out to minorities, even though there is no means of measuring this accomplishment.[43] Balogh has pointed out that the League system contributed significantly to the development of the moral consciousness (*Rechtsbewusstsein*) of mankind, and of the general recognition that the international community must be concerned with the maintenance of the rights of national minorities.[44] The operation of the system was an important phase of the essential process of breaking down the concept of the sovereign, irresponsible state, and erecting in its stead the concept of a universal legal order. In some cases, the Council obtained tangible redress for mistreated minorities, or successfully enjoined governments from carrying out oppressive policies. In other cases, generally unpublicized, it used informal and friendly negotiation to obtain improvements in the position of minorities.[45]

The League system undoubtedly helped to minimize international friction by providing a regularized, multilateral method of dealing with minority problems, and thus discouraging — and making less necessary — the arbitrary, unilateral intervention of kin-states in the affairs of minority states. In undertaking the task of protecting minorities, the League contributed to world peace "by diverting to itself the many currents of irritation, ill-will and disappointment which would otherwise have done increasing harm to interstate relations. . . ."[46]

However great the tangible and the conjectural accomplishments of the League system, its failures and deficiencies were much more formidable. It is impossible to maintain that the minorities obtained an adequate and impartial hearing of their grievances and demands, or prompt, effective, and reliable measures of protection. The record is spotty and uneven, but the general verdict of failure was inevitable even before the virtual denunciation of minority obligations by Poland on 13 September 1934, when Colonel Beck declared before the Assembly:

> Pending the introduction of a general and uniform system for the protection of minorities, my Government is compelled to refuse . . . all coöperation with the international organisations in the matter of the supervision of the application by Poland of the system of minority protection.[47]

Following this pronouncement, the system became increasingly dormant and ineffectual, until it was finally swept away by the impact of the Second World War. The minorities were not reconciled to their position, the exacerbation of majority-minority relations was not prevented, and the minority problem was not eliminated as a factor making for the destruction of international stability.

The League system was superior to possible alternative arrangements relying exclusively upon internal constitutional guarantees of minority rights, or resting upon bilateral agreements unsupported by an international guarantee, or leaving the protection of minorities dependent upon the unregulated and capricious intervention of kin-states; but it was unable to solve the difficult problem with which it came to grips.

CHAPTER 3

THE FAILURE OF THE LEAGUE
MINORITY SYSTEM

CRITICISMS OF THE SYSTEM

The analysis of the failure of the League minority system must take into account the criticism and demands for alteration which were showered upon the League from all sides. In so far as this criticism was valid, it helped to explain the failure; in so far as it was invalid and unreasonable, it was itself a cause of the failure.

The attack of the minority states began at the Peace Conference and continued without respite, reaching a climax in the Polish repudiation of the system in 1934. There were exceptional points of view among the minority states,[1] but in general, those states may be said to have constituted a bloc which was sharply critical of both the fundamental nature of the system and its method of operation.[2]

The system was held, in the first place, to violate the essential attributes of the sovereign state. The leaders of the new and enlarged states tended to think of sovereignty as an unalterable and irreducible quantity of rights and immunities which automatically accrue to any state. Either a sovereign state exists or it does not; if the existence of a state is conceded, then there is no alternative but to treat it as the possessor of a standard set of sovereign attributes, identical with that possessed by all other states.

It was this kind of thinking about sovereignty which lay at the root of the most vociferous opposition to the system by minority states. They argued that it was inadmissible that sovereign states should have external restraints placed upon their freedom to determine and alter their own constitutional forms and procedures, and to regulate internal relationships.

Speaking for Poland, Paderewski insisted that the sovereign state has the right to pursue the ideal of the national state by taking measures aimed at the denationalization and assimilation of minorities; he thus expressed fundamental disagreement with the purpose of the League minority system and denied the competence of the international community to promote that purpose by controlling the minority policy of sovereign states.[3]

The concept of the equality of states provided another basis of attack. This concept is closely related to the theory of sovereignty; if sovereignty is a monolithic chunk of rights, which must be possessed in full or not at all, then it follows that every political entity possessing that attribute must be considered the equal of every other such entity. It is understandable that the League system, imposing restraints upon a limited number of states, should be anathema to those leaders of minority states who thought in these terms. They denounced it as a discriminatory and unjust plan, an insult to the dignity of sovereign states, and an intolerable attempt to fasten upon them the stigma of moral inferiority. The minority states objected to being singled out as the most likely oppressors of national minorities, and were particularly indignant at the exemption of Germany and Italy. They were not impressed by the legalistic fiction that "voluntary" acceptance would make minority treaties less derogatory to their sovereignty and equality; they knew that the treaties were in fact differential obligations imposed upon them by the great powers.

The sensitivity of the minority states on the score of equality led them to raise an insistent demand for the generalization of the system, so as to make all states equally liable to international intervention on behalf of minority groups.[4] Under such sponsorship, this was a device for discrediting and undermining the existent scheme; minority states aimed not so much at generalizing the system as at destroying it. Their status would have been less humiliating if it had been more widely shared, but even universal application would not have made the system compatible with their doctrine of sovereignty.

The minority states criticized the system on grounds of policy as well as of principle. They argued that it was unnecessary, since they had every intention of treating their minorities in a liberal and humane manner. They inveighed against it as a detriment to their internal tranquillity and stability, maintaining that it impeded the process of natural assimilation, encouraged minority groups to perpetuate their sense of separateness, diminished popular respect for government by allowing minorities to go over its head to a "foreign court of appeal," and created popular animosity against minorities by emphasizing their distinctiveness and making them a privileged class. They argued that vitally necessary economic and social reforms, notably the redistribution of agricultural lands, were impeded by the special immunities guaranteed to national minorities, which were in many cases comprised largely of great landlords.[5] They professed to fear that the system, as established, would permit minority groups to act with impunity as foreign-dominated "states within the state," subverting the state in the interest of irredentist kin-states. This apprehension led minority states to press for acceptance of the "clean hands" doctrine, which denied international protection to any minority failing to give evidence of loyalty to its host state.

The general position typical of the minority states was that the League system tended to concede too much to minority groups. The minority treaties should be construed and applied in a spirit reflecting the assumption that the interests of states were paramount, and that it was the function of the League system "to grant to minorities such satisfaction as is legitimate and *compatible with the interests of the State.*" [6] Better still than the minimization of the internationally guaranteed rights of minorities would be the abolition of the League system, or failing that, its generalization — for in a system of universal application, all states would have a stake in combating the efforts of minorities to expand their rights under the system.

The points of view of national minorities, expressed through sympathetic governments and a variety of private associations, showed great diversity, reflecting differences in the size and compactness of minority groups, the intensity of their national feeling, their political and cultural maturity and economic status, the degree of external support which they received, and the inherent limitations of their positions. Some groups desired only guarantees of nondiscrimination, and looked upon differential treatment as a disability; others were preoccupied with resistance to assimilation, and strongly demanded the maximum enjoyment of positive minority rights. Some groups were accustomed to minority status, and expected nothing better in the future; others regarded their minority status as merely a temporary misfortune or injustice, soon to be remedied.

The general tone of the public expressions of minority sentiment was set primarily by those large and highly developed minorities which were disappointed and resentful at having been denied the right of self-determination, profoundly disturbed at the prospect of losing privileged economic positions, and disinclined to accept the loss of their traditional hegemony over the "inferior" peoples into whose hands they had been placed. Their dissatisfaction was even more bitter than that of the treaty-bound states, and they produced, in alliance with their kin-states, a steady stream of criticism and proposals for fundamental revision of the League's approach to minority protection.

The minorities denied the adequacy of the substantive rights guaranteed to them, particularly of the group rights which were essential to the cultivation of national feeling and the fostering of national culture. Linguistic and academic rights had been too narrowly circumscribed. The right of participation in the control and administration of cultural and political institutions had been guaranteed to an unduly limited number of national groups. There had been no provision establishing the freedom of national minorities, as corporate entities, to maintain cultural relations with their co-nationals in other states. The minorities constantly harped on the inconsistency in the effort to protect minorities while declining to recognize their group status.[7]

The treaties were criticized as being unduly vague and ambiguous. The minorities wanted explicit provision for the right of individuals to declare membership in national groups, excluding governmental determination of such questions, and precisely defined rights relating to educational facilities and public subventions. They demanded clear establishment of the competence of the Council to exercise constant supervision rather than merely sporadic intervention on their behalf, and unequivocal recognition that the system was designed as a permanent support for the efforts of minorities to perpetuate their national cultures, rather than as a transitional device to pave the way for eventual assimilation. The treaties were lacking in precision on these points, and the minorities were profoundly disquieted by the fact that ambiguities might be, and often were, exploited to the detriment of their interests.

Minority organizations deplored the restricted range of the League system, not only because it left many minority groups without protection, but also because it stimulated the resentment of the states which were subjected to international supervision and minimized the moral authority of the system, thereby diminishing the effectiveness of the protection enjoyed by those minorities which were included within its scope. Minorities and their allies supported the generalization of minority obligations, because they were convinced that the international protection of national minorities could survive and develop only if it were recognized as a general principle of positive international law, resting solidly on moral foundations, and having universal applicability.[8]

In short, the minorities were persistently, and sometimes vehemently, critical of the League system because it fulfilled neither their expectations nor their demands. They found fault with details of the system and the manner of its operation, and, as their demands were formulated and expounded, it became increasingly clear that they would not have been satisfied with the system, even if it had worked perfectly. Their demands were far-reaching and perpetually expansive; from their point of view, the League system was fundamentally defective and hopelessly inadequate, both in theory and in practice, in principle and in detail.

FUNDAMENTAL DEFECTS OF THE SYSTEM

Criticism of the system was strongly infused with the bias of its sources, and tended to be immoderate and polemical, rather than measured and analytical. Nevertheless, the vast and comprehensive mass of derogatory comment served to elucidate a number of defects in the system which were in no small measure contributory to its failure.

The confinement of the application of the system to the small states of Eastern and Central Europe was one of the most striking of its defects. The failure of the Peace Conference to impose general minority provisions upon Germany, and to insist that Belgium, Denmark, France, and Italy undertake similar obligations at least in respect of the populations of their newly acquired territories, demonstrated conclusively that the international protection of national minorities was not accepted as a fundamental principle of international law, applicable to great as well as to small powers, and to Western as well as to Eastern and Central European countries. It was treated as a mere expedient, to be adopted with discriminatory effect, not as an expression of a universally valid, normative approach to problems of human relations.

It is true that the generalization of minority obligations was not politically feasible, either in 1919 or subsequently; the alternative to a system of limited scope was not a universal system, but rather no system at all. It is also true that external supervision of the treatment of minorities was not everywhere equally necessary, and that no standard set of provisions would have been universally appropriate. It may even be that generalization would have compromised the effectiveness of the League system by making all states reluctant to support the vigorous application of its provisions, for fear of setting precedents which might be used to their own embarrassment.

Nevertheless, the fact remains that the restriction of the League system stimulated the acute resentment of those states which were within its compass, left many minority groups unprotected, diminished its moral authority, and gave it the appearance of tentativeness and the prospect of instability.

The League system bore the marks of the failure of its originators to appreciate the complexity of the problem with which they were dealing, and to arrive at carefully considered and definite decisions on matters of principle; it also bore the marks of necessary compromises which sometimes substituted agreements on ambiguities for disagreements on clear statements of principle.

No authoritative answer was available for the important question whether the League guarantee was intended to serve as a permanent means of supporting the maintenance by minorities of their national-cultural individuality, or as an ephemeral measure to facilitate their gradual assimilation. This issue was the focus of a bitter controversy, marked especially by the apparent endorsement of the assimilationist thesis by Mello-Franco and Sir Austen Chamberlain, the Brazilian and British members of the Council in 1925,[9] and by subsequent denunciations of this interpretation made by Stresemann[10] and other supporters of the claims of minorities. It was a gravely defective system which failed to make its fundamental purpose clear.

As minority spokesmen frequently complained, the League system was hopelessly indecisive in regard to the recognition of the collective rights of minority groups. The creators of the system had been compelled by the obvious necessities of the situation to make some effort to safeguard certain positive minority rights which were intrinsically group rights, requiring for their implementation institutions under the control of minorities, acting as corporate groups; yet, they had been so unaccustomed to thinking in terms of the autonomy of distinct national communities within the state that they had treated these rights primarily as individual rights. The fundamental inconsistency of the attempt to guarantee collective rights without full recognition of the concept of collective existence was a source of much confusion.

Many problems arose out of the fact that the League system was frequently torn between the two purposes of dispensing justice and preserving peace. No provision had been made for deciding between demands for continuous supervision, wide publicity, and judicial technique, in the interests of justice, and opposing demands for mere sporadic action to effect political compromise, within an atmosphere of secrecy suitable to negotiation, in the interests of peace. The operation of the system was constantly confused by the uncertainty of the balance between the ideals of strict justice and political conciliation.

Another defect was the complete absence of provisions concerning the duties correlative to the rights of minorities. It was freely assumed and officially asserted by League organs that members of minorities owed full allegiance to the states of which they were nationals,[11] but the minority treaties and declarations failed to state the relationship between the performance of duties and the enjoyment of rights. As a result, there was persistent controversy in regard to the question of priority, with the minorities arguing that loyalty could be expected only as a consequence of just treatment, and the minority states claiming that the enjoyment of rights must be contingent upon prior demonstrations of loyalty.

In operation, the system reflected a pro-state bias which was understandable in view of the fact that the guarantee was entrusted to a body of representatives of states, but which nevertheless diminished its value. It was unrealistic to expect minorities to have confidence in a system which weighted the scales against them. The procedure was too slow, too solicitous of the susceptibilities of states, and too closely dependent upon political considerations; protection and redress were always uncertain and frequently inadequate.

One of the fundamental purposes of the statesmen who constructed the League system was to eliminate bilateral disputes over the treatment of minorities, by making the guarantee of the rights of minorities the function of an international agency. The internationalization of minority problems was by no means perfectly achieved. Under the League system, it was still possible for a controversy over the rights of minorities to assume the character of a bilateral dispute, and this frequently occurred, especially when kin-states took advantage of membership on the Council to seize that body of cases involving minorities in which they had a special interest.[12] Even such a multilateral action as a request by the Council for the advisory opinion of the Permanent Court led to the introduction of elements of bilateralism into the proceedings, for the Court heard the arguments of the accused state and of the state which asserted an interest in the welfare of the particular minority involved in the case.[13]

The effort to internationalize the protection of national minorities had been inspired by the conviction that it would jeopardize the maintenance of friendly and peaceful international relations to allow kin-states to make the treatment of particular minorities an issue between themselves and the states to which the minorities owed allegiance. This conviction, however, was unable completely to supplant the deep-rooted belief that a state did in fact have a special and legitimate interest in the fate of ethnically related minority groups in other states. The territorial settlement and the minority system erected at Paris were based on the acceptance of the validity of the principle of nationalism; it would have been inconsistent with that principle to deny absolutely that Germany or Greece, to cite typical examples, had any more interest than other states in the fate of German and Greek minorities. If the validity of the "we-feeling," the sense of cohesiveness, characteristic of nationalism is accepted, then it is totally unreasonable to expect or demand that the body of a nation will disinterest itself completely in the destiny of its fragments in other states.

In accordance with the implications of the principle of nationality, national states continued after the Peace Conference to manifest a special concern for the welfare of kindred minorities, and, except for the states to which the minorities concerned owed allegiance, most states exhibited a tendency to accept those manifestations as natural and legitimate, despite the premise of the League system that such matters had become the exclusive concern of international agencies. There was a subtle inclination to assimilate the protection of national minorities to the protection of aliens — that is, to regard a member of a minority group, even though he were a national of the state wherein he resided, as a "quasi-alien," a person on whose behalf a particular foreign state might intercede if he were subjected to unjust treatment.[14]

Finally, kin-states which were members of the Council tended, with the approval of the relatively disinterested members, to take the initiative in implementing the League guarantee. "In the annual League debate on minorities of 1930 the British delegates frankly adopted the view that where German minorities were concerned it was for the German Government to look after their interests."[15] The outcome was that the interests of minorities which had no friend on the Council were generally neglected, and that when the League did act with effect, it was usually in cases "where pressure [was] put upon it by some power which could have championed the minority in question even without the League. . . ."[16]

This failure to eradicate vestiges of bilateralism and to effect a genuine internationalization of the protection of national minorities was a major defect of the League system.

THE BEHAVIOR OF PARTICIPANTS IN THE SYSTEM

A decisive factor in the ineffectiveness and ultimate collapse of the League system was the failure of the various parties and agencies involved to coöperate in good faith to make it work. There was nothing automatic and inexorable about the operation of the League system. It was not a magic formula for the solution of the minority problem, but a device which could be operated successfully only through the coöperative effort of the states, groups, individuals, and international agencies concerned with the problem. The failure was not so much that of an inherently defective tool, as of the human beings — too often perverse, quarrelsome, hypocritical, and designing human beings — whose function it was to use the tool.

The Minority States. The primary responsibility for making the League system work devolved upon the minority states. It was incumbent upon them to treat their minorities fairly and liberally, and to coöperate with the League in making the international guarantee a reality, so that the minorities might enjoy a sense of well-being and a sense of *security* in that well-being. In such circumstances, there was reason to hope that the minorities and the nations to which they stood in the relation of severed fragments would become reconciled to the political *status quo*, and that internal stability in the minority states and peace and harmony in international relations would be the happy result.

The record of the minority states was not a uniform one. It is generally conceded that Czechoslovakia was extraordinarily liberal in its treatment of minority groups and coöperative in its attitude toward the League system.[17] The policy of Estonia toward minorities also drew widespread praise.[18] The policies of these states were definitely exceptional, even though other host states did on occasion exhibit a liberal attitude toward their minority groups.[19]

Seen as a whole, the record of the minority states was discreditable. Newly liberated peoples, succumbing to the temptation to seek vengeance for past wrongs, seized upon the pretext of eliminating the special privileges which some minorities held as vestiges of their bygone hegemony in order to reduce those minorities to impotence. Obsessed by the ideal of national uniformity, minority states erected centralized administrative regimes, undertook to denationalize minorities, and in other ways used the power of the state to serve the interests of the majority nationality, at the expense of the rights of minorities. On grounds of national security, they persecuted "disloyal" minorities, and thereby stimulated the disaffection which they allegedly sought to suppress. They resorted to every possible evasion, and even to flagrant violations, of their international obligations. The oppression of minorities assumed a variety of forms, ranging from officially sponsored or officially tolerated violence, to refusal to implement commitments to grant positive economic, political, or cultural rights to minority groups.[20]

The treaty-bound states not only failed, on the whole, to treat their minority groups in the prescribed manner, but they also seized every opportunity to nullify the international guarantee. Even when they professed willingness and determination to respect the rights of minorities, they demonstrated hostility to the principle of international supervision by attempting to undermine the right of petition and impede the development of an effective and impartial minority procedure by the League. Since the Council could make no substantive decision on a minority question without the assent of the state concerned, voting as an *ad hoc* member of the Council,[21] there was no possibility of using coercion against minority states to enforce fulfillment of their obligations. The Council was, in minority questions, an agency of conciliation and mediation; by adopting an intransigent and uncoöperative attitude, the minority states were able to reduce the guarantee of the Council to futility.

The minority states were in large measure responsible for the creation of the conditions which frequently required the minority machinery of the League to go into operation; they were also largely responsible for the creation of the conditions which prevented that machinery from operating properly.

It ought not to be too readily assumed that the minority states which obstructed the functioning of the League system of minority protection were abnormally wicked and perverse. These states were faced with genuinely complex problems of intergroup relationships, and if their records were deplorably bad, there is no evidence that the policies of other states would have been more enlightened and humane if they had been forced to grapple with nationality problems of equal magnitude under similar economic and psychological conditions.

Moreover, the urge of the treaty-bound states to achieve national homogeneity despite the resistance of minority groups should be ascribed not so much to moral depravity as to their acceptance of the principle of nationality, which had served as the cornerstone of the peace settlement. The logic of the national state ideal impelled them to try to incorporate all the elements of their population into a single national body which should serve as the basis of the state, and of which the state should serve as the political expression and embodiment.

The resistance of the minority states to external supervision of their internal affairs, based on the plea of sovereignty, was not an exceptional phenomenon; despite the premises and implications of the League Covenant, the states of the world continued in general to act as if the principle of sovereignty were the fundamental precept of the international order.

The behavior of the minority states was in fact a reflection of the inconsistencies which ran through the postwar scheme of things. These states had been included in a family of presumably sovereign, equal, national states; yet, they were forbidden to realize the implications of the nature with which they were supposedly endowed. Their attitude toward minorities and the League guarantee was thus explicable in terms of ideological dilemmas as well as of bad faith.

The Minorities. Another factor in the ineffectiveness and collapse of the League system was the attitude and behavior of the minorities themselves. While they had no legal standing as participants in the system, it was nevertheless true that moderation and coöperation on their part were essential to its success. Their pattern of behavior, like that of the states concerned, was marked by considerable variations, but it is clear that the minorities contributed substantially to the failure of the system which had been created for their own protection.

Many of the minority groups were accustomed to the enjoyment of a specially privileged position, and sought to utilize the immunities provided by the League system for the perpetuation of that position. For instance, great landowners who were members of minorities frequently invoked the protection of the League against legitimate agrarian reforms, in an apparent effort "to abuse the application of the protection of minorities by using it not in the interests of a national minority, but in those of a social class." [22] The moral authority of the League system was undermined by such efforts to use it for the support of entrenched privilege which rested in many cases on the iniquitous policies of colonization and confiscation which had long been applied by the former masters of the newly liberated peoples.

Members of former ruling peoples who had been abruptly transformed into members of national minorities had difficulty in adjusting to their novel situation. All too often, they exhibited a firm belief in their cultural and intellectual superiority and inherent right to rule the "inferior" peoples of Europe, thus raising an important obstacle to the development of harmonious relationships between majority and minority nationalities.

The attitude of the minorities toward the League system was so critical, and their demands for substantive and procedural reform so far-reaching and insistent, that they tended to reject that system as utterly worthless, thereby making it so. Many of their criticisms were well-grounded, and their lack of confidence in the system was understandable. But the protection afforded by the League was better than no protection at all, and the League system had possibilities of development and effective operation which were not exploited, in part at least because the minorities chose to agitate for an ideal system which was unobtainable at the time, rather than to concentrate on the practical task of maximizing the usefulness of the defective system which was available to them. The League system, representing a compromise between the demands of national minorities and of national states, required a spirit of accommodation on both sides; the uncompromising attitude of the minorities was not conducive to its success.

The problem of loyalty to the state was of crucial importance. There was no possibility that states would grant liberal treatment to disloyal minorities, or that the agencies of the League would insist that they do so. Even though the rights of minorities under the treaties and declarations were not formally conditional upon manifestations of loyalty to the state, it was an underlying premise of the system that satisfactory relationships could be established only between tolerant majorities and loyal minorities.

Disloyalty and persecution formed a vicious circle which ultimately shattered the League system. It was frequently impossible to determine which was cause and which was effect. There can be no doubt that minority states sometimes used trumped-up charges of disloyalty as a pretext for persecution – and succeeded in stimulating genuine disaffection. On the other hand, minorities sometimes employed false allegations of persecution to justify activities directed against the integrity of the state – and suffered actual oppression in retaliation.

It is probably true that "the majority of the great variety of national fragments were loyal and law-abiding persons who desired no more than to be assured of the full rights of citizenship and national freedom. . . ." [23] The European Nationalities Congress, meeting for the first time at Geneva in 1925, declared its adherence to the political *status quo* and barred all revisionist agitation.[24] However, certain groups among the protected minorities were unwilling to accept their status on any terms; they could not be reconciled either by liberal treatment or by effective protection. Such groups, notably the Germans of the various minority states, the Hungarians of Rumania, and the Macedonians of Yugoslavia, strove relentlessly to embarrass and undermine their host states.[25] They engaged in activities detrimental to internal stability, infected such international associations as the European Nationalities Congress with the virus of their discontent,[26] and turned increasingly to clandestine collusion with revisionist states of kindred nationalities. Thus, they brought suspicion upon all minorities, loyal and disloyal alike, and provided a convenient pretext for indiscriminate oppression.

> [The minorities] were themselves not completely innocent parties in the breakdown of the international system of protection. Those groups which permitted themselves to be used as tools for the disruptive plans of their powerful co-nationals unwittingly sacrificed their own interests, as well as the cause of all minorities.[27]

The Kin-States. The League minority system required the sympathetic support of those states which were connected with groups outside their borders by the bonds of ethnic kinship. Such states as Germany, Austria, Hungary, and Bulgaria could contribute greatly to the success of the system by accepting the political *status quo*, respecting the internationalization of minority protection, and encouraging coöperative and moderate attitudes among their co-nationals in the minority states; they could destroy it by adopting a contrary policy.

These states took the lead in combating the tendency of the Council to neglect the interests of national minorities, and in pressing for the adoption of broad interpretations and effective procedural devices which would make the international guarantee an instrument of impartial justice upon which minority groups could rely. Germany, in particular, after its admission to the League in 1926, countered the arguments and demands of the minority states, and helped to prevent the League system from degenerating into a meaningless farce. Germany became "almost the sole champion of the aggrieved groups." [28]

Unfortunately, however, the kin-states did not genuinely accept the internationalization of minority problems. They persisted in regarding the oppression of their co-nationals as an affront to themselves, rather than to the international community, and in attempting, with frequent success, to inject into the procedure just those elements of bilateral conflict which the League system had been intended to exclude.

It became increasingly clear, as the years passed, that Germany and the other champions of particular minorities were not at all sympathetic with the aims of the League system or its basic principles. They were influenced, in the first place, by the deterministic implications of the principle of nationality. If that principle be valid, then national minorities are anomalous. The only proper destiny of a fragment of a nation is to be reunited with the body of the nation. Even though a national minority may be treated in a thoroughly just and liberal manner, and be assured by the international community that it will continue to enjoy such treatment, its position is not satisfactory, because it is deprived of the possibility of real life and development by the fact of its separation from the nation to which it belongs.[29] Moreover, a national minority can owe no allegiance to an alien state, since nationality is the only legitimate basis of political obligation.[30] According to this theory of nationalism, the body of a nation from which fragments have been severed is a mutilated organism, unable to function or to develop normally until it has been made whole again. It cannot be bound to acquiesce in the perpetuation of its condition, since it inexorably, and legitimately, strives to attain the supreme goal of national integrity. Given this kind of thinking and feeling, it is understandable that the kin-states should have been fundamentally out of sympathy with a system which was based on the idea that the legitimate aspirations of national minorities could be satisfied by an international guarantee of decent and humane treatment.

The attitude of the kin-states was also influenced by extraneous political considerations. These states, defeated in the First World War, had been required to accept peace treaties which they regarded as incompatible with their political, economic, and strategic interests, as well as their aspirations stemming from nationalist ideology. Being fundamentally committed to the revision of the Paris settlement, they could not give their wholehearted support to the League minority system which was designed to aid in the perpetuation of the *status quo* by making it tolerable. The revisionist states sought rather to abuse the principle of minority protection by using it as an instrument of their political ambitions.

Actuated by nationalist and political motives, the bloc of states led by Germany undermined the League system by encouraging national minorities to be discontented with their position and immoderate in their demands. They went on to deal the system a fatal blow by promoting disloyalty and using disaffected minorities as pawns in the game of disrupting their host states and disintegrating the European order.

Germany gave active support to associations of Germans who lived in the minority states, ostensibly to aid them in their legitimate efforts to develop their cultural life and to press their demands for effective protection against oppression. These minority organizations became centers of German irredentist propaganda, and, after the advent of the Nazi regime in Germany, they clearly served as instruments of the foreign policy of the German state.[31] Germans in the minority states were impregnated with the ultra-nationalist doctrines of Nazism, and were induced to repudiate the ideal of the League system — that they should become loyal minorities sharing with tolerant majorities in the building of a stable European order along the lines laid down at

Paris — in favor of the ideal of union with their co-nationals in a Greater German State. The Hitlerian regime did not succeed in winning over all the *Auslandsdeutsche* to its cause, but it did weld large numbers of them into charges of "human dynamite," ready to be detonated at the command of the *Führer*.[32] Long before Hitler brought German minority groups into active service as units of a wartime "fifth column," Germany had discredited the League system for minority protection by encouraging and underwriting disloyal activities among its beneficiaries.

Similarly, Hungary utilized its co-nationals to stir up trouble in Rumania, and Bulgaria and Italy undermined the authority of Yugoslavia by supporting Macedonian unrest.[33] Abuses of this sort were fatal to the experiment in the international protection of national minorities.

The Neutral States. A considerable share of the responsibility for the failure of the protective system must be assigned to those "neutral" states which were its potential leaders. The first blow was dealt by the United States, when it reverted to isolationism and sacrificed its opportunity to serve as a universally respected neutral participant. France was disqualified for leadership by its alliances with minority states; its sympathy with their point of view precluded support of a vigorous and impartial enforcement of the rights of minorities.[34] France was so completely devoted to the preservation of the *status quo* that it was inclined to regard any concessions to the demands of minorities as dangerous compromises with revisionism, and to insist that the ideal of justice to minorities be subordinated to the purpose of keeping the peace.[35] Italy had neither the desire nor the moral authority to play a leading role in the system, since it contained important national minorities to which the Fascist government applied a policy of oppression and Italianization.[36]

It was incumbent upon Great Britain to assume the lead in implementing the League gurantee of minority rights, as it alone had the requisite stature and prestige, direct interest in European stability, and neutrality. Non-European members of the Council were able to serve usefully in the mediatorial role of rapporteur on minorities,[37] but only Britain was in a position to breathe the spirit of vitality into the system.

Unfortunately, Britain's leadership was extremely reluctant and halting, and the other neutral members of the Council displayed very little enthusiasm for their task. Hesitance to accept the obligation of enforcing the minority provisions was evident as early as 22 October 1920, when Balfour complained that the responsibility of holding the minority states to their commitments was a thankless and invidious one for the powers represented on the Council.[38] The members of the Council were acutely aware of the danger that diplomatic relations with the minority states might become strained as a result of efforts on their part to champion the cause of oppressed minorities. Their attitude was inevitably shaped by the fact that they were representatives of *states;* hence, they tended to be chary of treading too roughly upon the principle of sovereignty, of intervening without extreme provocation in the relations between the minority states and their citizens, and of encouraging unduly the pretensions of national minorities to rank as recognizable entities on the international scene. These considerations tended to outweigh the humanitarian and pacificatory purposes of the League system, and thus to militate against vigorous efforts to implement the international guarantee.

The neutral members generally took the attitude "that the less the Council discussed minorities the better."[39] They chose to ignore violations of the minority treaties and declarations whenever possible, and to handle flagrant cases which were forced upon their attention with excessive regard for the sensitivity of the states concerned. A minority had little reason to be confident that its interests would be safeguarded by the Council unless it was fortunate enough to have strong and influential friends among the members of that body.

Despite its defects, the League system had significant possibilities; "when executed in good faith, the terms of the Minorities Treaties could afford effective protection, at least with regard to the main problems."[40] But the system was not executed in good faith; it was never given a fair trial, since none of the interested parties — neither minority states nor minorities nor kin-states nor neutral powers — entered into the great experiment with the spirit and attitude which were essential to its success.

THE GENERAL SETTING OF THE SYSTEM

Finally, the failure of the system for the international protection of national minorities was part of a larger failure — the failure of mankind to solve its fundamental economic, political, and spiritual problems. The collapse of the minority system was not an isolated phenomenon, but one aspect of a general breakdown of international law, institutions, and morality.

The troubles of minorities were in some cases not so much the troubles of national groups as of particular economic classes in an era of profound economic change. When minorities were composed predominantly of wealthy landowning or bourgeois elements, as they were in many cases, the national struggle became inextricably associated with economic conflict, and its intensity was intimately related to the failure of modern society to devise adequate means for effecting orderly economic adjustment.

In some cases, the economic difficulties of minorities were produced not so much by discriminatory treatment as by the deranged condition of the minority states. The First World War and the revision of frontiers at the Peace Conference played havoc with the European economy. Minorities shared with majorities the consequences of failure to restore their countries to sound economic health, and extraordinary tensions were engendered by the abnormal conditions of postwar existence.

The failure of minority protection was one aspect of the failure of liberal democracy to take firm root and to flourish in the Europe that emerged from the war. The oppression of national minorities was a manifestation of the general tendency to oppress all minorities. Intolerance toward national differences was symptomatic of a growing disposition to suppress all diversity. There could be no rights for national minorities when the rights of man were denied. The fate of minorities was bound up with the survival of constitutional ideals and institutions; when these succumbed before the rising tide of totalitarianism, the hopes of national minorities for a regime of tolerance and justice were doomed.

The fate of the League minority system was largely determined by its international political context. The problem of minorities was not a technical matter which could be handled in routine fashion by an agency isolated from the vicissitudes of political conflicts; it was a political problem of great moment, and it could be solved only in conjunction with other political problems. When the League failed to cope with the factors making for the disintegration of the world order, the collapse of the minority system was inevitable; it was an integral part of the League, and its destiny could not be divorced from that of the League.

The welfare of national minorities was dependent upon the maintenance of international peace, stability, and security. When the postwar hope of collective security proved illusory, and it became evident that war had not been eliminated as the ultimate fact of international life, the position of national minorities was vitally affected. They were regarded as potentially subversive elements by the states to which they owed allegiance; they were envisaged as possible allies by the states to which they were related by ethnic ties. As international tension increased, the freedom of national minorities was curtailed, and the possibility of concerted international action to protect them was progressively reduced.

The failure of the League minority system was the inevitable concomitant of the disintegration of the moral foundations of international order. The system was based on the premise that states would undertake in good faith to fulfill their commitments, acting in conformity with the norms of international law and morality. When this assumption became untenable, as a result of the anarchical and amoral tendencies which played havoc with the course of international relations in the 1930's, the regime of minority protection was deprived of its essential foundation. Minority treaties could carry no more weight than other treaties in a period when the norm, *pacta sunt servanda*, was cynically and flagrantly violated. There could be no security for the rights of minorities in a lawless world, where the very concept of right was displaced by the concept of might as the criterion of state behavior.

CONSIDERATION OF THE MINORITY PROBLEM DURING THE SECOND WORLD WAR

CHAPTER 4: *THE WARTIME SETTING OF THE PROBLEM*

The Second World War cannot be regarded as a consequence of the collapse of the League system for the protection of national minorities, or as a product of the conflicts engendered by unresolved minority problems. However, the problem of "racial, religious, or linguistic minorities" obtruded at a number of points into the complex network of factors involved in that colossal upheaval.

Minorities figured, in the first place, as victims of the evil political forces which were largely responsible for bringing the scourge of war upon mankind. Wherever fascist and ultra-nationalist dictatorships arose, they made life difficult for national minorities; the Nazi regime in Germany supplied the prime example of this policy in its ruthless campaign to make the German nation *Judenrein*. Only a few perspicacious individuals were able to see what sort of international policies were presaged by this domestic activity, but when war came it became apparent that Hitler's treatment of the Jews had been symptomatic of a profound immorality and fanaticism which had the gravest implications for the peace and order of the world. During the war, the unrelenting fury of the Nazi assault upon the existence of the

Jewish people served to dramatize the nature of the challenge with which civilization was confronted. The fate of the Jews— even Jews who had never considered themselves members of a minority in any significant sense — demonstrated that the treatment of minorities of race, religion, or culture may be usefully regarded as a clinical thermometer for ascertaining the surges of nationalistic fever which are dangerous to peace. A particular minority, which was impelled by adversity to consider itself more and more explicitly as a national minority, came to be recognized as the victim *par excellence* of Nazi barbarism; thus, the importance of the national minority problem became evident, and the claims of minorities for consideration of their interests in the future determination of a world order acquired new moral weight. Moreover, the tragic turn of events stimulated minority leaders to make an urgent search for a solution of the problems of minority existence.

Secondly, the minority question entered into the picture as an element in the propagandistic scheme used by Hitler to "justify" his expansive policy. Just as revisionist statesmen throughout the interwar period had frequently grounded demands for frontier changes on the argument that it was their national duty to rescue co-national minorities from oppression by "alien" masters, and to confer upon them the blessings of integration with the mother nation, so Hitler used this type of argument whenever it suited his purpose. Among the elements of the program of the Nazi Party, adopted at Munich on 24 February 1920, there appeared a demand for the union of all Germans in a Greater Germany, on the basis of the right of national self-determination.[1] Hitler relied upon the moral force of this doctrine to support his demands upon Czechoslovakia in 1938. At least one writer has speculated that regard for the principle of nationality was the psychological basis of Britain's policy of appeasement,[2] which culminated in acquiescence to Hitler's demand for the Sudetenland at the Munich Conference. In 1939, the *Führer* turned toward Poland, calling for the cession of the Corridor (along with Danzig) to the Reich, and for "the safeguarding of the existence of the German national groups in the territories remaining to Poland. . . ."[3] After war broke out, Hitler declared that a Polish terroristic campaign against German minorities had been a major provocation, forcing Germany to rise in the defence of its racial brothers.[4] Consistency was not one of the Nazi dictator's virtues; he switched easily from the principle of nationality to the concept of *Lebensraum* when he had exhausted the possibilities of the former. It is clear that Hitler was not concerned merely with the welfare of German minorities in other countries, or with the reintegration of all the elements of the German nation. However, the minority problem served Hitler well as a propaganda theme and a pretext for the launching of his career of aggression. Germany's transparent exploitation of the issue damaged the cause of minorities; it obscured the reality of the minority problem, making it seem an artificial issue concocted by a would-be conqueror to serve his ends.

Finally, national minorities assumed the role of villains in the piece. When war came, the Axis powers found numerous accomplices, and the opposing states found all too many traitors, among groups ethnically related to Germany and its satellites. The existence of the German International was confirmed by events, as members of German and other minorities served as "fifth columns" for the Axis armies, facilitating the conquest of the states to which they owed allegiance, and assisting in the imposition and maintenance of repressive and frequently barbarous regimes of occupation. This phenomenon gave weight to the view that it is dangerous for states to harbor minority elements; the disloyalty of some groups tended to support the stigmatization of national minorities *per se*.

Many issues were involved in the Second World War, and military and strategic problems quite naturally occupied the center of attention. Nevertheless, formulations of war aims and plans for the postwar world — official and unofficial, popular and scholarly, vague and precise, realistic and quixotic — were produced in unprecedented volume. These plans were devices for winning the war as well as for winning the peace; they were designed to serve as wartime propaganda and as postwar proposals. This duality of purpose did not apply to each individual scheme, but it was clearly characteristic of the body of planning, seen as a whole.

The agenda for the postwar world was crowded with problems competing for priority, and the problem of national minorities by no means headed the list. Indeed, it frequently seemed in imminent danger of being excluded altogether. But awareness of the problem was kept alive by the fact that minorities had served, and were serving, as victims, as pretexts, and as villains in the struggle. It was a problem with humanitarian, political, social, economic, and philosophical ramifications, and as such, it could not be ignored.

Planners of a postwar solution of the minority problem could examine the pattern of legal obligations, the structure of machinery for implementing the international guarantee, and the procedural methods which had been developed by the Council of the League of Nations. They had at their disposal the record of successes and failures of the defunct system, and an accumulation of proposals for revision. Just as plans for a new general international organization necessarily grew out of an appraising examination of the League which failed, so all sound thinking about the minority problem had to begin with an evaluation of the techniques by which the League had sought to solve that problem.

The first systematic effort on the international level to produce an adjustment of relations between national majorities and minorities had provided no certain answers, but it had done much to define the problems and elucidate the difficulties. Herein lay the greatest significance of the League experiment for the planners of future policy and organization.

Among the questions which were raised by an examination of the League experience, these were outstanding: Must group status and collective rights be explicitly recognized? Can a satisfactory procedure exclude the right of minorities to seize the guaranteeing agency of disputes and to participate in the ensuing investigations, debates, and negotiations? Can minority rights and duties be dissociated? What is the proper balance between political and judicial techniques, between considerations of peace and justice, in the treatment of minority disputes? Is it realistic to expect kin-states to become disinterested to the extent of allowing the protection of co-national minorities to be treated as an international problem rather than an issue between themselves and the alleged oppressors? Must an effective system of minority obligations apply equally to all states? Is any sort of group autonomy compatible with the demands of modern states for sovereignty, unity, and centralization? Can minorities reasonably expect to receive impartial justice from a guaranteeing organization made up of representatives of states? Is it possible for an international organization to act, and to appear to act, as an agency of the world community, rather than as a political instrument of particular powers or blocs? Can national minorities be satisfied by any arrangements short of independence or union with co-national states? Is a viable solution dependent upon world peace, security, and prosperity? Finally, these fundamental questions presented themselves: Can the problem of national minorities be solved within the framework of the national state system? Is it a problem that lends itself to solution by institutional devices, or does its resolution require a fundamental moral transformation of the bulk of the inhabitants of the earth?

Few of the statesmen, scholars, and publicists who drafted blueprints for a brave new world were fully aware of the range of problems suggested by the twenty-year experiment in international protection of minorities. Nevertheless, these basic, largely unanswered questions lay somewhere in the background as the plans for the future were produced.

CHAPTER 5:   *SOLUTION BY INTERNATIONAL ORGANIZATION: THE INTERNATIONAL GUARANTEE OF MINORITY RIGHTS*

If it is proposed to solve the problem of national minorities through the agency of a general international organization, two methods of utilizing such an organization are available: it may be assigned the task, as was the League of Nations, of serving as guarantor for special commitments to respect minority rights; or, it may be expected to uphold a universal standard of human rights for individuals, without reference to their membership in national groups. In either case, the assumption is made that national minorities will continue to exist in national states, in the literal sense that the physical mixture of populations will continue. While these two approaches are not mutually exclusive, they are different, in that one emphasizes the distinctiveness of the minority problem and the other treats it as merely one facet of the general problem of human rights.

In the present chapter we shall be concerned with the analysis of postwar plans which envisaged international action specifically directed at safeguarding the rights of national minorities.

It was not surprising that there were some wartime proposals to continue, without essential change, the prewar effort to protect minorities. It was true that the League minority system was generally regarded as a failure. The same was true of the entire League structure, but a major part of wartime thinking about the future was devoted to the formulation of plans for an organization not fundamentally dissimilar to the League of Nations, and this point of view prevailed at the San Francisco Conference. Thus, those who contemplated the erection of a new minority system patterned after the old one were not alone in assuming that the failures of international institutions are not necessarily conclusive.

However, wartime thinkers who advocated a return to the *status quo ante bellum* in this respect were decidedly in the minority. There was strong opposition, on several grounds, to a renewal of the League minority system.

In the first place, it was widely held that such a step would be dangerous, both to the security and internal peace of states containing minorities and to the peace of the world. Understandably, this view was expressed most passionately by representatives of Czechoslovakia, a state which had made a loyal effort to make the minority system work, and had been rewarded by betrayal, dismemberment, and occupation. President Benes and other members of his government in exile were thoroughly disillusioned and utterly determined that their country should never again take the risks involved in the policy of conceding a special status to national minorities.[1] Czechoslovak spokesmen were equivocal in their position as to the *competence* of the international community to impose upon them a new regime of protection for minorities,[2] but they made it perfectly clear that their fears for the security of their country precluded willing acceptance of such a regime.

Czechoslovakia was not alone in pointing to the danger that protected minorities might undermine the states in which they lived. The Polish Ministry of Information published a propaganda booklet, *The German Fifth Column in Poland*, alleging that even though the German minority in Poland had been treated with exceptional liberality, it had conspired with Germany, under the protective covering of the minority treaty, to destroy Poland. This polemic, containing a great deal of truth despite its exaggeration of the liberality of Poland's minority policy, was apparently designed to head off any possible movement to restore the system of minority treaties.

Fear of subversive activities by ethnically alien groups, stimulated by Hitler's use of Germans abroad, was reflected by resolutions adopted by the states of the Western Hemisphere at conferences in 1938, 1940, and 1942. In these documents, the position was maintained that the concept of national minorities and the principle of international protection of minorities had no possible application in the American Republics, and agreements were formulated on precautionary measures against disloyal activities by groups with foreign political connections.[3]

It is evident that Nazi exploitation of minorities created a general distrust of groups which were disposed to perpetuate their minority consciousness, and a strong reaction against the concept of international protection. As one observer warned, "Every protected minority will ultimately find its Henlein." [4]

The opinion existed in many quarters that restoration of the prewar protective arrangements would be impossible, or virtually so, at the conclusion of the war. It was recalled that most of the minority states had accepted special obligations after the First World War only under great pressure, and that the more recalcitrant of them had never ceased to rail against the system during the twenty years of its existence. Poland's gravest misgivings had apparently been confirmed (although it appeared that Poland had never tried to make the system work), and Czechoslovakia's hopes had been dashed. It seemed extremely doubtful that the minority states could again be induced to undertake special commitments for the protection of minorities, or that they would coöperate loyally in the execution of a renewed minority regime if it should be imposed upon them.

Furthermore, it was not apparent that the great powers were inclined to use their influence to promote the renewal of the system. The powers were impressed by the failures and the abuse of the defunct minority system. The viewpoint of the Soviet Union was a question mark: would it favor international supervision of treatment of national groups in those areas of Eastern and Central Europe where Soviet influence would probably be dominant at the end of the war? The United States was dominated by the "melting-pot" idea, and could hardly understand the desire of national minorities to perpetuate their collective peculiarities. Britain displayed no enthusiasm for undertaking again the difficult and thankless task of participating actively in international arrangements for safeguarding the rights of national minorities. Under these circumstances, it seemed unlikely that the international protection of minorities could be revived in anything like its old form.

There was a widespread tendency to decry the re-establishment of the League minority system as a futile expenditure of effort. Many champions of the rights of minorities had been so little impressed by the actual and potential benefits of the League system that they had come to believe that the game was hardly worth the candle. Some minorities were no longer inclined to base their hopes for liberal treatment on a system which, from their point of view, had promised too little and delivered even less. Persons who had considered the system primarily in terms of its peace-keeping value were also disillusioned. Neither the political nor the humanitarian aims of the system had been realized, and there was a general disposition to write off the experiment as a failure, not to be tried again.

Finally, there was the assumption that an international protective system would be rendered superfluous by changes in circumstances and by the utilization of other devices. There was some naive feeling that a conclusive victory over the Axis would inaugurate the supremacy of tolerant, humane democracy throughout the world, making the minority problem simply disappear. However, this apocalyptic vision was exceptional; a more rational reliance upon the argument of superfluity was characteristic of those who favored the adoption of new and different methods of solving the minority problem.

Despite these arguments against the continuation of the effort to provide an international guarantee of minority rights, a substantial body of opinion favored such continuation.

Some thinkers simply assumed that the effort would continue along established lines. Just as the League would be replaced by an analogous general organization, so the international protection of minorities would be resumed. Thus, a spokesman for Yugoslavia speculated that after the war "there will certainly be international guarantees of minority rights. We will naturally guarantee the rights of all minorities within our domains." [5] Such persons clearly underestimated the strength of demands for reconsideration of the decision concerning the minority problem which had been made in 1919, and overestimated the forces making for continuity in the functional development of international organization.

There was a related assumption that the League system had simply been suspended, and that the minority treaties and declarations would retain their validity at the conclusion of hostilities. According to this view, the minority system was dormant rather than defunct.

It is a striking fact that, during the war, this assumption was only occasionally mentioned in passing, [6] and its value as an argument for the continuation of international protection was not exploited. The explanation of this apparent lapse is not far to seek. The League minority system had satisfied no one; therefore, mere restoration of that system was the first choice of no one. Proponents of the re-establishment of the system invariably contemplated some sort of revision, designed to correct those features of the original arrangements which they regarded as crucial defects. [7] Thus, they chose to emphasize their proposals for change rather than the maintenance of the legal *status quo*.

The neglect of the argument of continuing validity of the minority instruments by wartime thinkers was a sound tactic. Even though they might have made a strong legal case for that position, it was clear that nothing was to be gained by proving that a protective system which had been generally ineffective, and virtually inoperative for several years preceding the outbreak of the war, was still theoretically in existence. To put the system into operation again, and still more to effect its modification, would require positive international decisions; it mattered little whether those decisions purported to reaffirm and modify the old system or to erect a new one.

Most wartime thinkers who favored the international protection of minorities recognized that the future was not to be bound by the past, and that the League minority system would probably prove to be a negative rather than a positive factor in shaping the new approach to the minority problem.

GENERAL PROPOSALS

The concept of the international guarantee of minority rights was frequently endorsed during the war in very general and sometimes quite vague terms which left room for considerable doubt as to whether their authors were seriously dedicated to the proposition that the League experiment in safeguarding minorities must be continued.

In 1944, a group of American and Canadian scholars produced a statement of views entitled *The International Law of the Future*, in which the principle was enunciated that:

> Each State has a legal duty to see that conditions prevailing within its own territory do not menace international peace and order, and to this end it must treat its own population in a way which will not violate the dictates of humanity and justice or shock the conscience of mankind.[8]

They proposed that an international executive agency be empowered to consider violations of this principle and to take remedial action if the situation menaced international peace and order. This provision was designed to remove the need or the excuse for arbitrary intervention by interested states.[9]

This scheme neither precludes nor specifically provides for international protection of national minorities. It does not define a minimum standard of justice, or state whether special minority rights are involved. It does not suggest international supervision of minority treatment except at the emergency stage. However, it does affirm a principle which is vital to the concept of international minority protection — the principle that the state's freedom in relation to its own people is limited by international standards. This plan is clearly concerned with human rights; it is not so evidently concerned with the rights of national minorities as such.

The Commission to Study the Organization of Peace exhibited a similar uncertainty in regard to protection of minorities. It accepted the view that the state's freedom in relation to its own nationals must be limited.[10] Its Fourth Report contained a proposal that "A permanent international commission should be created . . . to formulate from time to time the principles and procedures of international justice with respect to *groups* or individuals." [11] Somewhat later, the Executive Committee of its Committee on Human Rights suggested the possible desirability of special conventions to buttress human rights in areas where racial, religious, or linguistic minorities have been persecuted, but it viewed the concept of minority rights as narrow and discriminatory, and therefore as less acceptable than the more general concept of human rights.[12] Thus, it appears that the Commission was not firmly committed to the safeguarding of the rights of national minorities *per se*.

Pope Pius XII declared, on 24 December 1939, that the framing of a peace would require the "benevolent examination" of the needs and demands of ethnic minorities,[13] and two years later, he asserted that within the limits of a new order based on moral principles, there would be no place for suppression of the cultural or linguistic characteristics of national minorities.[14] Catholic thought is further exemplified by a bill of rights, drafted by the Rev. Wilfred Parsons, S.J., in which provision is made for "the right of ethnic and religious minorities to enjoy equal opportunities for the development of their common humanity." [15] We have found no evidence of papal or other specifically Catholic concern with the problem in any other terms than these exceedingly general statements of principle.

A conference of Protestant churchmen of the United States agreed on the principle that the rights of racial and religious minorities in all lands should be recognized and safeguarded.[16] A group of leading Catholics, Protestants, and Jews issued a statement on 6 October 1943, calling for the guarantee by an international organization of the rights of ethnic, religious, and cultural minorities.[17] In these statements, we find definite acceptance of the principle of international protection of minorities, but complete failure to spell out the application of the principle or to specify the scope of minority rights.

There was a considerable degree of tentativeness in the early stages of Jewish wartime thought. Salo W. Baron confined himself, in an article written in 1940, to stating that "the minorities clauses of the last treaties ought to be greatly modified and improved upon, rather than blindly discarded." [18] Jacob Robinson suggested in 1943 that the international guarantee of the rights of national groups might take the form of improved minority treaties or a general bill of rights.[19] In the case of leaders of Jewish thought, this vagueness merely reflected a disposition to wait until the general shape of the postwar world could be ascertained before going on the record with detailed proposals.

A few influential political voices in the United States and Britain were heard during the war years, supporting the principle of minority protection but going no farther. In 1945, Senator Wagner advocated that the new international organization should include only states which would subscribe to the principle of maintaining "that equality for minority groups which is at the basis of all justice." [20] Clement Attlee, leader of the British Labour Party in the House of Commons, declared that the rights of national, racial, and religious minorities must be recognized, and that the sovereign rights of states containing such groups must be subordinated to the effective authority of an international body.[21] His party accepted that principle at its Thirty-Ninth Annual Conference, in 1940.[22] Viscount Cecil of Chelwood expressed the hope that something analogous to the League minority system would come after the war.[23]

The import of such general, unelaborated endorsements of the concept of minority guarantees is difficult to determine. In some cases, they were probably no more significant than statements of opposition to sin. In other cases, they were preliminary to serious consideration of the problems involved in safeguarding minorities. In any event, broad statements of principle were not in themselves very meaningful; it was necessary, before anything constructive could be done or realistic approaches to a solution put forward, to ask the crucial questions: what rights, of what groups, in what countries, were to be safeguarded, by whom, and by what means?

PROPOSALS FOR A SYSTEM OF LIMITED SCOPE

There were a number of proposals during the war that the future minority system should be applicable only to Eastern and Central Europe, i.e., that its sphere of operation should be roughly the same as that of the previous system.[24] Strikingly, most of these proposals emanated from Jewish thinkers, who were motivated by the fact that few Jews outside that region desired to maintain communal status or special rights outside the scope of a general system for guaranteeing individual human rights.

Suggestions that internationally enforceable obligations to respect the special rights of minority groups should be imposed upon the Axis states in the peace treaties [25] indicated the conviction that it was feasible and desirable to erect again a minority system affecting only a limited number of European states. The specific inclusion of Germany in a system to be erected on the basis of the peace treaties was suggested by the Interim Committee of the American Jewish Conference.[26]

The writings of Oscar Janowsky constituted an interesting case study in the development of postwar plans. In 1942, he advocated a generalized regime of guaranteed minority rights, with subjective determination of membership in national groups and recognition of minorities as legal entities competent to tax their members and to operate cultural institutions which should share proportionately in public subventions. He proposed that the system should be explicitly based on the nonassimilative ideal, and that redress for violations of minority rights should first be sought on the domestic level, retaining the possibility of international intervention as a final resort.[27]

In 1943, Janowsky reiterated this plan, limiting its application to the area of Eastern and Central Europe.[28] Two years later, he presented a carefully elaborated version calling for the erection in that area of one or more regional federations, the constituent elements of which would be multinational states, within which the various national groups would figure as legally recognized entities, enjoying cultural autonomy and functioning as organic elements in the state structure. There would be an international guarantee of the position and rights of national groups in this part of Europe, and the protective system would be extended to cover Germany and Italy, as well as possible new or enlarged states. The international machinery would function on the spot, with control agencies extending in pyramidal fashion from the local level to the highest political and judicial levels of the new world organization.[29]

Thus, Janowsky appeared to abandon the ideal of a universal minority system in favor of one of limited scope. By introducing the concepts of federalism and multinationalism, he really proposed a radical change in approach to the minority problem, shifting from the effort to protect minorities in national states to a new scheme of guaranteeing minorities a status of equal partnership in the structure of multinational states. Despite this fundamental innovation in principle, his plan was evidently based on the League system, with improvements and certain supplementary features drawn from the Upper Silesian regional system, which had functioned from 1922 to 1937 under the German-Polish Convention of Geneva. Hence, it may be treated here as a proposal for the reconstitution of an international protective system of restricted territorial coverage.

The proposals of Max Laserson fell somewhere in between the categories of limited and universal systems. He favored a flexible system, whereby some states — those bound by the League system, with the addition of Germany, Italy, and Spain — would be permanently under international supervision, and all others would be subject to exceptional intervention on behalf of minorities whenever the international organization should recognize an emergency situation.[30]

A planning agency of the United States Government suggested in 1944 that a revised version of the League minority system might be adopted, with possible expansion to cover Germany and Italy, elevation of the standards of minority treatment, and development of improved machinery which might include "a permanent minorities commission or other agency of the international organization with powers of investigation, conciliation, and recommendation. . . ." Evidence that this proposal did not reflect a definite commitment to such a scheme as the solution of the minority problem was provided by the inclusion in the same document of a very limited and cautious endorsement of the idea of population transfer, support for the development of regional solutions along the lines of the former Upper Silesian system, and a final statement to the effect that the United States should favor action to promote general human rights, "(1) in order eventually to eliminate the problem of minorities as such, (2) to pave the way for the eventual termination of special minorities treaties, and (3) to place this question on the broader foundation of the protection of basic human rights." [31]

PROPOSALS FOR A UNIVERSAL SYSTEM

The American Jewish Conference adopted, on 2 September 1943, a resolution calling for an international bill of rights which should in addition to assuring the equal enjoyment of human rights by all citizens of every country, embody recognition of "the inalienable right of all religious, ethnic and cultural groups to maintain and foster their respective group identities on the basis of equality." [32] The Conference submitted this draft bill of rights to the Department of State, with a specific proviso for "the establishment of appropriate and adequate national and international machinery to secure the enforcement of these rights." [33] This principle was further developed at the 1946 session of the organization, when it was resolved that the international bill of rights should include provisions for "the protection of specific group rights of ethnic, cultural and religious groups. Among such rights are rights in the field of education, welfare, and religious and cultural activities." [34]

Dr. Max Gottschalk, Director of the Research Institute on Peace and Post-War Problems of the American Jewish Committee, rejected the idea of relying on individual countries to treat their Jewish citizens in a satisfactory manner, and declared: "It would be much wiser, therefore, for the United Nations collectively to provide special guarantees for all minorities everywhere and at the same time also to create the instruments for the immediate and lasting enforcement of these guarantees." [35]

A carefully elaborated plan for the creation and enforcement of a universal regime of human rights, including positive minority rights for all groups which desired them, was produced by Hersh Lauterpacht.[36] Another prominent international lawyer, Hans Kelsen, proposed the universalization of minority protection, supported by the definitive establishment of the new concept that minority groups should have the legal personality requisite for bringing complaints directly before an international court.[37]

A somewhat more conservative plan, not involving an attack on the tradition that only states can be competent participants in the international legal system, was adopted in 1942 by the League of Nations Union of New Zealand. This resolution urged the protection of minorities in all member states of the future world organization, and suggested a pattern of machinery for supervision and enforcement extending from the local area of tension to the highest political level of the international agency.[38]

Viscount Cranborne, speaking on behalf of the British Government in the House of Lords, on 8 March 1944, suggested the adoption of:

> . . . some broad general declaration by the United Nations reprobating ill-treatment by a State of its minorities — some general statement of a standard to which they would be expected as members of the United Nations to conform, and indicating that if they did not conform to it certain sanctions would have to be applied to them.[39]

In so doing, he seemed to propose the universal protection of the rights of minorities. However, this endorsement was extremely weak and tentative, since it did not envisage the establishment of definite and precise legal obligations, or allow for protective action except in cases of drastic abuse. It was further qualified by a warning against the dangers of political friction which might be engendered by "continual interference with the ordinary processes of internal law and administration" by an international guarantor, and by an indication that the goal should be to promote assimilation rather than the perpetuation by minorities of their sense of differentiation.[40]

FEDERALISTIC PROPOSALS

Proponents of federalism — global or regional — theoretically eliminated the issue of international protection for national minorities, by postulating the destruction of the context within which that concept has meaning, i.e., the pattern of independent national states, joined loosely in some organization analogous to the League of Nations. Within a federation of nationalities, the categories of national majority (the state-forming and state-possessing group) and national minority (the group of quasi-aliens, people in the state but not of the state) are presumably discarded. Thus, it seems that federalistic thinking would place the problem of relationships among nationalities in a conceptual setting so radically different from the old context that its disposition of the problem would have no relevance to the type of solution which was attempted by the League of Nations.

This theoretical differentiation was not always apparent in actual schematic planning. Advocates of limited federations frequently proposed arrangements for minority protection which differed little from the League system except that the guarantee was to be entrusted to a regional or continental agency.[41] Janowsky's plan provided for supervision by a global organization of the treatment of minorities within regional federations of multinational states.[42] Even proponents of world federation drew heavily from the concepts and experience of the League minority system, and displayed marked differences of approach primarily in regard to the mechanisms of enforcement and guarantee which they envisaged.[43] The explanation of this apparent anomaly probably lies in the fact that the distinction between federation and mere association has become somewhat blurred. There may be no fundamental difference between a scheme for a "weak federation" and a plan for a "strong organization of sovereign states"; in such circumstances, it would be unrealistic to expect the two plans to exhibit a fundamental difference in approach to the minority problem.

CONCLUSION

One of the most striking features of this phase of wartime thought is the almost complete failure of the type of solution which we have discussed in this chapter to command the support of governmental leaders and influential political figures. There were a few gestures of support from these sources, but they were fairly insubstantial; it became increasingly clear during the war that responsible statesmen and officials had largely discarded the premise that there should be a systematic attempt to establish new provisions for the international protection of national minorities.

Many of the proposals which we have examined were vague statements of principle, unaccompanied by real plans for effectuation. Some thinkers proceeded blithely to elaborate plans for international guarantees, with little concern for the crucial problem of their political acceptability. Others got themselves impaled on the opposite horn of the dilemma, when they went to such lengths to obviate the objections of statesmen whose consent was vital that they destroyed the effectiveness and usefulness of their plans, making them unattractive to minorities whose coöperation was vital.

A few wartime thinkers produced plans for international protection of minorities which reflected awareness of the problems involved, appreciation of the lessons of the League experience, and determination to find a balance between conflicting interests and demands of majorities and minorities, of states and national groups. Yet the basic problems were not solved. In particular, the choice between a universal and a limited system of minority obligations remained unsettled. Max Laserson sought to combine the advantages and eliminate the disadvantages of both types,[44] but without marked success; in a system which subjects some states to permanent supervision and others to temporary, emergency intervention, the stigma of discrimination persists, so far as the permanently bound states are concerned, and the difficulty arises of determining both the legal justification and the moral and political necessity for exceptional international intervention in other states, whenever such action may be proposed.

Equally little progress was made in finding a practical basis of agreement upon the scope and character of the minority rights which might be guaranteed. Champions of minorities pressed for more extensive rights than they had previously enjoyed, including, in many cases, recognition of collective legal status and competence. The hard fact was that statesmen, generally backed by a public opinion which was deeply impressed by the perfidy of irredentist and disloyal minorities, were disposed to curtail, rather than to expand, the rights of minorities.

Even the best of wartime proposals for repetition of the League experiment in minority protection failed to show the way in which the system could be made both workable and acceptable. This does not mean that the proposals were not worthy of consideration and perhaps of acceptance by an international community whose problems are not generally susceptible of perfect solution. It does mean that the proponents of a new protective regime failed to dispel the skepticism which had been produced in the minds of statesmen and peoples by the failure and abuse of the League system.

Few of those who were concerned with the minority problem relied exclusively on the hope that international protection would be revived. Most of the plans which we have examined were put forward in combination with other methods of solution which we shall discuss in the chapters which follow.

CHAPTER 6:   *SOLUTION BY INTERNATIONAL ORGANIZATION: AN INTERNATIONAL BILL OF HUMAN RIGHTS*

The guarantee by international organization of a uniform set of basic rights for all human beings may be regarded as a full and sufficient solution of the problem of national minorities, as an essential supplement to other partial solutions, or as the admittedly inadequate but only feasible concession to the demands of minorities for protection against the majorities with which they find themselves associated in national states. In any case, wartime proposals for an international bill of human rights reflected a distinctive approach to the minority problem, in their emphasis upon the relevance of universal human rights to that problem.

The idea of an international bill of rights was a prominent and almost ubiquitous feature of unofficial postwar planning. In many cases, the bare proposal was put forward that there should be such a codification of human rights, without any attempt at specification of the rights which should be included. Proposals of this sort have little interest for us here, since we are concerned with the relevance of the substantive provisions of a bill of rights to the minority problem.

A number of thinkers combined the concepts of special protection for minorities and of recognition of human rights for all individuals. For instance, Jacob Robinson proposed a general bill of rights of universal applicability, together with a special regime of minority rights for specific danger zones,[1] and Joseph Tenenbaum argued for a universal bill of individual rights containing special provisions "granting and enforcing the safety of the Jewish minority and the national cultural rights of the Jewish people everywhere." [2]

Various explanations may be given for this advocacy of a dualistic approach to the problem. Some spokesmen for minorities were inclined to grasp at every straw; they appealed for every conceivable sort of protective device, in the desperate hope that some of their suggestions would be accepted. They were not concerned with the logical compatibility of the concepts of individual rights and minority rights, or with the specific manner in which the two might be fitted together. They advocated both, hoping for at least one.

In the second place, this position was supported by minority thinkers on the ground that all human rights are interdependent. They doubted that a government which violated the basic rights of its ordinary citizens could be induced to respect any set of special rights which might be claimed by national minorities. While they did not feel that ordinary human rights were sufficient to satisfy the legitimate aspirations of all national minorities, they did think that the international guarantee of those rights was essential to the creation of a world context within which minorities could hope for the exceptional rights which they considered vital to their collective survival.

The dualistic approach was sometimes used as a tactical device to overcome the objection of minority states to being singled out again as the objects of a system which they regarded as discriminatory. It would establish the principle that all states are obligated to respect international standards in their relation-ships with their own nationals; this would presumably remove some of the sting from the requirement that certain states should submit to external supervision of their policy toward national minorities.

Finally, there was the view that uniform individual rights and special minority rights are logically correlative. An international bill of individual rights would provide the negative protection of which members of minority nationalities stand in particular need — the right not to be subjected to discrimination or to be treated arbitrarily. Positive minority rights could be provided for in specific articles, applicable only where there were groups needing and desiring such rights. Thus, all minorities would have a negative guarantee, and those which required it would have a positive regime of special minority rights.

A considerable part of wartime thinking was based on the premise that there was no problem of national minorities as such; there was only the problem of individuals, struggling to have their rights recognized and respected. Members of national minorities might have exceptional difficulties, but their problem was fundamentally the same as that of other individuals, and their only legitimate aspiration was to enjoy equality of rights with their fellow citizens. This kind of thinking expressed itself in proposals for international bills of rights, based exclusively on the concept of individual human rights.

Proposals of this character were often the reflections of the wide moral horizons of their authors. To some Jews, for instance, it seemed narrow and selfish, and in the long run suicidal, to think only of improving the lot of the Jews; it seemed self-evident that the future of Jewish rights was linked with the future of the rights of all human beings, and the problem was therefore not that of making a certain spot or spots safe for the Jews, but "that of making the entire world safe for a decent design for human living." [3]

The elements of danger in the concept of minority rights

served to push some thinkers into the individualistic camp. C. J. Hambro was typical of those who feared that the granting of special rights to minorities would equip them for playing a disruptive role in the life of the state, and who therefore advocated the recognition of the rights of human beings in their individual capacities only.[4]

Some minority thinkers believed that it would be a disservice to national groups to single them out as the objects of international protection. If they alone among the citizens of a state could appeal over the head of the government to an international agency, the suspicion might seem to be confirmed that they were extraneous elements in the body politic. An example of this kind of thinking is found in the warning of a Jewish publicist that Jews must not be beneficiaries of laws of exception or wards of external agencies, lest they become marked and mistrusted. This fear led to the suggestion that the future regime of international protection should be concerned with the guarantee of basic human rights to all people of all countries.[5]

Advocacy of an international bill of individual human rights as a substitute for the League system of minority guarantees was sometimes founded on the ill-considered assumption that the former type of system could succeed where the latter had failed. Thus, Morris D. Waldman, asserting that minority rights were a "proved failure," argued for the protection of all human beings, without regard for their majority or minority status.[6] Granted that the argument of discrimination against particular states cannot be employed in opposition to the system envisaged here, and that the cause of humanity in general may have a stronger ideological attraction than the cause of particular national groups, it is still not self-evident that the protection of all men everywhere is a more feasible project than the protection of limited categories of men. The magnitude of the undertaking is incomparably greater; all states, great and small, are placed in a position analogous to that of the minority states of the League system, and thereby presumably acquire an interest in minimizing the effectiveness of the system, lest it interfere unduly in their own domestic affairs. The defiant and intransigent object of the international guarantor's pressure may well be, in a given case, not a relatively small and weak state like those bound by the League system, but a major world power with strength to reinforce its pride and dignity. The failure of the League system does not disprove the practicability of a more ambitious system, but it certainly does not suggest that it is reasonable lightly to assume that the more ambitious system can succeed.

The case for the substitution of human rights for minority rights also took the form of assertions that the enjoyment of equal individual rights rendered superfluous any demand for a special minority regime. As Judge John J. Parker put it, "If every citizen is given equal justice under law, governmental oppression of minorities cannot arise." [7] This point of view failed to consider the strength of the conviction held by some minorities that their collective existence requires the recognition of certain exceptional rights of a positive character, the denial of which is tantamount to oppression. Certain Jewish groups, for instance, seemed to fear the assimilative tendencies which might be engendered by complete emancipation — i.e., enjoyment of full equality as individuals — almost as much as the tragic effects of group persecution.[8] It could be argued that minorities *ought* not to desire differential treatment, but it was unrealistic to ignore the fact that many minorities would regard as seriously deficient any list of rights omitting provision for group facilities to guard against assimilation.

OFFICIAL THOUGHT

The concept of human rights figured prominently in the wartime proclamations and postwar plans of the official leaders of the United Nations, who repeatedly endorsed the ideal of greater human freedom. Winston Churchill described the conflict, at its very beginning, as a war "to establish, on impregnable rocks, the rights of the individual. . . ." [9] President Roosevelt declared as early as 3 January 1940, that America could never be wholly safe unless other governments recognized certain freedoms which he believed to be essential everywhere,[10] and a year later he defined the American objective in terms of building a new world founded upon the enjoyment by all men of the "Four Freedoms": freedom of speech and expression, freedom of worship, freedom from want, and freedom from fear.[11]

Through the Atlantic Charter and the Declaration by United Nations,[12] the doctrine of human rights became officially a fundamental element of the credo of the anti-Axis coalition.

It should be noted that these official expressions of concern for human rights neglected any consideration of the question whether there should be special treatment of the problem of national minorities. Even though the emphasis was clearly placed upon the concept of individualism, the concept of minority rights was not repudiated; it was simply not mentioned.

There was, however, a school of official thought which supported the idea of an international bill of rights and explicitly rejected the notion that national minorities should be in any sense the special beneficiaries of such an instrument.

President Benes of Czechoslovakia declared on several occasions his belief in the necessity and desirability of a charter of individual human rights, universally applicable.[13] He was careful to elaborate his position as follows:

> The protection of minorities in the future should consist primarily in the defense of human democratic rights and not of national rights. Minorities in individual states must never again be given the character of internationally recognized political and legal units, with the possibility of again becoming sources of disturbance.[14]

This opposition to the granting of minority rights was obviously motivated by concern for the security of the Czechoslovak state; however, at another time, he shifted the argument to slightly different ground, expressing interest in the safety of minorities and observing that they had no need for anything more than ordinary democratic rights.[15]

Sumner Welles, American Undersecretary of State, stated on 31 May 1943:

> Finally, in the kind of world for which we fight, there must cease to exist any need for the use of that accursed term "racial or religious minority." If the peoples of the earth are fighting and dying to preserve and to secure the liberty of the individual under law, is it conceivable that the peoples of the United Nations can consent to the re-

establishment of any system where human beings will still be regarded as belonging to such "minorities"? [16]

This clear repudiation of the philosophy of the League minority system betrayed a failure to understand the profound difference between the shape of the minority problem in the United States (and to a certain extent, in most other Western democracies), and in various other areas, notably Eastern and Central Europe. Welles' view ignored the fact that segregation, so bitterly opposed by members of minority groups in this country who wish to be admitted to full membership in an integrated American community, is regarded not as a disability but, when it takes certain forms, as a valued right by many minorities elsewhere, who attach great importance to the ideal of preserving and fostering their sense of corporate identity and differentiation from the "alien" peoples among whom they live. In its opposition to the evil of discrimination, the position assumed by Welles was in complete harmony with the negative aspirations of all national minorities. Its deficiency lay in its blindness to the existence of the *positive* aspirations of those national groups for whom "racial or religious minority" is not an "accursed term," but a category for which international recognition is desired.

The leading tendency of Pan-American thought was decidedly Wellesian. There was great interest in the project of establishing human rights for all individuals without distinction as to race, creed, language, or other factors. However, there was constant reiteration of the principle enunciated at the Eighth International Conference of American States in 1938, that the concept of national minorities had no meaning in the Americas,[17] and there was a tendency to treat the international recognition of minority rights anywhere in the world as an unnecessary and potentially dangerous measure. Thus, when the Inter-American Juridical Committee endorsed the idea of an international bill containing the rights fundamental for the protection of the individual, it went on to suggest that such an instrument, "if sufficiently comprehensive," might "preclude the necessity of making provision for the protection of minorities in countries where there are large minority groups that have long possessed a separate national character." [18]

As we have seen, the official wartime leaders of the United Nations substantially agreed that the postwar international system should give recognition to the rights of man, but exhibited little conviction that it would be either necessary or desirable to include supplementary provisions or arrangements for the benefit of national minorities. Many champions of minority interests deplored this attitude, but they could all agree that provisions for equality in the enjoyment of individual rights were essential, even though they fell short of satisfying the positive aspirations of many groups.

However, it was far from clear that the statesmen of the United Nations had an unwavering determination to *guarantee* even those rights which minority leaders regarded as an irreducible minimum. Strong statements of such intention occasionally appeared. Sumner Welles asserted that the charter of the new world organization should contain specific obligations relating to the fundamental rights of individuals in member states, and enforcement provisions incapable of nullification by pleas of sovereignty or domestic jurisdiction.[19] The American Republics, in a resolution calling for the drafting of a charter of human rights, declared their support "of a system of international protection of these rights."[20] President Roosevelt, reporting to Congress on the Crimea Conference, said that the peace would be "based on . . . the *guaranties* of tolerance and freedom of religious worship."[21]

Vagueness and indecision were more characteristic of official statements concerning the enforcement of human rights. Roosevelt's stronger assertions must be placed alongside such statements as the one he included in his State of the Union Message to Congress, on 7 January 1943: "We *hope* that these blessings [the Four Freedoms] will be granted to all men everywhere."[22] The United States, the United Kingdom, the Soviet Union, and China, in the Dumbarton Oaks proposals relating to the organization of the postwar world, confined themselves to providing that the projected organization, acting through organs with only the power of recommendation, should "promote respect for human rights and fundamental freedoms."[23]

Indeed, the principle of nonintervention was sometimes invoked by Allied spokesmen in such a manner as to suggest that they

might positively disapprove of any international effort to supervise the treatment by states of their own nationals, either as individuals or as minority groups. Anthony Eden, British Foreign
Minister, stated in a broadcast on 4 January 1942: "What matters
in foreign affairs is not the form of internal government of any
nation but its international behavior. The trouble with Hitler . . .
was not that he was a Nazi at home. The trouble with him was
that he would not stay at home." [24] In similar vein, Prime Minister Churchill said: "I presume we do not include in our programme of world renovation any forcible action against any
Government whose internal form of administration does not
come up to our own ideas. . . ." [25]

Governmental leaders in the Western Hemisphere were quite
as busy affirming the principle of nonintervention as declaring
their support of the international protection of the rights of man,
since the former doctrine was dear to the hearts of Latin Americans, who had only recently succeeded in inducing representatives of the United States to repeat it with them as a part of the
American credo.[26]

There is no necessary conflict between the principle of nonintervention and the international protection of the rights either
of individuals in general or of minorities in particular, if the
former principle is interpreted as precluding merely the arbitrary interference by one state in the affairs of another. However, since this interpretation was not specified, the doctrinal
endorsements of nonintervention seemed to imply rejection of
the possibility that the international community, acting in accordance with a prescribed procedure, might intervene for the purpose of compelling states to respect the internationally recognized
rights of individuals or of groups.

SUMMARY

We have found that the idea of an international bill of rights
received a great deal of emphasis in both official and unofficial
circles during the Second World War. In many cases, the assumption was made, implicitly or explicitly, that the guarantee of
rights to all individuals would obviate the need for the special
protection of minorities. Behind this assumption there lay sometimes a fear of minorities, and sometimes a failure to compre-

hend the phenomenon of self-conscious minorities. Seldom did this assumption appear to rest on a reasoned rejection of the contention that something more than ordinary individual rights was necessary to enable some national minorities to maintain the collective existence and foster the development of the ethnic and cultural values which seemed so vital to them and to their champions.

In other cases, the guarantee of equal rights to all individuals was envisaged as only a partial solution of the minority problem, to be supplemented by the application of other methods of solution.

Advocacy of an international bill of rights was frequently unaccompanied by a realistic appreciation of the difficulties involved in such a project. No evidence was put forward to show that the problems of formulation, of securing ratification, and of arranging for enforcement would be less formidable in connection with this project than with a plan for the guarantee of minority rights.

Spokesmen for minorities generally supported this approach; the objections which were raised by some of them took the form of denials that the guarantee of individual rights was in itself an adequate solution of the minority problem.

CHAPTER 7:   *SOLUTION BY MORAL TRANSFORMA-
TION: ASSIMILATION AND CUL-
TURAL PLURALISM*

The two groups of wartime proposals with which we have dealt in Chapters 5 and 6 are similar in that they both treat the national minority question as a problem to be solved by legalistic, organizational methods. They recognize that the problem would become more manageable if the human beings concerned, majorities and minorities alike, should become more reasonable, more tractable, more humane. But they do not anticipate or require such transformation. Majorities may continue to be selfish, domineering, and perhaps ruthless; minorities may continue to be demanding, troublesome, and perhaps perfidious; but regulations can be established in international law, and procedures and agencies can be set up in international organization, to control the oppressive tendencies of majorities and the disloyal machinations of minorities. Thus, the minority problem can be solved, even while human beings retain the unfortunate characteristics which gave rise to the problem.

We come now to two groups of wartime proposals — schemes for assimilation and for cultural pluralism — which seek a solution of the difficulties of majority-minority relations in the moral transformation of the human participants. They are not unconcerned with legal provisions and organizational arrangements, but they are basically interested in and dependent upon fundamental changes in the minds and spirits of men. Their similarity lies in this common reliance upon human mutability; their difference, which is profound, lies in the specific moral changes which they require.

Assimilation demands that minorities consent to abandon the ethnic, cultural, and linguistic characteristics which distinguish them from the national majorities with whom they live, and to become merged into nationally uniform communities with the majorities. It demands also that the majorities concerned accept and facilitate this merger. Cultural pluralism, on the other hand, requires that majorities respect the peculiar characteristics of minorities, foster their development, and learn to think of them as politically irrelevant, and that minorities accept the obligation of being temperate in their autonomistic demands and of restricting the scope of the implications of their particularism. In the one case, minorities are expected to relinquish their insistence on being different; in the other, majorities are expected to abandon their intolerance of those who are different.

The distinction is not always so precise. There may be schemes envisaging the disappearance of the minority problem, without making it clear whether minorities are expected to cease being different, or majorities are to stop acting as if the distinguishing characteristics of minorities make any material difference. There may well be a middle ground, requiring minorities to curtail their determination to remain distinct entities and majorities to curb their zeal for suppressing heterogeneous elements in the body politic.

ASSIMILATION

A significant school of wartime thought started with the premise that the national state would or should continue to be the "normal" unit of political organization, reasoned that national states and national minorities were ultimately incompatible, and concluded that it was necessary to eliminate the minority problem by eliminating minorities. Abjuring the most drastic Hitlerian method of physical extermination, supporters of this view had two alternative methods to consider: the transfer of populations, and the policy of assimilation.

Both these policies were widely considered, and they were frequently not disentangled. The proposal that national minorities should be reduced in size by the physical removal of some of their numbers, and then obliterated by assimilation of the remnant, was characteristic of a large body of postwar planning.[1] President Benes of Czechoslovakia expressed his policy as follows: "Members of minorities who refuse to return to their national state . . . will be definitively sacrificed and given up to national assimilation in the other state."[2] Joseph B. Schechtman supported á similar combination of the evacuationist and assimilative methods.[3] We shall reserve the problem of transfer for consideration in Chapter 8, and turn now to an examination of the wartime sentiment for utilization of assimilation as a means of solving the minority problem.

The proposal that national minorities be assimilated was usually put forward by statesmen and publicists within whose frame of reference the interests of the national state ranked as supreme values. Minorities might raise anguished cries against their "spiritual emasculation" and protest that sacred cultural values were being violated; but the welfare and security of the state were prior considerations. Allied with this concern for the state, and sometimes indistinguishable from it, was a concern for the alleged interests and rights of the majority nationality. The national group which forms the bulk of the population of a country has the right to a national state, a political entity which can serve as the embodiment of the nation and the instrument of national aspirations. It has an interest in making its national state secure and its institutions stable, even at the cost of obliterating minority cultures and imposing an enforced homogeneity upon the population.

Czechoslovak leaders provided an example of this line of thought. Benes declared that: "Before we begin to define the rights of minorities we must define the *rights of majorities* and the obligations of minorities." [4] Minister of State Ripka held that: "The new international organization . . . must be based on the nation-State which is the expression and consequence of modern nationalism." [5] In a statement of policy before the Constituent National Assembly on 8 July 1946, Prime Minister Gottwald asserted: "The new Constitution will emphasize that the Republic is a national state of the Czechs and Slovaks." [6] Governmental leaders of Czechoslovakia contemplated the assimilation not only of the remnants of the irredentist and dangerously disloyal minorities, but also of the Jews who might remain in the state,[7] thus indicating that they were motivated by nationalist aspirations as well as by considerations of security.

Assimilationist sentiment naturally found a sympathetic reception in the United States. There were groups in this country which understood and supported the demands for corporate survival which were pressed by some minorities elsewhere, but America as a whole was proud of its "melting-pot" tradition, sure that ethnic masses could be "melted," unable to comprehend why such masses should desire to avoid being "melted," and inclined to assume that its method of solving the minority problem had universal validity.

Woodrow Wilson had said: "America does not consist of groups. A man who thinks of himself as belonging to a particular national group in America has not yet become an American." [8] American insistence on assimilation had rested in part on agreement with the thesis of John Stuart Mill, that "Free institutions are next to impossible in a country made up of different nationalities." With Mill, Americans had assumed that the operation of representative government and the formulation of a united public opinion were not feasible in a setting of national, cultural, and linguistic diversity.[9] Thus, it had been argued that statehood could not be extended to Hawaii until its various national and racial groups had been adequately Americanized.[10]

Considerations of national strength and security entered into American support for the principle of assimilation. Hitler's use of self-conscious German minorities abroad for subversive purposes occasioned some alarm. America's mistrust of its Japanese minority was expressed in the compulsory evacuation of that group from the vulnerable Pacific Coast area. There was a tendency to reason as follows: America has a right to be strong and safe; splinter groups may be elements of disunity and perhaps of disloyalty; therefore, if members of national minorities are to remain in the country, they ought to be fully Americanized.[11]

Finally, the American assimilationist tradition had been based on the conviction that assimilation was in the best interests of the minority concerned. There was an element of national arrogance in this view; those who come to our shores should be willing and anxious to relinquish their old national cultures in exchange for the better one which America has to offer. Why should anyone not wish to partake of the "American way of life"?

On a more rational level, and one more susceptible of generalization, it was argued during the war that people who are singled out by obvious nonconformity inevitably suffer ill-treatment in some degree. As minorities become assimilated, their "social visibility" is reduced, with a consequent decline in their liability to discrimination.[12] There were minorities and sections of minority groups which adopted this point of view. For instance, the Reformist Anti-Zionists among American Jews deplored any recognition of Jews as distinct groups, even in Eastern Europe, and favored the complete assimilation of Jews into the national communities in which they lived, with Jewry being treated as a religious sect only. In 1942, this group formed the American Council for Judaism, aiming "to combat nationalistic and secularistic trends in Jewish life." [13] Indeed, the minority problem in the United States consisted largely in .the reluctance of the national majority to permit the full assimilation of certain minority groups whose members were desirous of incorporating themselves in the American community.

We can only pause to point out that the ethnographic situation in the United States is virtually *sui generis*. The nature of the

American minority problem is largely determined by the fact that most minority groups in the United States originated as aggregations of immigrants, who voluntarily relinquished membership in the national states of their ethnic groups, and abandoned their cultural communities in order to seek for themselves and their descendants the values of membership in another national community. The problems implicit in that situation are not comparable to those arising in states where substantial portions of the autochthonous population insist on retaining the cultural and linguistic characteristics which differentiate them from their neighbors, refusing to concede that they should abandon valued national traditions in favor of cultural patterns which they regard as alien and inferior. This is not to say that the American method of assimilation cannot be applied elsewhere. It is to say that the setting of the American minority problem is unique in many respects, that the intrinsic difficulties of carrying out the assimilative process are greater in most other ethnographic situations, and that the solution of the world minority problem is not to be sought in a superficial imitation of American techniques. The essential point for our purposes is that the wartime consideration of the assimilative solution received a powerful impetus from the fact that that solution had been markedly successful in the United States and was in accord with American preconceptions.

The method of assimilation had a great deal of appeal in Great Britain, where there was a strong consciousness of the fact that the British nationality was the product of a long process of combining diverse ethnic strains. Viscount Cranborne, speaking in the House of Lords on 8 March 1944, indicated that whatever specific method might be used for the solution of the minority problem, the ultimate aim of policy must be the welding together of ethnic groups. The minorities "must try and merge themselves in the general population." The interest of the international community in the stabilization and pacification of political relationships is the focal point of attention here. As Viscount Cranborne put it, "A policy which by the very act of protecting minorities kept alive these problems, and even extended them to areas where they do not exist at present, would be a very poor thing indeed." [14]

Opposition to the concept of assimilation was raised in many quarters and on various grounds. In the first place, it was frequently considered illusory for minorities to hope that by acquiescing in assimilation they might escape discrimination and persecution. This argument was usually buttressed by a reference to the German Jews, who had largely cast off Jewishness in favor of genuine membership in the German national community, but had not thereby rendered themselves immune to Nazi persecution.[15] The irrationality of anti-Semitism was such that it might turn against assimilated Jews quite as readily as against Jews who insisted on maintaining their particularistic self-consciousness. Thus, the argument of futility was directed against the assimilative solution.

Secondly, it was contended that assimilation was inherently undesirable. The old liberal concept of the nation was introduced at this point. The nation has a right to exist. Reinhold Niebuhr declared that "a collective survival impulse is as legitimate a 'right' as an individual one. Justice, in history, is concerned with collective, as well as with individual, rights," and he condemned the liberal-democratic world because it is "implicitly making collective extinction the price of its provisional tolerance." [16] Even Benes, who was prepared to insist on the assimilation of vestigial national minorities in Czechoslovakia, proclaimed: "Nationhood — I emphasize it — nationhood, like personal freedom, is an absolute value." [17] The World Jewish Congress asserted the right of the Jewish nation to collective existence;[18] the American Jewish Committee, although it represented at most a very mild nationalism, nevertheless advocated the "freedom of groups to develop their own cultures and traditions." [19] Jewish criticism of the nationality policy of the Soviet Union concentrated on its assimilative aspects, which were regarded as violations of the right of Jewry to survive as a distinct nation.[20] Jewish nationalists were inclined to regard assimilation as a policy "completing spiritually what Hitler has not completed physically. . . ." [21]

The destruction of minority nationalities by assimilation was held by some to violate the interests of the individuals concerned. The national culture was treasured as a priceless heritage; deprived of it, the individual would become a sort of spiritual eunuch, culturally impoverished and incapable of normal human development.

The undesirability of assimilation was also posited on the basis of civilization's need for the distinctive contributions of every national group. Each nation has a unique tone to sound in the symphony of human culture; each nation is an indispensable and irreplaceable player in the orchestra of humanity. Some nations, notably the Jewish nation (so long as no Jewish state existed), would die if the policy of assimilation were carried out against all national minorities, and others would become disabled as contributors to human culture.

A third school of thought denied the feasibility of this solution, on the grounds that some national minorities were passionately determined not to be assimilated,[22] and that most previous attempts at compulsion had merely stimulated the national consciousness and reinforced the intractability of minority groups. Supporters of this argument could simply reiterate the verdict reached by Macartney in 1934 in considering the possible solutions of the minority problem: "forcible denationalization is not one of them." [23] They could add that no other method of assimilation gave greater promise of success, in view of the undiminished devotion of many groups to the ideal of collective survival.

Indeed, it is difficult to take the proposal of assimilation seriously as an immediate, short-run approach to a solution of the minority problem. Proposals of this nature were seldom accompanied by positive plans for implementation. Negatively, special linguistic, associational, and cultural rights might be denied to minority groups, and resort might be had even to heavy-handed methods of repression. Positively, members of national minorities might be pressed into an educational mold which would, superficially at least, make them conforming members of the majority community. However, the educational process is slow and uncertain, even in this era of mass media of communication. No wartime assimilationist provided evidence that his proposal represented an adequate means of dealing with immediately pressing minority problems.

As a long term solution, assimilation had greater relevance, even though its practicability, justice, and desirability might be challenged as we have indicated above. It was not unrealistic to expect that evolutionary social development might eventuate in the fusion of national groups living in close association with each other, and perhaps, ultimately, in the creation of a cosmopolitan culture and community consciousness. This process might be aided and accelerated by definite techniques and organizational mechanisms. In the final analysis, however, this millennial solution demanded not a mere mechanistic adjustment of human relationships, but a fundamental moral transformation of both majorities and minorities, involving the development and implementation of a freely accepted agreement to integrate members of minorities fully into the national communities of the majorities among whom they lived.

CULTURAL PLURALISM

It is essential to establish the fact that the concept of cultural pluralism offers a distinctive approach to the solution of minority problems. Neither the rejection of assimilation, nor the advocacy of guaranteed individual or group rights, is equivalent to the endorsement of cultural pluralism. In examining the wartime assertions of the pluralist thesis, we shall find that, consciously or not, proponents of cultural pluralism are advocating a revision of political concepts which goes far beyond that implicit in the mere demand that minorities be protected against discriminatory treatment or granted rights designed to facilitate group survival and development.

In the first place, cultural pluralism requires the elimination of the concept of the national state, and with it, the concepts of national majorities and minorities. The state is a political organization of a group of human beings, without concern for their ethnic distinctions; it is not the embodiment or the instrument of a particular nation. This concept involves the rejection of the view that a national majority constitutes the state-forming and state-possessing core of a body politic, while members of national minorities are quasi-aliens, in but not of the state.

The inadequacy of the national state idea, in application to areas of extreme ethnic heterogeneity at least, has long been obvious to many thinkers. Lord Acton inveighed against the principle of nationality, on the ground that it was destructive of the rights of national minorities, the security of the values of freedom and liberalism, and the vitality and progressiveness of the state.[24] A. E. Zimmern argued that the theory of the national state did not correspond to the realities and needs of Europe, and predicted that it would "go the way of Henry VIII's and Luther's theory of a National Church." [25] Writing in 1934, Macartney despaired of solving the minority problem within the national state framework, and declared: "The troubles of our day arise out of the modern conception of the national state: out of the identification of the political ideals of all the inhabitants of the state with the national-cultural ideals of the majority in it." [26]

Many thinkers who concerned themselves with the minority problem during the Second World War came to agree with Macartney's conclusion: national states and national minorities are incompatible; it is unlikely that national minorities can be adequately protected within national states; it is unlikely that minorities will become reconciled even to a securely protected minority status so long as the philosophy of the national state dominates political thought and is partially realized in the political organization of the world; therefore, the concept of the national state must be abandoned, before an approach can be made to the solution of the nationality problems of the modern world.[27]

Correlative to the requirement that the concept of the national state be abandoned is the assumption of the cultural pluralist that there can and must be a clear and definite separation between nation and state, between nationality and politics. Nationality must be restricted to the cultural sphere; it must not have, and must not be thought to have, any political implications. It must be de-politicized, disestablished, made irrelevant so far as affairs of state are concerned; membership in a particular national group must be as immaterial, politically, as membership in a particular church ideally is in the United States. Nationalism must be "cultural in content and ethical in expression." [28] National loyalties must play their role in the cultural sphere, remaining subsidiary to and compatible with a larger community of political allegiance. This theme, the de-politicization of nationalism, appeared frequently in wartime thought.[29]

The divorce between nationality and politics imposes requirements upon the state as well as upon national groups within the state. If the scope of national activity is to exclude political affairs, then the scope of state activity must exclude cultural affairs. Cultural pluralism assumes a dichotomy of human affairs; just as the nation serves as an instrument of cultural life, and must accept de-politicization, so the state serves as a mechanism of political and economic control, and must accept de-culturization. The state must not attempt to force its citizens into a standard mold, nor should it infringe upon the cultural autonomy of any national group. Its goal must be not the elimination of differences, nor even the toleration of diversity, but "the reception of the differences into the unity of the whole society." [30]

Out of the ferment of wartime thought with regard to the minority question, there came a number of concrete plans, elaborated in more or less detail, for the realization of the concept of cultural pluralism. One of the most carefully developed schemes was that presented by Oscar Janowsky,[31] who proposed the organization in Eastern and Central Europe of one or more regional federations of multinational states, within the framework of a general international organization. The attempt to solve the nationality problem on the basis of cultural pluralism would be carried out on the level of the multinational state, which would consist not of a state-possessing national majority and tolerated national minorities, but of many national groups, each of which would be an equal partner in the state, organically incorporated in the multinational structure, and administering the cultural affairs of its members through its own autonomous agency. A precautionary international guarantee of the rights and status of national groups would be superimposed upon this structure, but the main reliance would be upon the multinational, or national federative, aspects of the basic state organization.

The Anti-Fascist Council of National Liberation of Yugoslavia announced, on 29 November 1943, its decision to reconstitute the Yugoslav state as a federative organization assuring the full equality of the constituent national groups.[32] The plan put forward for Yugoslavia was an adaptation of the Soviet nationality regime, which theoretically accords to national groups an autonomy of limited substantive content within the framework of a multinational, or unnational, state.

Projects for the solution of the nationality problems of that region of extreme ethnic complexity, Eastern and Central Europe, along the basic lines of the Janowsky plan were produced by a number of wartime thinkers.[33] Similarly, the *Ihud* group of Palestinian Jews proposed the erection of a bi-national state in Palestine.[34]

A variant of the usual type of cultural pluralist doctrine, the Bauer-Renner plan, received some attention during the war. This plan, developed by the Austrian Social Democrats Otto Bauer and Karl Renner shortly before the First World War, envisaged the formation of national groups on the basis of the personality principle, as distinguished from the territorial principle; these organized groups would administer the cultural affairs and look after the peculiarly national interests of their members, operating autonomously in their nonterritorial, functional spheres of competence, within the framework of a multinational state which would superimpose political and economic unity upon the constitutionally established pluralism of national-cultural entities.[35] The application of this version of cultural pluralism to Eastern and Central Europe had some appeal to theorists, in view of the obvious difficulties of realizing the national state ideal in that region, or even of establishing a regime of local autonomy for minorities so dispersed as were the various peoples of that area.[36]

Wartime drafters of blueprints for the institutional implementation of the cultural pluralist ideal exhibited a great deal of vagueness and confusion. Their writings revealed a rather desperate search for examples of states which had succeeded in achieving a pluralist solution; the accolade was given at one time or another to the Soviet Union, the United States, the United Kingdom, Canada, South Africa, Switzerland, and Belgium. This rather indiscriminate citing of examples seemed to indicate not so much an open mind concerning methods of establishing pluralist systems as a basic confusion about the meaning and import of the principle of cultural pluralism. In wartime thought, the principle became vague and ambiguous; it came to mean little more than the establishment, by almost any means, of reasonably stable and pacific relationships between diverse peoples inhabiting the same country.

The problem of establishing cultural pluralism is not, in essence, the legal and organizational problem of securing the acceptance of constitutionally or internationally binding provisions and the contrivance of mechanisms of administration and enforcement. It is rather a problem of effecting a profound moral change in human beings. Some wartime thinkers showed awareness of the essential nature of this problem, by stressing the need for a spiritual transformation of majorities and minorities, involving the growth of mutual tolerance and the rediscovery of common ethical principles by conflicting national groups.[37]

Legal and mechanical devices are not irrelevant. They may be instrumental in bringing about the necessary moral changes. But the minority problem is not solved by labelling a heterogeneous political unit a "multinational state" and declaring that minority groups have now been allotted the status of "equal partners" in a structure established on the basis of "national federalism." Wartime cultural pluralists had a tendency to treat as a terminological and mechanical problem, a problem which really involves the difficult task of persuading majorities to accept members of minorities as full members of the political community, while respecting their right to maintain and foster their ethnic and cultural traditions, and persuading minorities to give full allegiance to the states of which they are members, restricting their activities as ethnic groups to the pursuit of cultural values compatible with political loyalty to a non-national state. There is no difficulty in establishing multinational states. The difficulty lies in the establishment of multinational states whose citizens are conceptually and spiritually prepared to abandon the desire for a national state and to combine a pluralism of ethnic and cultural loyalties with a unity of political allegiance.

The cultural pluralist variety of wartime thought offered no short-run solution of the minority problem. Its concepts, terminology, and machinery might be adopted at the end of the war, but the problem of alleviating the tensions of majority-minority relationships would remain.

In the long run, this solution had much to recommend it. It was not necessarily impracticable. Men of different religions had learned to live together peacefully, belying the old notion that political unity was impossible in the presence of religious diversity. Just as the principle, *cuius regio eius religio*, had been supplanted by religious freedom, so the principle, *cuius regio eius natio*, might give way to the principle of ethnic-cultural freedom.[38] The history of the slow and tortuous development of religious freedom might throw some light on the problems and requirements which would have to be met in the development of national freedom.

Assuming its ultimate feasibility, the desirability of a system of cultural diversity within a framework of political and economic unity can hardly be contested. Such a system would be compatible with the existence of a healthful variety conducive to the enrichment of human civilization. It would not preclude the blending of national cultures, but would provide the noncompulsive circumstances most propitious for that sort of development. The realization of that ideal, however, lies far in the future. Wartime cultural pluralists erred by neglecting to formulate immediately practical approaches to the minority problem, in their zeal to secure the formal establishment of the concepts and mechanisms of a system which could become effective only as a result of the gradual operation of a process of moral transformation of human beings.

CHAPTER 8:   *SOLUTION BY PHYSICAL ELIMINA-*
TION OF MINORITIES: FRONTIER
REVISION, TRANSFER, AND ZIONISM

The third general type of solution for the minority problem which found a place in plans and proposals formulated during the Second World War may be characterized as the method of the physical elimination of national minorities from national states. More accurately, this is a method, not of *solving* the minority problem, but of *eradicating* that problem by the alteration of the ethnographic conditions which give rise to it. This concept, in itself, does not contemplate the utilization of international legal provisions and organizational devices to make the position of national minorities tenable; it does not envisage the moral transformation of majorities and minorities in order to harmonize their relations, on the basis either of assimilation or of cultural pluralism; rather, it relies on the more drastic solution of discontinuing the coexistence of diverse national groups within the same states. However, it is not necessarily an exclusivistic method. It may be, and has been, suggested as a supplement to other methods, and its limited use has been envisioned as an indispensable prerequisite to the successful operation of other types of solution.

In common with the assimilationist approach, the method of physical elimination assumes the desirability, or the probability or inevitability, of the continuation of the national state as the "normal" unit of human political organization. These two methods differ as to the technique of eradicating minorities, but they both assume the necessity of carrying out that operation, so as to arrive at a system of ethnically homogeneous national states. Thus, both imply an endorsement, motivated either by philosophical preference or by a sense of practical necessity, of the principle of nationality – of the nineteenth century slogan, *"Jede Nation soll einen Staat bilden: Jeder Staat soll nur eine Nation umfassen."* [1]

FRONTIER REVISION

The idea of manipulating boundaries so as to unite within a given state *all* parts of a particular nation and *no* segments of any other nation, thus achieving the ideal application of the principle of nationality, occupied a minor place in wartime thought.

Leading statesmen of the United Nations made pronouncements which they regarded as endorsements of the principle of national self-determination,[2] and their frequent statements upholding the principle of national freedom could be construed as indications, however vague, of support for the idea of changing frontiers in order to incorporate peoples in states appropriate to their national feeling.

However, there were obvious political limits to the applicability of the method of frontier revision. The wartime thinking with which we are concerned here postulated the military victory of the United Nations. It was doubtful whether victorious states would consent to cede territory to their allies. It was completely unrealistic to suppose that they would reward their prostrate attackers by granting them a favorable revision of boundaries. Furthermore, the general political mood of the great powers was not such as to encourage the hope that they would automatically support territorial adjustments proposed merely on the basis of the principle of nationality.

It was clear that economic and strategic factors would enter prominently into the determination of postwar boundaries. Calculated concern for world stability and the economic and military interests of national states made hard-headed statesmen unwilling to contemplate the full application of the principle of national self-determination. Moreover, the moral sanctity of the principle was challenged; it was generally regarded as merely one principle among many which ought to be considered. The fundamental moral desirability of the homogeneous national state was no longer universally accepted as a dogma of liberalism.

Finally, the inherent inadequacy of the method of frontier revision was fully recognized. Statesmen and publicists had become aware of the complexity of the ethnographic picture, not only in Eastern and Central Europe, but in many other areas as well. It was obvious that no conceivable shifting of boundaries could make all states ethnically homogeneous.

These limitations combined to minimize the significance of frontier revision in wartime conceptions of a general solution of the minority problem. In regard to specific areas, demands for territorial adjustment were prominent, or even dominant, elements in proposals for solution; there was general agreement that frontier revision might play a useful, but necessarily limited, role in a larger program.

THE TRANSFER OF POPULATIONS

The idea of the transfer of populations was the dominant element in wartime thought regarding approaches to a solution of the minority problem. It was highly controversial, and was opposed by some as strenuously as it was espoused by others. Yet, an analysis of the various strands of thought and opinion leads us to the conclusion that the principle of transfer was definitely in the ascendant.

There were many evident variations among the supporters of

this method. Some supported it enthusiastically and unreservedly; others saw it regretfully as a last resort, and accepted it with misgivings. Some seemed to regard it as a principle of universal applicability; others would limit its application to a few minority groups. Some considered transfer the complete and exclusive solution; others favored its use in combination with other methods. Motivations varied widely, as we shall point out subsequently. But the idea of transfer — in some form, and to some extent — assumed far greater importance during the Second World War than ever before.

The concept of the exchange of minority populations as a modern idea was first put forward by Turkey in 1913,[3] and the post–World War I conventions between Greece and Bulgaria and Greece and Turkey, which "confirmed or caused the uprooting of over two million people," [4] provided the major precedents for the implementation of that idea. Both supporters and opponents of transfer relied heavily upon arguments derived from those experiments.

The most recent examples of physical removal and resettlement of minorities were provided largely by Nazi Germany.[5] Hitler's attitude toward transfer was markedly inconsistent. In a speech to the *Reichstag* on 6 October 1939, he declared his intention of securing the resettlement of German splinter groups from various European countries, so as to establish "a new order of ethnographical conditions." [6] This aim was fully consistent with the standing demand of the Nazi Party for "the union of all Germans to form a Great Germany on the basis of the right of self-determination of nations," [7] and with the concept of the race-nation which would be a mutilated organism so long as some of its blood-members remained detached from it. However, it violated the concept of *Lebensraum* and implied abandonment of the claim that all land ever held historically by Germans must of right come under German political control; it would appear that Hitler reluctantly evacuated the Germans from some European outposts as a concession to the demands of his allies. His policy was determined by the exigencies of the moment, on the basis of calculation as to where and how German minorities might be most useful to the Nazi cause. At any rate, Hitler conducted a large-scale transfer of German minorities to their ethnic Fatherland during the early years of the war, and also intervened in Central Europe to promote the partial unscrambling of Rumanians, Hungarians, and Bulgarians.[8]

Hitler's transfers perhaps stimulated interest in that method of solving minority problems, although they also made it liable to stigmatization as a "Nazi method," too close for comfort to Hitler's ultimate device of sheer physical extermination. Moreover, the evacuation of substantial numbers of minority peoples under Nazi sponsorship reduced the size of the task which might be faced by a postwar Europe bent on eradicating heterogeneity within states, thereby making that task appear more feasible.

There were many wartime expressions, from unofficial sources, of tentative or limited support for the policy of transferring minorities to states dominated by their ethnic kinsmen. A number of students of the minority problem, including some whose general position was unfavorable to the concept of achieving national homogeneity by this means, suggested the transfer of selected groups: peoples who had been most consistently abused by host states, co-nationals of Axis states, demonstrably troublesome and perfidious groups, or minorities concentrated along the frontiers of their kin-states.[9]

Another version of limited support for the transfer principle was the approval of the *voluntary* migration of peoples. In modern times, it has become virtually standard procedure in international treaties involving the cession of territory to grant to affected individuals the right to opt for retention of their former citizenship at the price of moving to the newly defined territory of their old state. However, the increasingly restrictive regulation of migration by modern governments has tended to prevent the operation of the principle of voluntary transfer except when it has a basis in specific international arrangements. Proposals for the facilitation of optional transfer of minorities were acceptable to the great majority of students of the problem.

Indeed, the concept of transfer in wartime thought was somewhat clouded by a general failure to apprehend the vital distinction between *optional* and *compulsory* transfer. The former has an appeal because it does not involve resort to ruthless measures of eviction so easily castigated as violations of elementary human rights but it has the disadvantage of ineffectiveness; "experience has shown that a voluntary exchange simply does not take place, except under conditions which amount, in reality, to compulsion." [10] Compulsory transfer, on the other hand, can be an effective remedy, actually eliminating minorities, but it has to face the charges of inhumanitarianism.

Some postwar planners tried to have the best of both worlds. A prime example is Sumner Welles, who, in preaching the positive advantages of transfer, implicitly assumed the thorough-going elimination of minorities which could be achieved only through compulsion,[11] but who, in defending transfer against the charge that it violated human rights, deftly shifted his ground and intimated that it was a system of voluntary movement which he was advocating.[12] Those who envisaged transfer as a radical solution, a surgical operation, could not validly describe their proposals in voluntaristic terms. Those who were unwilling to contemplate the compulsory expulsion of minorities were not entitled to pretend that they were advocating a policy which would produce the results that might be expected from, and held to justify, a policy of obligatory migration.

There was a considerable body of unofficial wartime thought which supported the transfer principle without apparent reserve or limitation, looking to compulsory transfer for a general solution of the minority problem. Sumner Welles regarded the League minority system as a mistake, declaring: "The minority problem could have been corrected only by courageous and radical steps providing for the orderly transfer of populations." [13] He felt that the minority problem could be solved only by the method of physical elimination, and he proposed specific transfers not only in Europe, but also in India, if the partition of the subcontinent should become a reality.[14] L. B. Namier, among others, believed that "Transfers of population carried through in a sensible manner will have to form the basis of future arrangements." [15]

The pronouncements of President Benes and other official leaders of Czechoslovakia constitute one of the most interesting and significant chapters in expulsionist thought during the war. Benes, the old liberal, exhibited a great deal of wavering and ambiguity, making it rather difficult for the observer to believe that his sense of political morality ever became fully reconciled to the implications of the doctrine which his sense of political realism impelled him to preach. He alternately declared in categorical terms his resolve to carry out large-scale expulsions of minorities from Czechoslovakia, and embraced the principle of transfer diffidently and tentatively.[16]

Despite these vacillations, it appears that Benes was firmly, albeit reluctantly, devoted to the principle of transfer; the only real question was the degree of thoroughness with which it would be applied to the minorities of Czechoslovakia. Benes was torn between the passionate conviction that Czechoslovakia could survive only as an ethnically homogeneous state,[17] and the equally compelling moral scruple against indiscriminate penalization of loyal and disloyal members of minority groups. By stipulating that members of national minorities who had proved their loyalty to the state would be permitted to remain but that they would be required to submit to assimilation,[18] he sought to safeguard the principle of justice to individuals while adhering to the ideal of the eventual elimination of national minorities.

The same ambiguity as to the thoroughness of the contemplated expulsive process appeared in the statements of other members of the Czechoslovak government in exile.[19] Nevertheless, the general intent was clear: Czechoslovakia would become a national state of Czechs and Slovaks, without national minorities; this ethnic homogeneity would be achieved primarily by the expulsion of minorities; the process would be completed by compulsory assimilation of the few individual members of minorities who would be permitted to remain.

A plan for postwar Poland, drafted by underground leaders and submitted to the Polish National Council in London, envisaged the evacuation of all Germans from that country, except those who had clearly demonstrated their loyalty to the state.[20] On 5 February 1945, the Provisional Government of Poland declared its conviction that the German minority must be ousted.[21]

In general, the governmental leaders of the major Allied powers encouraged the Czechoslovaks and Poles to believe that their expulsionist plans would be approved.[22] Prime Minister Churchill told the House of Commons, on 15 December 1944, that contemplated revisions of Poland's boundaries would involve the shifting of several millions of people, and added:

> . . . expulsion is the method which, so far as we have been able to see, will be the most satisfactory and lasting. There will be no mixture of populations to cause endless trouble. . . . A clean sweep will be made. I am not alarmed by these large transferences, which are more possible in modern conditions than they ever were before.[23]

British parliamentary debates revealed considerable support among leading political figures for the general concept of expulsion of minorities.[24] The planning agencies of the United States Government exhibited great interest in the possibilities of that method of dealing with the minority problem,[25] although they clearly regarded transfer as strong medicine, to be administered only to selected patients and under the supervision of a physician.[26]

The Case for Transfer. The case for transfer was based on a variety of arguments, reflecting the different value considerations which were uppermost in the minds of its various proponents.

Public and private spokesmen for states which had suffered at the hands of treasonable minorities, or which had been assaulted by other states on the ground that their co-nationals required external protection, were led by concern for the welfare and security of the state to demand mass expulsion. Despite some attempts to avoid undue generalization, they tended to accept the sweeping propositions that all heterogeneous elements were potentially subversive, and that maximum security could be obtained only by sweeping the state clean of minority peoples.

The case for state security merged, almost imperceptibly, with the case for realization of the national aspirations of the majority people. The ideal of the complete identification of nation and state was not dead. Ethnic homogeneity frequently appeared as a value in itself; the majority nation had the moral right to a state which would not be cluttered up with "alien" groups.

Considerations of the interests of the minority groups themselves formed the basis of another school of evacuationist
thought. Transfer was put forward as a preventive device.
Minorities living as "guests" in the national states of other
peoples would probably, perhaps inevitably, always suffer persecution in some form and to some degree, and would be
vulnerable to sudden, violent campaigns of oppression and extermination. Therefore, it was in their best interest to move. The
discomfiture and loss incident to transfer would be negligible,
compared with the suffering and insecurity which might otherwise be their lot.

The ethnic interests of expellees and the states which would
receive them were sometimes stressed by supporters of transfer.
Minorities in an "alien" state faced the prospect of assimilation,
either by artificial imposition or by a natural evolutionary
process. The viability of national cultures would be enhanced
by the reunion of the scattered parts of nations into integrated
communities. This argument took at face value — though sometimes with tongue in cheek — the insistent demands for national
integration which had been put forward before the war by
certain irredentist minorities and their revisionist co-national
states. Some advocates of transfer made, or pretended to make,
the assumption that national minorities and their parent nations
placed the value of living together and fostering the development of their ethnic cultures above all other considerations; this
assumption was seldom valid, as was evidenced by the widespread opposition to transfer which was raised by both minorities
and potential receiving states.

Actually, the transfer of minorities was, in many cases, conceived as a means of punishing aggressive states and their accomplices in other countries. This motivation was most evident
in proposals for expelling German minorities; if transfer involved suffering, that could only be considered just retribution
for the sins of the Third Reich and the *Auslandsdeutsche*.

A major basis of support for the principle of transfer was the
contention that this radical, definitive, and foolproof solution
of the nationality question was necessary in the interest of the
international community. The method might have its disadvantages and its secondary injustices, but it would conduce to

the greatest good of the greatest number, in the long run, by eliminating one of the important causes of war. A world of nationally homogeneous states would not be troubled by real and alleged persecution of national minorities, upheavals engendered by dissident ethnic groups within states, or interventionist adventures launched on the pretext of protecting the interests of co-national fragments. Thus, a significant source of international friction would be eliminated. The Greco-Turkish precedent was frequently cited to prove that beneficial effects on interstate relations might be anticipated from a general disentanglement of populations.

The minority problem was clearly one which involved the interests of states containing minorities, of national minorities, of co-national states, and of the international community. The principle of transfer affected the interests of these various parties. It might be called into play by the decision of minority states, thus assuming the character of unilateral expulsion. It might take the form of a reciprocal exchange of minorities, arranged by bilateral agreement. Finally, the operation of the transfer principle might be authorized by an international decision, and carried out under the direction and with the assistance of an agency of the international community. The choice of method of authorization and implementation was evidently a significant factor, and aside from occasional expressions of absolute determination to be rid of minorities which emanated from such countries as Poland and Czechoslovakia, the bulk of the support which the transfer principle enjoyed was contingent upon the utilization of the bilateral or multilateral methods of approach. By and large, the transfer of populations was envisaged as an international task, which could be carried out with a maximum of efficiency and a minimum of suffering and inhumanity only under the auspices of an international organization.

The Case Against Transfer. Opponents of the principle of transfer marshalled an imposing array of arguments against that method of dealing with the problem of national minorities.

In the eyes of one who was completely committed to another type of solution, the transfer of minority populations was unnecessary, and the mere proposal was undesirable, since it implied the repudiation of the particular method which was held to give promise of a satisfactory solution. However, not all champions of other methods were categorically opposed to transfer; many of them accepted the necessity of its limited application to prepare the way for the successful operation of their proposals.

There was a tendency in some quarters to disparage the idea of transfer, on the ground that its realization was impossible. It was difficult to avoid that conclusion, if one perceived the vast entanglement of racial, religious, linguistic, and ethnic groups throughout the world; it might be held that, for better or for worse, the eggs were scrambled and must remain so. The argument of impossibility was raised by men who were considering even limited segments of the problem. Stefan Osusky asserted that "broadly speaking, the map of Europe cannot be ethnographically remade." [27] Maritain limited his ground even more, arguing rather circuitously that the removal of all Jews from Eastern and Central Europe was "absolutely out of the question because it is impossible." [28]

These conclusions of Osusky and Maritain appear untenable. It may be undesirable, and it may involve serious difficulties, to separate the various nationalities of Europe, but it hardly seems realistic to assume the utter physical impossibility of that project.

Moreover, transfer is not necessarily an "all or nothing" doctrine. The case for transfer as a means of coping with problems arising out of ethnic heterogeneity is not undermined by the observation that its global application is infeasible.

The humanitarian objection to transfer possessed the initial advantage that the compulsory movement of populations was associated in the popular mind with the ruthless activities of the Nazis. Much of the opposition centered around the contention that the uprooting of human groups was a barbarous procedure, inevitably accompanied by a vast amount of suffering. The Greco-Bulgarian and Greco-Turkish transfers after the First World War, despite their relative smallness in comparison with the transfers projected for the post–World War II period, and despite the degree of international supervision which had been involved, had nevertheless produced "a great toll of human tragedy." [29] Humanitarians adverted to the physical discomfort and hunger which would be difficult to avoid in any mass migration, the economic loss and maladjustment which would be experienced by expellees even in a well planned and well executed transfer, and the moral and psychological shock which would be involved in the transplantation of peoples deeply rooted in the land and social milieu of one country to the new environment of a strange land and a perhaps inhospitable society.

Mass expulsions had been listed in 1942 as one of the war crimes for which the Nazi leaders would be punished by a morally indignant world.[30] In the years that followed, however, public opinion in the allied countries became somewhat inured to the fact of colossal human tragedy. As Winston Churchill put it: "We are, of course, cauterised by all that we ourselves have passed through. Our faculty for wonder is ruptured, our faculty for horror is numbed. . . . [Perhaps we have lost] the physical and psychic strength to react against these shocking tidings." [31]

Opponents of transfer attempted the task of stirring the conscience of the peoples of the United Nations into revolt against the allegedly brutal concept of transfer. Their task was made difficult by two factors: first, the strength of the argument that in the long run, the total of human suffering would be greater if minorities were not evacuated than if they were subjected to the temporary distress incident to transfer; second, the growing insensitivity to human pain, which was particularly prominent in this case because of the fact that many of the minority peoples who would be affected were co-nationals of, and to some degree collaborators of, the Axis states.

The practical difficulties of carrying out the wholesale resettlement of national minorities, especially in the anticipated chaos of postwar Europe, received great emphasis. Europe would have more refugees and displaced persons than it could properly care for, without the addition of millions of transferees. The European economy would be seriously deranged; why complicate the problem of rehabilitation by adding the economic maladjustments incident to mass transfer? Europe's shattered transport system might be hopelessly overburdened by a large-scale shift of national minorities. This line of argument led to the conclusion that it would be economically ruinous to attempt wholesale transfers in Europe at the close of the war, and that such transfers, if instituted, could not possibly be carried out within an humanitarian framework, because of the economic problems involved.

It was evident that the disentanglement of peoples, to be permanently effective, would have to be followed up by the imposition of stringent controls on migration, to *keep* peoples disentangled. The world would be divided up into water-tight compartments; the international mobility of labor would be completely precluded. The political ideal of national homogeneity could be achieved only at the cost of initial economic dislocations of a serious nature, and of long-run economic catastrophe, produced by the rigidity of ethnic barriers to the flow of population from areas of labor surplus to areas of labor scarcity. Barriers to migration were already formidable; the development of a sound world economy required a trend toward freedom of movement in response to economic stimuli, not toward perpetual segregation of ethnic groups.[32]

Another phase of the case against transfer consisted in the consideration of the rights of national minorities. It was frequently suggested that the human individual has an inherent right to live where he is born; no political authority has the moral right to declare a certain portion of the earth the exclusive preserve of a particular nation, and to expel therefrom members of the autochthonous population who exhibit the characteristics of other ethnic groups. Sumner Welles, a strong advocate of the *policy* of transfer, seemed to undermine the moral foundations of that *principle* when he wrote: "To every believer in the moral values for which the United States has fought, the right of every individual to live safely, without fear and without discrimination, in the land of his birth must be safeguarded as one of the essential foundations upon which a free world can be constructed." [33] This right was most often cited in reference to Jews, probably because there was then no Jewish national state to which they might be consigned; if they had no right to live in their native lands, their right to live anywhere might be negated, at least in theory.

The fallacy of the argument that the transfer of national minorities was a process of "repatriation," involving the return of peoples to "their own natural territory," [34] was easily exposed. The minority problem was not a matter of dealing with alien invaders; it involved ethnic groups which, in many cases, had been rooted in particular areas for centuries, and individuals who were generally entitled to claim their countries of residence as "homeland," equally with members of national majorities. As one writer put it, the expulsion of the Germans from the Sudetenland would be "not the expulsion of a horde of intruders but the destruction of an ancient and respectable element of Bohemian civilization." [35] The assumption that an indigenous peasant of Eastern Europe, whose ancestors had lived in the same village for generations, "belonged" in Germany simply because of his name, language, or other ethnic factors, implied a conception of extreme national determinism. It imputed to the nation an organic character completely inconsistent with individualism, and elevated to the status of an eternal law of nature, the modern and arbitrary notion that "Germans" or "Hungarians" — objectively determined by officials, without consideration of subjective factors — ought to live within the area which is at any given time designated as "Germany" or "Hungary." Thus, the concept of transfer violated both the right of the individual to live in the land of his birth, and his right to subjective determination of nationality.

In so far as transfer, in theory or in practice, involved the indiscriminate ousting of members of national minorities, operating as a punitive measure against loyal as well as disloyal citizens, it was subject to criticism as a violation of the basic right of the individual to be judged on his own merits, and not to be condemned by association.

The basic philosophical objection to the concept of transfer arose out of the repudiation of the national state ideal. It was held that transfer reflected defeatism, a profound pessimism concerning the ability of mankind to work out a means for the peaceful coexistence of different peoples.[36] The quest for ethnic homogeneity implied capitulation to a nationalist philosophy which denied the essential unity of humanity, a philosophy in which the nation, a concept tending to take on racialistic connotations, was ranked as a supreme and eternal value, and in which the individual was degraded to an appurtenance of the nation to which he was supposed to belong. The desire for ethnic uniformity within the state was condemned as a primitive urge, logically implying the stamping out of all diversity, and thus leading to totalitarian government and stagnant, tribalistic culture.[37] Internationally, the transfer philosophy, with its drastic insistence on the rigidification of national lines of division, loomed as an obstacle to the realization of forward-looking plans for evolving political and economic unity and ultimate world government; it was described as a "defiant gesture of uncompromising political nationalism," which "implies that any solution which points beyond the national State is impossible." [38]

The wartime case against transfer, composed as it was of a variety of arguments resting on different premises, cannot be evaluated as a whole. Some of the arguments were relevant only in certain contingencies; they were applicable to unilateral, or indiscriminately vengeful, or poorly organized transfers, but not necessarily to movements of population carried out under international authorization and supervision, with adequate safeguards for guaranteeing justice to individuals and minimizing attendant suffering. Some of the objections were valid only if transfer were treated as an exclusive solution of the minority problem, to be applied immediately after the war on a global scale. Finally, there were objections in principle, directed not at abuses or unwise applications of the policy of transfer, but at the underlying philosophical assumptions of the case for the uprooting and resettlement of minorities.

The difficulty and complexity of the task of transfer were not exaggerated. Emphasis on the limits of physical and economic feasibility was a useful counterweight to unrealistic projects. Insistence on the importance of humanitarian considerations was essential to counter the passion of outraged majorities and the cynicism of those who applied the analogy of a surgical operation to a process which involved the excision not of passive tissue, devoid of consciousness, but of human beings possessed of mind and will and whatever rights and dignity we may be able to claim for the individual in modern society.

The philosophical case against transfer was based on high

moral values and profound insight into the inadequacy of the national state idea for the modern world. It correctly character-ized the concept of transfer as a reactionary doctrine inconsistent with the ideal of building a new world on the basis of a trans-cendent unity enveloping but not attempting to obliterate di-versity. However, the world was apparently not ready for this ideal, and its advocates found themselves prophets crying in the wilderness, while statesmen prepared to re-establish a system in which the national state idea should be dominant, albeit im-perfectly realized and somewhat restricted by an overriding principle of international law and organization.

ZIONISM

The Zionist approach to the solution of the problem of Jewish minorities is a specialized version of the concept of solution by physical elimination of minorities. Zionism has two assumptions in common with the methods of frontier revision and transfer: the assumption of the continuance of the national state system, and the assumption that the basic element in a solution of the minority problem must be the removal of minorities from the national states of other ethnic groups.

Zionism has distinguishing characteristics which justify its separate treatment: it is concerned with the problems of only one people, the Jews; it aims at the establishment of a new national state; and it is a movement for transfer initiated by the minority concerned.

The concept of a Jewish state in Palestine occupied a pre-dominant place in Jewish thought during the Second World War. There were dissenters, who hoped for a solution of the Jewish problem which would not involve the migration of Jews from their countries of residence and citizenship. Zionism was seldom put forward as a complete solution of the Jewish problem, justifying indifference toward other proposals, for it did not contemplate the concentration of *all* Jews in the pro-jected Jewish national state. Nevertheless, the outstanding char-acteristic of Jewish wartime thought was the conviction that the establishment of a Jewish state was the *sine qua non* of a suc-cessful attack on the problems of Jewry; it was the indispensable foundation of a solution.

Zionism was not a new doctrine, but the strength of its appeal to Jews and non-Jews alike was immensely increased by the Nazi campaign of persecution and murder to which European Jewry was subjected. This catastrophic phenomenon provided the impetus for the movement on the part of Jews to abandon Europe, relinquishing the hope that any means could be found for making their minority position tenable. It produced widespread sympathy for the notion that a Jewish national state should be established, and furnished dramatic evidence of the urgency of that project.

The demand for a Jewish state was motivated, in the first place, by the humanitarian purpose of providing a refuge for Jews who might find it impossible, or deem it unwise from a rational point of view or unthinkable from an emotional standpoint, to return to their homes after the war. A Jewish state would accord those refugees from persecution a welcome which could not be expected elsewhere and an assurance that they would never again suffer the indignity and insecurity which had been their unhappy lot as "guests" in the national states of other peoples. To give them a state of their own, in the traditional homeland of their people, would provide a psychological compensation, making their flight seem less like expulsion and more like liberation.[39]

The humanitarian purpose shaded over into a nationalistic purpose. The man who felt himself to be a member of a Jewish nation need no longer suffer abuse or discrimination because of his Jewishness, nor need he be subjected to either subtle or crudely compulsive methods of assimilation. The abnormality, the spiritual and cultural anomaly, the moral humiliation of his permanent minority status could be ended; by migrating to the Jewish state in Palestine, the Jew who treasured his ethnic heritage could achieve a deep spiritual gain as well as mere physical relief and security, for now his status would be normalized and he could be a Jew, fully, proudly, and confidently.[40]

Zionist proposals were concerned not only with the individual interests of Jews who were actual or potential victims of oppression, but also with a set of impersonal values — the values of the Jewish nation. Quite aside from the humanitarian urge to save the lives of Jews, there was a nationalistic urge to ensure the survival and foster the development of Jewry as an ethnic entity.

It was true that many Jews denied the reality of a Jewish nation and favored the complete incorporation of Jews in other national communities, with the retention of no other differentiating characteristics than those incident to membership in a distinctive religious sect. However, Jewish nationalism was strengthened by oppression, and the appeal of assimilation to individual Jews was lessened by the demonstration that it did not necessarily provide immunity to the brutal attacks of anti-Semites. Community of fear and suffering produced new bonds of unity among Jews — bonds which came to be regarded more and more explicitly as national ties. Jewish nationalism was articulated during the Second World War as never before, and it played a major role in the campaign for a Jewish state.

The existence of a Jewish nation was proclaimed: "We are a separate nationality; one nation in diversity, one people in the diaspora; one ethnic, cultural and national entity. . . ." Jewry is a nation because its members have "the will to live as a people." [41] A nation transcends its individual members, and possesses values of its own; a nation has a right to survive and develop. These national rights cannot be realized by a people in diaspora, broken down into a myriad of minority groups; majority status somewhere, the possession of a national home, the erection of a state to serve as an instrument of the nation — these are absolute requirements for collective survival and development, and they are therefore the rights of the nation.[42] Jews might survive without a Jewish state, but the Jewish nation could not. This line of thought indicated that concern for the interests of that collective entity was one of the major factors motivating the demand for a Jewish state in Palestine.

Jewish nationalistic thought exhibited many of the characteristics of the classical brand of liberal nationalism. There was a harmony of interests between the Jewish nation and the international community. The flowering of its distinctive culture within the framework of its own state would enable the Jewish nation to make its indispensable contribution to human civilization.[43] The prospects for world peace would be enhanced if the legitimate aspiration of the Jewish nation for embodiment in a national state were satisfied, thus eliminating the "abnormal" factor of "Jewish homelessness" from the world scene.

Finally, the projected erection of a Jewish state in Palestine was seen as a boon to those Jews who might remain in their former status as citizens of other states. The development of Jewish culture in Palestine would serve their spiritual interests; the new state would be a reservoir from which the Jew anywhere in the world might draw "cultural enrichment, religious guidance and inspiration, and a new pride to sustain his status as a man." [44] Those who struggled in other countries to escape assimilation and maintain their Jewishness would find spiritual sustenance in cultural emanations from the Jewish state.

Moreover, the Jewish state could and would utilize its position in international law, diplomacy, and organization to insist on the protection of Jews in other states. Perhaps the thinning out of Jewish minorities by emigration to Palestine would take the edge off the problem of anti-Semitism, making the problem of protection less formidable. At any rate, the existence of a Jewish state "would be a guarantee to the Jews of Europe that any future aggression against them will not be ignored by the community of nations." [45] No longer would the initiation of international action to protect Jews depend upon the vagaries of the mood and political motives of other states; the cause of Jewish rights would have a permanent spokesman and reliable champion in international councils.[46]

This final argument served to clarify the essential nature of the solution envisaged by Zionists. It was only partially an evacuationist solution. The Jewish minority problem would be reduced to manageable proportions by the voluntary movement of large numbers of Jews to Palestine. A Jewish state would do what it could, within the restrictions imposed by international law, to ensure the survival of Jews and their Jewishness in other countries. Finally, a Jewish state would urge the erection of international machinery for the protection of minority and human rights, and would use its influence and authority to see that the rights and interests of Jews were not neglected by the operative agencies of the international protective system.

3

INTERNATIONAL TREATMENT OF
THE MINORITY PROBLEM IN
THE POSTWAR WORLD

CHAPTER 9:   *THE POSTWAR AGENDA*

As the Second World War moved inexorably toward the conclusion of a victory for the United Nations forces, the era of postwar planning merged into the era of actual construction of what it was hoped would prove to be a lasting world order. The transition from purely preparatory thinking to the stage of preliminary efforts to determine the shape of the new order began even before hostilities ended.

The problem of national minorities was one of the many items on the agenda of postwar statesmanship. Its objective basis, the intermixture of peoples, and its subjective basis, the complex of attitudes toward that factual situation, persisted despite the profound changes wrought by the war. It was a matter of international concern, requiring, as clearly and urgently as it had at the end of the First World War, an international solution.

The task of re-establishing peace after a global conflict has come to consist, in the twentieth century, of two imperfectly distinguishable aspects: the formulation of a substantive political settlement, involving the adjustment of the interests and claims of states, and the erection of a general international organization, involving the determination of the basic institutional and procedural patterns of international relations. In contrast to the

Allies of the First World War, who had undertaken to deal with both these matters simultaneously, the United Nations gave priority to the organizational task.

The United Nations Conference on International Organization was convened at San Francisco, on 25 April 1945, in order to give final form to the project for a general institutional system which had been developed by the leading members of the coalition at their Dumbarton Oaks conversations in 1944.[1]

This conference provided the first major opportunity for accumulation of evidence as to how seriously the problem of national minorities would be regarded in postwar international councils and what approaches to a solution might be contemplated by the statesmen responsible for shaping the new world structure.

From this standpoint, the most striking positive aspect of the conference's work was its attention to the general problem of human rights. While this subject had been accorded but cursory treatment in the Dumbarton Oaks Proposals,[2] it became a matter of major concern at San Francisco.

Much of the discussion concerning human rights could be dismissed as platitudinous oratory, and many proposals were made which reflected little more than an awareness of the ideological necessity to endorse the concept of the dignity of the individual. The unanimity of sentiment for providing in the Charter of the United Nations that the organization should be concerned with promoting respect for human rights did not extend to the proposition that member states should be unambiguously bound to observe a set of clearly defined rights or that an agency of the United Nations should be granted definite competence to intervene in the internal affairs of states for the purpose of enforcing respect for human rights.

In the final result, the Charter produced at San Francisco indicated, at a number of points, an international interest in the problem of ensuring human rights for all individuals on a nondiscriminatory basis.[3] It improved upon the Dumbarton Oaks treatment of the subject primarily by reiterated reference rather than strengthened provision. Without establishing a clear and comprehensive legal basis for an international system for the protection of human rights,[4] the Charter declared the purpose of the United Nations to promote respect for such rights, provided for the erection of machinery for the realization of this objective, and established a potential basis for the argument that governmental trampling on human rights constitutes a violation of international law with which an agency of the international community is competent to deal.

The Charter made no explicit reference to the problem of national minorities or provision for positive minority rights. This issue had hardly been injected into the debates at San Francisco. Public discussion of the Dumbarton Oaks Proposals had produced occasional demands that the new world organization should be entrusted with the function of safeguarding the right of minorities to preserve their group identities.[5] Nevertheless, aside from a casual French reference to the possibility that international intervention to prevent abuse of minorities might sometimes be necessary to maintain the peace,[6] and a Panamanian proposal that the United Nations should create an International Educational Office to promote, *inter alia*, "the nationalization by the school of foreign groups or colonies so that they may not become minorities with foreign ideals and languages," [7] the minority problem was ignored at San Francisco.

It might be argued that the conference subsumed the minority problem under the general heading of human rights, not so much ignoring that problem as opting for the position that it could best be solved by the international promotion of basic rights for all individuals. Granted that the human rights provisions of the Charter were relevant to the minority problem, the inference might seem to be justified that the conference did treat the minority problem as a segment of the more comprehensive problem of human rights.

However, there is no evidence that this was a consciously adopted approach to solution of the minority problem. In view of the failure of the conference to debate possible alternative approaches, the conclusion is inescapable that it acted without deliberate intent to choose a definite method of dealing with postwar minority problems; the only certain implication of the conference's silence is that there was no present intention to resume the efforts of the League to uphold a regime of positive minority rights. Nor can it be said that the delegates at San

Francisco evinced a will to postpone consideration of the minority issue until negotiations for substantive political adjustments should be undertaken, following the pattern of 1919, when decisions on minority questions had been made in connection with interstate settlements rather than with the formulation of the League Covenant.

The fact is that the United Nations Charter was formulated without consideration of the questions of principle which are presented by the existence of national minorities in a world dominated by the concept of the national state as the basic unit of political organization. It was drafted without recognition of the minority problem as a significant item on the agenda of international relations. The first major stage of the process of postwar settlement was completed without indication that the international community would again undertake seriously to deal with this source of international discord.

Even so, the San Francisco Conference did not foreclose the possibility that the minority problem might be subjected to systematic international treatment. The role of the new world organization in the field of individual human rights remained uncertain, but it was conceivable that it might prove to be significant enough to provide the indispensable basis of a tolerable status for members of minority groups. So far as the special problems of national minorities were concerned — problems related to their group consciousness and urge for cultural survival — it should be noted that the Charter did not *preclude*, even though it did not promise, the subsequent construction of an international framework within which those problems might be systematically solved. The Charter pointed the way to an international bill of rights, which might make provision for the recognition of the collective rights deemed so important by self-conscious national groups. The United Nations might serve in the future as the guarantor and focal point of a revived or a completely new minority system.

Moreover, the omission of explicit consideration of the minority problem did not mean that the issue would be ignored in subsequent stages of the postwar settlement. Other conferences, more specifically concerned with arrangements relating to areas where the minority question was especially prominent, lay in the future. We shall see in the following chapters how this question figured in postwar negotiations other than those at San Francisco.

The second phase of the process of shaping a new world order was initiated at the Tripartite Conference of Berlin, commonly referred to as the Potsdam Conference, from 17 July to 2 August 1945.[1] The prewar European *status quo* had been supplanted by the Hitlerian New Order, which had in its turn been overthrown by the invading armies of the United Nations. In the interregnum which followed, with Europe suspended between war and peace, political control of the Continent was divided between the governments of resurrected national states and authorities of the great powers — the United States, the United Kingdom, and the Soviet Union — which had led the coalition to victory. The Big Three constituted a kind of European directorate, a latter-day Concert of Europe, with *de facto* competence to exercise leadership in the interim between the demolition of the old order and the construction of a new one. This was a period of transitional arrangements and preliminary settlements. Yet, however tentative and provisional the policies put into operation during this period may have been in theory and intent, they in fact set into motion trends which could not easily be reversed, and thereby contributed significantly to the determination of the ultimate form of the postwar European system.

The European triumvirate reached two agreements in 1945 which had an important bearing on the problem of national minorities. The first related to the adjustment of the Soviet, Polish, and German boundaries. Roosevelt, Churchill, and Stalin agreed at Yalta that the eastern frontier of Poland should follow the Curzon Line, with slight digressions in favor of Poland, and recognized the necessity of allowing Poland compensatory accessions of former German territory, adding that "the final delimitation of the Western frontier of Poland should . . . await the Peace Conference." [2] At the Potsdam Conference, the Big Three (now consisting of Truman, Attlee, and Stalin) agreed to the tentative assignment of Königsberg and its adjacent area to the Soviet Union, and the placing of the former German area east of the Oder-Neisse line under the provisional administration of Poland, while reaffirming the principle that no final territorial decisions should be made before the peace conference. [3] The great powers thus committed themselves, clearly if not conclusively, to politically motivated frontier revisions which were in violation of the ideal of minimizing the incidence of national minorities and consolidating ethnic groups in their own national states.

The second element of the position assumed by the Big Three in 1945 which related to the minority problem appeared in Section XII of the Potsdam Protocol:

> The Three Governments . . . recognize that the transfer to Germany of German populations, or elements thereof, remaining in Poland, Czechoslovakia and Hungary, will have to be undertaken. They agree that any transfers that take place should be effected in an orderly and humane manner.

The powers decided that their representatives on the Control Council in Germany would make plans for the reception and distribution of the expelled German minorities, and that in the meantime Czechoslovakia, Poland, and Hungary would be requested to suspend expulsions.

This endorsement of the transfer principle apparently was intended to apply to the area provisionally assigned to Polish administration, as well as to the prewar territory of Poland, Czechoslovakia, and Hungary. In discussing the Polish settlement at Yalta, the leaders of the three major members of the United Nations coalition had seemed to assume that transfer would automatically follow frontier changes; Churchill was reported to have said that the placing of the Polish-German frontier at the Neisse River would entail the transfer of nearly nine million Germans. [4] Barbara Ward has held that the Potsdam decision involved British and American acquiescence in the Russian policy of settling the boundary along the Oder-Neisse line "and removing some 9 million Germans permanently westward." [5] Whatever may have been the actual intention at Potsdam, the great powers subsequently acquiesced in the expulsion of the native German population of the eastern provinces by Polish authorities, and thus confirmed the view that the Potsdam decision had as its corollary the elimination of Germans from the area tentatively assigned to Poland. [6]

It does not appear that the agreement to support the mass transfer of German minorities was regarded as a particularly momentous decision by the assembled statesmen. In the published account of the proceedings by James F. Byrnes, who attended as the American Secretary of State, there is no indication that the principle of transfer was the subject of controversy or searching discussion; the only reference to this decision is the statement that, in the later stages of the conference, "agreement quickly followed" on several matters, including the matter of transfer. [7]

Section XII of the Potsdam Protocol did not constitute an unlimited endorsement of the principle of transfer of national minorities. It did not advocate or initiate the policy of transfer. It simply recognized the necessity of certain specified transfers, and gave the qualified approval of the powers occupying and administering Germany to the continuation of movements already in progress.

In actuality, however, the real significance of the Potsdam Protocol for the problem of national minorities lay not in the restricted nature of its endorsement of the transfer principle, but in the fact that it contained the first formal, public indication that the statesmen who were in a position to dominate the framing of the postwar settlement were prepared to accept the transfer of populations as a respectable and useful device for the solution of minority problems. The limited acceptance of transfer was not so stated as to preclude unlimited acceptance; the principle had achieved recognition, and the restrictions laid around it at Potsdam might subsequently be ignored or removed, permitting it to become the basis of the postwar approach to the minority problem. [8] This anticipated result was not fully realized, but the Potsdam decision did in fact provide a quasi-authoritative basis for a great surge of postwar transfer activity.

It is difficult to draw a clear line between wartime and postwar movements of populations in Europe, or between voluntary and forced, planned and unplanned, or authorized and unauthorized movements. The population of the Continent was in chaotic flux during the final stages of military operations and the early postwar period. Formal transfer agreements sometimes merely confirmed migrations already accomplished. Efforts were made to control population movements, but spontaneous transfers continued to take place simultaneously with organized movements, throwing records into confusion and making it impossible to chart with any degree of accuracy the precise course of intra-European population transfers.

On 20 November 1945, the Allied Control Council for Germany approved a schedule for the reception of six and a half million members of the German minorities of Czechoslovakia, Poland, and Hungary, and an additional 150,000 Germans from Austria. In accordance with this plan, the transfers envisaged at Potsdam were substantially carried out.[9]

Both Czechoslovakia and Poland had anticipated the Potsdam decision and its supporting arrangements by laying the groundwork for, and to some extent initiating the implementation of, the policy of expelling Germans, on the basis of wartime understandings with the major powers and unilateral determination to achieve national homogeneity. Czechoslovak and Polish leaders welcomed the formal endorsement of transfer by the Big Three in conference, even though they did not seriously believe that international authorization was necessary. The Potsdam decision gave impetus to the process of expulsion and its restrictive features had some effect, but it did not genuinely transform the movement of population into an internationally directed and controlled program.

Czechoslovakia moved relentlessly to reduce to the merest fragment the German minority which had been established in the Sudetenland since the twelfth century, with little regard for the moral consideration that loyal Germans should not suffer the same penalties as traitors,[10] or for the practical consideration that its economy would be seriously dislocated by the loss of man-power.[11]

Poland effectively eliminated Germans from its established territory and from the eastern German provinces under its provisional rule, to the accompaniment of boasting by Hilary Minc, Minister of Industry, that his country was acquiring valuable economic assets under a program which involved the right of Poland to liquidate the Germanic remnant "in such time and by such means as we shall deem proper." [12]

In accordance with the Potsdam authorization, Hungary launched a campaign to expel its German population. The press organ of the National Peasant Party, *Szabad Szo*, contained this declaration on 22 August 1945: "We Hungarians and the Germans have lived side by side for a thousand years, and a thousand years have not sufficed to build up a friendship . . . there can be no hope that the two peoples will be on peaceful terms with each other. One of them must go, and it cannot be in doubt which is the one to go." [13] Motivated by this sentiment, by the desire to confiscate German land, and by the need to make room for incoming refugees, the Hungarian Government resorted to the wholesale expulsion of the German minority, which had included some 500,000 persons before the war.[14] This transfer went slowly, but by July 1947, some 178,000 Germans had been evacuated, and a month later 170,000 others were denied voting rights on the ground that their expatriation was pending.[15]

The expulsion of German minorities was not limited to those states whose transfer programs had been specifically sanctioned at Potsdam. By various methods, Rumania and Yugoslavia contrived to effect the substantial elimination of Germans who had remained in their territory at the end of the war.[16]

The Hitlerian projects for the "repatriation" of Germans, the flight of German minorities — spontaneously and otherwise — before the advancing Red armies, and the postwar expulsions had the combined result of virtually eliminating the problem of German minorities in Europe. Eastern and Southeastern Europe had been dotted with German colonies comprising some three and a half million members. "Some of these colonies dated from the twelfth century; as a matter of fact, they no longer exist." [17] The bulk of the German population of the South Tyrol remained under Italian rule, and vestigial German minorities persisted elsewhere, but the German minority problem had been reduced to an item of minor importance in European politics.

The corollary of the elimination of German minorities from non-German states was the crowding of some nine and a half or ten million refugees into a Germany shorn of one-fourth of its prewar area.[18] The immediate problem was that of providing the means of subsistence for this mass of homeless people, in a land that was devastated and chaotic and presumably condemned to long-term industrial restrictions. This was more than a problem of relief to be solved by the occupying powers. The neighbors of the Reich, in divesting themselves of German minorities, had produced a dilemma which might plague them for generations to come: if rump Germany were deprived of the opportunity to develop an industrial economy adequate to provide its swollen population with a decent standard of living, Germany would become a festering sore, dangerous to the economic and political health of the Continent; if the German economy were rebuilt to the level necessary for the sustenance of the millions of refugees, then the consolidated German nation, the largest in Europe, might once again become a threat to the security of its neighbors. If one assumes — as the proponents of transfer frequently did — that Germans are inherently dangerous, then it does not necessarily appear that they will constitute a lesser threat as an integrated national-political body than as a nation and a series of national minorities.

At a meeting of the Council of Foreign Ministers in Moscow, on 9 April 1947, representatives of France and the United States pointed out that the policy of concentrating a large German population in a reduced area in the geographical center of Europe might produce a danger to the peace.[19] The fear of the military power which might be developed by a tightly integrated German nation stimulated suggestions that the transfer of *Volksdeutsche* to Germany be suspended and that the contrary policy of promoting the *dispersion* of the German nation be inaugurated.[20] This caution was *ex post facto;* for better or for worse, the states of Europe had substantially eliminated their German minorities by sending them to Germany.

The transfer policy of European governments in the immediate postwar period affected many other peoples than the German minority groups. This was almost literally a nomadic era in human history, and a significant contribution to the bulk of population movements was made by calculated policies of shifting human beings about in accordance with ethnic considerations. Some of these movements had the character of bilateral exchanges. For instance, Czechoslovakia and the USSR concluded formal agreements in 1945 and 1946 for the reciprocal transfer of minorities.[21] In other cases, unidirectional movements were launched by states which desired to purge themselves of heterogeneous ethnic elements or by states wishing to receive ethnic kinsmen.[22]

THE CZECHOSLOVAK-HUNGARIAN CONTROVERSY

The supremacy of the concept of transfer in postwar European minority policy met its gravest test in the relations between Czechoslovakia and Hungary. The government of the former expressed, both during and immediately after the war, its intention of expelling the bulk of the Hungarian minority along with the Germans,[23] and it began in 1945 to take definite preparatory steps.[24]

The contemplation of the unilateral expulsion of Hungarians by Czechoslovakia met with the sharp disapproval of the United States Government. The American mission in Budapest asserted on 12 June 1945, that the United States could approve only agreed transfers, carried out with regard for European peace and security.[25] In the same vein, the State Department announced: "It is this Government's view that problems involving the large-scale transfer or exchange of populations are susceptible of solution only on the basis of international agreement and not by unilateral action."[26] This attitude forced Czechoslovakia to treat the disposition of its Magyar minority as a problem to be worked out in agreement with Hungary.

The Hungarian Government was adamantly opposed to the method of solving the Magyar minority problem which Czechoslovakia was determined to set into operation. It was by no means disinterested in the fate of its co-nationals; it repeatedly protested to the great powers against the alleged persecution of Magyars in Czechoslovakia, asserting that the abuse of those people was a grave offense "against the entire Hungarian nation."[27] But Hungary proposed to promote the welfare of its kinsmen in other ways than by taking them in as refugees.

The objections raised by Hungary included the claim that it was economically unable to absorb a large mass of immigrants. If the small Slovak minority of Hungary were exchanged for the much larger Magyar minority of Czechoslovakia, the net result would be a diminution of the population of the latter state, exacerbating its labor shortage, and an intolerable overcrowding of Hungary, creating insoluble economic problems.[28]

This argument led directly to the expression of sentiments reminiscent of prewar Hungarian revisionism. In this case, the revisionist position was adopted rather cautiously, in the contention that if the Magyar minority of Czechoslovakia should be forced upon Hungary, it would be necessary to cede to Hungary the land which those people had inhabited, in order to provide an economic basis for their existence.[29]

Subsequently, however, Hungary adopted a more assertive attitude toward the issue of territorial adjustment. In an *Aide Memoire* addressed to the Big Three on 25 January 1946, it scored the errors and injustices of the post–World War I settlement, complaining that vast numbers of Magyars had been unnecessarily placed under foreign domination, and vigorously demanded that the new settlement should promote both the ethnic interests of Hungarians who were compactly settled in areas adjacent to Hungary and the economic interests of the Hungarian State, by providing for the cession of those areas to Hungary.[30] This brand of unabashed revisionism was further expressed in a proposal that the problem of the Magyar minority in Rumania be solved by attaching those people, together with the territory where they lived, to Hungary.[31] It would appear that Hungary opposed the transfer of population because it much preferred the transfer of *land;* it was continuing to wage its prewar campaign for frontier changes.

Hungary stated the additional objection that the wholesale ejection of minorities from their homes, without regard for the loyalty or disloyalty of individuals, was a violation of human rights, an undemocratic measure which should be condemned in principle.[32]

Finally, the Hungarian Government resisted the Czechoslovakian demand by asserting that its neighbor was still bound by the minority treaty of 1919, and that the necessity as well as the legal basis existed for renewing the League minority system.[33] Czechoslovakia should observe its obligation to respect the rights of Magyars, rather than subjecting them to the drastic policy of expulsion.

Specifically, Hungary proposed to the great powers the establishment of an international commission to study the Czechoslovak-Hungarian minority problem, and of an international regime over the parts of Slovakia inhabited by Hungarians, in order to stabilize the situation until a permanent solution could be arranged.[34] By this method, the Hungarian Government sought to secure acceptance of its view that the treatment of the Magyar minority in Czechoslovakia was an issue to be determined neither by unilateral action nor by bilateral agreement, but by a multilateral decision. It was an international problem, for which the great powers should assume primary responsibility.

The response of the Big Three to this overture was completely negative. Czechoslovak leaders had already received assurances of Soviet support in regard to its policy of transfer.[35] Both the United States and Britain rejected the Hungarian proposals, declaring that they regarded the question as one to be settled bilaterally by the interested parties.[36] The great powers who constituted the *de facto* governing board of the international community were thoroughly unwilling to admit this vexed minority problem to their agenda.

Confronted with this attitude, Hungary had no alternative but to deal directly with Czechoslovakia. A series of embittered negotiations between the two states produced an agreement concerning a limited exchange of population, signed on 27 February 1946.[37] The terms of this convention were not carried out,[38] and even if they had been, the dispute would not have been terminated thereby, for it was recognized on both sides that the agreement constituted only a partial solution of the problem, a preliminary to further negotiations.

Czechoslovakia continued to insist on a free hand in eliminating its Magyar minority. On the same day that the exchange convention was signed, the Czechoslovak Government addressed a letter to Hungary, reiterating an earlier proposal that all members of the Magyar minority who were not covered by that agreement and who were not restored to Czechoslovak citizenship should be transferred to Hungary.[39] It is notable that this document introduced a new criterion for the restoration of citizenship, in addition to the test of proved loyalty to the state; it indicated that this boon might be conferred upon some members of the Hungarian minority who were "of Slovak origin (ancestry)." Apparently, Czechoslovakia now felt that it was not enough to have *loyal* citizens; it must have citizens of appropriate racial background. In a homogeneous Czechoslovak state, there might be a place for Magyarized Slovaks who would consent to be re-Slovakized, but not for genuine Magyars. This bit of racialism indicates how the basis for the desire to eliminate national minorities from Czechoslovakia was transformed, almost imperceptibly, from a quest for state security into an ideal of national homogeneity for its own sake.

Hungary maintained its refusal to accept its co-nationals from Czechoslovakia, unless perchance they might bring their territory with them, and did not abandon its efforts to secure the intervention of the great powers in the case.[40]

CONCLUSION

This survey of preliminary developments in postwar European minority policy has revealed a general disposition to utilize the principle of transfer as the basic element in the solution of the problem of national minorities. The initiative in the movement to eliminate national minorities in this drastic manner came from the small states of Eastern and Central Europe. It began as a drive to punish disloyal minorities and make the states secure against the threat of future "fifth columns," and it became a campaign to achieve the ideal of national homogeneity.

This movement apparently had the full support of the Soviet Union. Moscow could hardly endorse the nationalist ideology which came to play such a significant role in the process of eliminating minorities, but it had adequate political motivation for giving its general support to the policy which was so insistently demanded by the states along its western fringe.

The United States and Britain acquiesced in the execution of this policy, within fairly definite limits. They were impelled by the humanitarian sensitivity of their people to urge that transfers should be carried out in an orderly and humane manner. They frowned upon unilateral expulsion of minorities and the indiscriminate subjection of individual members of minorities to the harsh penalty of being uprooted from their homes. They insisted that transfers should be undertaken only by the mutual agreement of the expelling and receiving states.

The only dissenter among the states concerned with the transfer policy was Hungary, which objected as a potential recipient of refugees. Hungary agreed that disloyal members of minority groups should be expelled — it ousted the bulk of its own German population — but its government adhered to the view that the major approach to a solution of the minority problem should be the renewal of the system of international protection of national minorities.

The second major trend discernible in this analysis is the repudiation of the internationalization of the minority problem. European states proceeded on the assumption that it was a vital part of their national business to dispose of minority problems in a manner calculated to satisfy their security needs and ideological aspirations. States exhibited an active interest in the future of their co-nationals, rejecting the assumption of the League minority system that the welfare of national minorities was pre-eminently a matter of international concern.

Most significantly, the great powers made a deliberate effort to push the problem of national minorities back into the realm of domestic policy and bilateral negotiation. As the leaders of the international community, they rejected the tentative internationalization of the problem which had been effected in 1919. They did not wish to be bothered with the problem of the Hungarian minority in Czechoslovakia; they did not choose to study the problem, to supervise an exchange of population, to establish an interim control over majority-minority relations, or to assume responsibility, as leading participants in an international organization, for the operation of a new system of international protection for national minorities.

This attitude qualified the significance of the humanitarian sentiments which the United States and the United Kingdom attached to their limited endorsement of the principle of transfer, reducing them to the level of moral preachments. These powers urged the humane settlement of the minority problem, but declined to play an active role in that settlement except as they provided assistance to ethnic expellees along with other refugees and displaced persons.

It had been the ideal of the League minority system to remove the minority problem from the sphere of bilateral negotiation, and to establish the principle that the problem was the concern of the organized international community. The great powers, after the Second World War, reversed this trend by handing the problem back to the states directly concerned with the fate of particular minority groups.

CHAPTER II: *THE PARIS PEACE CONFERENCE AND THE MINORITY PROBLEM*

The tortuous process of re-establishing the legal framework of European order after the Second World War reached a minor climax on 29 July 1946, when representatives of twenty-one members of the United Nations coalition met in Paris to consider draft treaties of peace with Italy, Rumania, Bulgaria, Hungary, and Finland. This was not a peace conference in the traditional sense of the term, convened to bring about at one stroke a definitive settlement. It was merely the penultimate stage of a peacemaking process which had been initiated with the conclusion of military armistices, given direction in some degree by the policies of the occupying powers, and carried through the treaty-drafting stage by the Council of Foreign Ministers and their deputies.[1] It was the function of the conference to examine the drafts and submit its recommendations to the Council, which would be responsible for the final shaping of the treaties. Thus, the conference had only an advisory role to play in the framing of the new European settlement.

Despite its limited competence, the Paris Conference had great significance. It permitted the presentation and discussion of the views of the smaller states, including the defeated satellite states. It offered a new setting for hammering out agreements on issues about which the great powers had found themselves in conflict, and facilitated the raising of problems which they had tended to neglect. For these reasons, the conference was a crucial point in the process of determining the nature of postwar international policy concerning national minorities. It provided the nearest approach, thus far, to a systematic examination of the minority problem as it existed at the end of the war, and to the formulation of an international decision as to methods for dealing with that problem.

FRONTIER REVISION

The problem of national minorities first entered into the peace-making process as a factor involved in the definition of frontiers. The notion that the boundaries of states should ideally coincide with the boundaries of nations was not so dominant in the international thought of 1946 as it had been in Wilsonian ideology. Yet, even though many other factors were admitted as legitimate elements in the determination of frontiers, the weight of the ethnic principle was still substantial, and it was thrown into every controversy regarding territorial settlement.

One of the most difficult problems which the Council of Foreign Ministers encountered was the establishment of the boundary between Italy and Yugoslavia. The ethnic issue figured in the discussion of this problem from the beginning; the Council agreed, on 19 September 1945, to have the deputies study the Italo-Yugoslav frontier in order to find the line "which will in the main be the ethnic line leaving a minimum under alien rule. . . ." [2] It could be inferred from this communiqué that the great powers approached their task with a firm adherence to the concept of the national state. The use of the term "alien rule" suggested that national minority status is intrinsically abnormal, and the adoption of the principle of the ethnic line indicated a belief that the ideal solution of the nationality problem is to refrain, so far as possible, from placing people in that anomalous position.

The ethnic principle did not prove to be a clear and simple

guide in this case. At the session of the Council in Paris, 25 April to 16 May 1946, the Soviet Union espoused the claim of Yugoslavia that Venezia Giulia should be treated as an inseparable whole, which should then be assigned, on ethnic and other grounds, to Yugoslavia. The United States, the United Kingdom, and France, on the other hand, objected to this interpretation of the ethnic principle, which would have the effect of incorporating a large Italian minority in Yugoslavia, and proposed instead a partition of the area which would satisfy, in approximately equal measure, the ethnic claims of the two states, leaving the smallest possible minority groups on each side.[3]

The issue was resolved at the second part of the Council session in Paris, 15 June to 12 July 1946, in an agreement to divide the disputed area along a line proposed by France, essentially a line of ethnic balance, and to establish the city of Trieste and its environs as a Free Territory under an international regime.[4]

There was no general disposition among the delegates to the Paris Conference to reopen this issue. The Italian Government expressed the sentiment that to have Italians cut off from Italy would be to suffer some kind of national wound,[5] but it was in no position to attack a settlement which represented the maximum concession to Italian ethnic claims that the Western powers had been able to secure after months of wrangling with the Soviet Union.

Yugoslavia, supported by Czechoslovakia, continued to press its ethnic demands, declaring defiantly that its people would never acquiesce in a settlement which frustrated the unification of all Yugoslavs in their own state.[6] The conference was not moved by these threats, however, and Yugoslavia reluctantly accepted the compromise arrangement, participating in the signing of the Italian Treaty on 10 February 1947.[7]

The Council of Foreign Ministers agreed at the first part of its Paris session that the South Tyrol should remain under Italian sovereignty.[8] This decision was attacked in some quarters as an indefensible violation of the principle of nationality; for instance, Churchill declared that there should be a plebiscite to determine whether the population of the South Tyrol might desire to be incorporated in Austria.[9]

The foreign minister of Austria, addressing the Paris Conference on 21 August 1946, asked for the cession of the South Tyrol, "where the people have been deprived of the most primitive human rights. . . ."[10] Subsequently, Austria submitted a memorandum in which Italy's treatment of its German minority was denounced, and a plebiscite was proposed.[11] Despite the strength of Austria's ethnic claim to the South Tyrol, the conference does not seem to have considered this proposal. In this case, there was no balancing of competitive ethnic claims; there was simply a reaffirmation of prewar boundaries, a continuation of the minority status of a large group living on the frontier of its co-national state, without serious examination of the question of frontier revision.

Hungary brought before the Paris Conference its demands for favorable revision of boundaries with Czechoslovakia and Rumania, arguing that frontier adjustments should be used wherever possible to reunite Magyars with their parent nation and in other cases to divide areas of mixed population according to the principle of ethnic balance.[12]

Czechoslovakia charged that Hungary was using the minority problem as a pretext for expansionist ambitions; it was attempting, by appealing to the ethnic principle, to gain the territorial ends which it had failed to make good as a partner of Nazi Germany.[13]

The conference appeared to agree with Czechoslovakia. It approved the restoration of the prewar frontiers, depriving Hungary of its wartime territorial gains; the one exception which it recommended involved the transfer of a small area from Hungary to Czechoslovakia. Hungary's revisionist proposals, veiled and direct, were not considered on their ethnic merits, but were pushed aside as presumptuous emanations from a defeated Axis state.

This analysis of the major territorial questions which arose during the formulation of the satellite treaties reveals the persistent intrusion of the problem of national minorities; at least one party to every controversy stressed the relationship of the territorial to the national problem and urged consideration of the effect which a given boundary change would have upon the size and probable treatment of national minorities. In the case of the Italo-Yugoslav frontier, the ethnic principle was treated as a factor of predominant importance, and the decision was justified on the ground that it divorced a minimum number of people from their appropriate national states and provided an approximate ethnic balance. This attention to the concept of ethnic balance indicated the conviction that national minorities would be regarded as *hostages;* if Italy and Yugoslavia possessed them in equal numbers, it might be hoped that the two states would treat them with prudent restraint.

In no other case, however, was the ethnic factor given great weight in territorial decisions. Political, economic, geographical, and strategic factors were allowed to override ethnic considerations. Austria's suggestion that the shifting of a frontier could accomplish the desirable end of eliminating the troublesome problem of the Tyrolean minority in Italy went unheeded. Hungary's contention that a readjustment of its boundaries would reduce the tensions generated by the minority problem was brusquely rejected.

The conservatism of the conference prevented any general attempt to refashion the boundaries of Europe for the purpose of eliminating national minorities. By and large, the peacemakers were inclined to restore the prewar frontiers, leaving national minorities resident in "alien" states and therefore dependent upon whatever arrangements might be made for ensuring their just treatment.

THE TRANSFER OF NATIONAL MINORITIES

The Paris Conference agreed without difficulty to the principle of transfer of minority populations in its loosest, least drastic sense, by approving a conventional option clause for the Italian Treaty, permitting Italian-speaking residents of areas cut off from Italy to opt for retention of Italian citizenship and movement to Italy.[14] It went beyond this by recommending, at the instance of Yugoslavia, that Italian citizens whose customary language is Serb, Croat, or Slovene, should be entitled to opt for transfer to Yugoslavia.[15] An endorsement of the transfer of peoples in ceded areas to their "proper" national states was written into the recommendation concerning rectifications of the Czechoslovak-Hungarian frontier.[16]

These decisions indicated general agreement on the desirability of the unscrambling of populations, at least when the process is voluntarily initiated by the persons affected. The restriction of the right of option to persons whose customary language was that of the state to which they desired to migrate made it apparent that the conference was interested in facilitating voluntary movement of individuals only for the purpose of reducing the size of national minorities.

The problem of large-scale, compulsory transfer of national minorities was introduced by Czechoslovakia, which sought to gain the backing of the international gathering at Paris for its position in the unsolved minority dispute with Hungary. Czechoslovakia proposed to add to the draft treaty with Hungary an article authorizing the transfer of 200,000 Magyars from Czechoslovakia to Hungary, and binding the latter state to receive and confer nationality upon them whether or not bilateral agreement could be reached concerning detailed arrangements for execution of the transfer.[17] Czechoslovak representatives expressed the intention to retain and subject to complete assimilation those apparent Magyars who were in reality Magyarized Slovaks, but insisted upon the absolute necessity of ejecting all genuine Magyars, in order to promote the internal security of the state, to remove the pretext for Hungarian revisionist activity, and to attain the ideal of national homogeneity. No other solution would provide Czechoslovak security, long-range friendship with Hungary, or peace in Central Europe.[18]

The Czechoslovak position was supported by the Soviet Union and the bloc of Slav states which it led. The representative of Byelorussia declared "that the presence of the Hungarian minority in Czechoslovakia could cause only difficulties, and that it would be a good thing for the Conference to dispose of such difficulties." [19] Vishinsky said with reference to Hungary that the Soviet Union "could not find acceptable the position of a country that considers her own children orphans whom she cannot accept," and upheld the Czechoslovak view that the transfer of the Magyar minority was the only solution of the problem.[20]

In view of strenuous Hungarian opposition to the Czechoslovak proposal,[21] American, British and Australian representatives took the lead in inducing the conference to refrain from authorizing Czechoslovakia to proceed unilaterally with the expulsion of its Magyar minority,[22] and to adopt a recommendation that the peace treaty with Hungary include an article binding that state to negotiate the issue with Czechoslovakia, with the proviso that the latter could bring the matter before the Council of Foreign Ministers in the event of failure to reach a bilateral accord within six months.[23]

Czechoslovakia and its supporters reluctantly accepted this recommendation, which was incorporated in Article 5 of the definitive treaty with Hungary, adhering to the belief that it would have been preferable to receive unqualified authority to expel the Magyar ethnic group. On the other hand, France, the United States, Britain, and Australia, while not impugning Czechoslovakia's motives, hailed the decision to insist on the bilateral approach. General Walter Bedell Smith, speaking for the United States, asserted that the problem was clearly a fit subject for Czechoslovak-Hungarian negotiation, and expressed the hope that the two states could achieve a success in solving this problem which would pave the way for similar negotiations between Hungary and Rumania.[24]

In view of the strength of eliminationist sentiment during the war and immediately thereafter, it is not surprising that the principle of transfer should have had its vehement champions at the Paris Conference. Outraged and ambitious nationalism quite understandably expressed itself in demands for ousting disloyal and ethnically alien groups (the distinction between these two terms was sometimes lost) from the state which was intended to be the embodiment and instrument of the nation.

The most striking and significant feature of the treatment of the transfer principle at Paris was the nature and extent of the opposition which was revealed. The opposition of Hungary was in a class by itself. The barbed comments of Czechoslovakia and its friends, to the effect that Hungary was a singularly unaffectionate mother to its scattered children, struck a telling blow at the Hungarian case. Hungary had unceasingly, since the end of the First World War, feigned grief because it was cut off from large ethnic groups which were a part of the Magyar nation; now, it adamantly refused to receive those groups. Many of Hungary's objections to the acceptance of a mass of refugees had great weight, but, valid as they were, they could not conceal the fact that Hungary was unprepared to act as if national integration were the supreme value which Hungarian nationalists had incessantly declared it to be. Nor could they dispel the suspicion that Hungary was interested in Magyar minorities primarily because of their usefulness as instruments of, and pretexts for, a revisionism which was motivated by more mundane considerations than the somewhat mystical desire to restore the integrity of the nation.

The opposition to the Czechoslovak transfer proposal which was raised by the United States, the United Kingdom, and Australia, bears close examination. It was not opposition to the principle of transfer; on the contrary, these states expressed sympathy with the Czechoslovak aim of achieving national homogeneity. It was not opposition, in principle, to the compulsory shifting of individuals; the United States hoped that this drastic action could be held to a minimum, but it did not dispute the right of the interested states, acting in concert, to resort to such action. Indeed, there was general satisfaction at the thought that Czechoslovakia and Hungary might be able to agree to a plan for settling the problem by obligatory transfer. When the opponents of the Czechoslovak scheme firmly declined to be parties to inserting in a peace treaty the principle of the forced transfer of populations, they were objecting to the policy of compelling a state unwillingly to receive its co-nationals from other countries, not to the principle of forcing members of national minorities to abandon their domiciles. Australia made this clear when it contended that "it would be wrong to attempt to write into this treaty [with Hungary] a clause permitting a forced transfer, *against the wishes of the receiving country*." [25] It was this rejection of the idea of coercing the receiving state which led the governments ranged against the Czechoslovak amendment to insist that transfer should be undertaken only in execution of a bilateral agreement between the two states directly concerned.

The interests and welfare of the human beings involved were matters of concern to opponents of transfer, even though it was felt that the *wishes* of those people might justly be disregarded. Movements of population should be orderly and humane, and, to this end, they should be conducted under carefully elaborated plans, adopted jointly by expelling and receiving states. Again, there was no evidence of rejection of the principle that human beings might be compulsorily uprooted; there was merely a reservation as to the manner in which that coercive process should be executed.

The two great powers of the West did not wish to concern themselves directly and actively with the problem. They felt that they had discharged their responsibility by admonishing Czechoslovakia to expel the Magyars only with the consent of Hungary and with precautions against needless suffering. There would be neither self-determination for these people nor an international decision as to their fate; their destiny would be placed in the hands of two quarreling governments, of which one passionately wished to be rid of them and the other passionately wished to avoid receiving them.

HUMAN RIGHTS

The third aspect of the work of the Paris Peace Conference which was closely related to the problem of national minorities was its treatment of the principle of human rights. It was held by the victors that the cynical aggressiveness of the Axis states had been the logical outgrowth of disregard for fundamental rights. Hence, concern for the establishment of a lasting peace, as well as for the realization of justice, made it legitimate and necessary for the conference to undertake to prevent future violations of human rights by the states which had been the cohorts of Nazi Germany. In laying down a minimum standard for the behavior of the defeated states toward their own people, the peacemakers would be promoting the cause of human rights. In requiring those states to accept the principle of nondiscrimination, they would be establishing safeguards against recurrence of the persecution of national minorities.

The great powers followed up their wartime declarations of intent to promote universal observance of human rights by utilizing their position as military victors and occupants of Axis territories to abolish repressive legislation, and by submitting to the Paris Conference draft treaties which contained provisions for obligating the satellite states to grant their peoples basic rights on a nondiscriminatory basis.[26]

Opposition to these provisions was raised by Italy and Rumania,[27] which observed that such a commitment was superfluous, in view of their spontaneous determination to uphold human rights. It carried an insulting implication which was offensive to national sensibilities, and it violated their sovereign equality, inasmuch as it purported to saddle upon them international obligations — subjecting them to the danger of intervention — which were not universally accepted by sovereign states. These protests were strikingly similar to the objections which had been made at Paris in 1919 by the states which had been asked to accept special minority obligations.

Paying little heed to these pleas, the conference readily approved the incorporation of the human rights provisions in the peace treaties. Members of the conference also found themselves in substantial agreement that the principle of the enjoyment of equal rights by all citizens should be written into the Statute of the Free Territory of Trieste.[28]

The first real human rights controversy arose in connection with a British attempt to amend the Rumanian, Hungarian, and Bulgarian draft treaties so as absolutely to preclude discrimination against nationals on the ground of their race, sex, language, or religion. Representatives of the United Kingdom stated frankly that this proposal was designed specifically to protect the status of Jews. Jewish organizations had expressed the conviction that special precautions were necessary to obviate the possibility that anti-Semitic practices might be continued or resumed in some of the former Axis states; Britain believed it advisable to reinforce the basic provisions on human rights, imposing a contractual obligation on the satellite states which would be proof against any future efforts to evade the requirement that they should afford completely equal treatment to their Jewish minorities. This view was supported by the United States, by members of the British Commonwealth, and, in the case of Hungary, by France.[29]

Despite strong opposition by the affected states, in which they were supported by the Soviet bloc, the conference approved the British proposal. In consequence, the special antidiscrimination provision appeared in the final versions of the Rumanian and Hungarian treaties,[30] although it was omitted from the definitive treaty with Bulgaria.[31]

The United States put through a proposal, which subsequently became Article 19, paragraph 4 of the Italian Treaty, binding states which received Italian territory under the treaty to secure to all inhabitants of that territory the enjoyment of basic human rights.[32] This American initiative, designed to restrict Yugoslavia's treatment of Italians in ceded areas, was defended as an application of the principle that peoples transferred to a new sovereignty are entitled to safeguards against discriminatory treatment.[33] It was opposed by the Soviet bloc and especially by Yugoslavia, which reacted in a manner typical of states which are requested to accept special international obligations to treat their citizens with fairness and justice.[34]

The conference endorsed that principle again, when it recommended that Czechoslovakia should be obligated to respect the human rights of the population acquired from Hungary as a result of a minor frontier rectification, in the event that the people involved were not returned to Hungary under an exchange arrangement.[35]

American gratification at the action of the conference in these cases was expressed by Secretary of State Byrnes: "It should not be overlooked that upon American insistence guaranties have been inserted to insure the full exercise of fundamental liberties and human rights to any people transferred to alien sovereignty."[36]

Even though the Paris Conference undertook to establish the legal duty of former enemy states to respect the human rights of their nationals and the obligation of successor states to uphold the rights of the population of ceded areas, it did not display enthusiasm for developing methods of enforcement. Certain nongovernmental associations had proposed that the treaties should create agencies for the systematic supervision of the observance of human rights commitments in former Axis countries,[37] but the only proposal to this effect which came before the conference, an ambitious Australian project for a European Court of Human Rights, was decisively rejected on the ostensible ground that such institution-building was a task for the United Nations.[38] With respect to the Trieste settlement, the conference did adopt a plan for implementation of the legal responsibility and institutional competence of the international community to secure the enjoyment of human rights by members of the various national groups,[39] but this was clearly an exceptional case. The human rights articles, as integral parts of the treaties, fell under the general scheme developed for the effectuation of the treaties as a whole,[40] but the conference gave no serious thought to the erection of the very different and much more elaborate machinery which would be required for a systematic international effort to protect individuals against violation of their human rights by governments.

In the debates concerning human rights at Paris, every delegation paid at least lip-service to the general principle that all governments should respect the human rights of all persons under their jurisdiction, without discrimination against national or other types of minorities.

When the question arose of imposing international obligations upon particular states to conform to that principle, a variety of attitudes became apparent. The United States and Britain led a group of states which favored seizing the opportunity to require pledges from the defeated powers and from states receiving territorial accessions. Moreover, they indicated an interest in the problem of national minorities by sponsoring proposals explicitly designed to buttress the human rights of Jews and of newly ceded ethnic groups which were believed to be in particular danger of suffering discrimination and persecution.

The Soviet Union insisted that special reinforcement for Jewish rights in Rumania, Hungary, and Bulgaria was unnecessary and that Yugoslavia, not being a defeated enemy, was entitled to consider its policy toward minority groups as a matter of domestic jurisdiction. The states which were called upon to accept special human rights obligations took the general attitude that such measures were justifiable and necessary in the case of *other* states, but not in their own cases. Nevertheless, the conference followed rather closely the Anglo-American line, recommending that the treaties include special human rights provisions.

It was not clear whether the failure of the conference to provide special arrangements for enforcement of the human rights articles stemmed from the belief that such action was unnecessary or undesirable, or impossible. There were clear indications that stiff political resistance would have been aroused by efforts to impose a system of supervision. The American Secretary of State, James F. Byrnes, seemed to believe that it was unnecessary to spell out the means by which paper guarantees of human rights might be transformed into concrete assurances.[41] The most likely explanation is that the great powers, although willing to exert themselves momentarily to contribute what they could to the future welfare of European peoples who might stand in jeopardy, were disinclined to accept a continuing responsibility for protecting those peoples against their own governments. It was one thing to participate in writing treaties, but it would be quite another thing to bear the burden of operating an institutionalized system for the protection of individuals, particularly members of national minorities, against persecution.

SPECIAL MINORITY RIGHTS

The Paris Conference found that it was impossible to dispose of the problem of national minorities by treating it simply as a special aspect of the problem of human rights. Minorities valued the provisions which would establish their claim to ordinary human rights on the basis of equality, but, in many cases, they felt that these provisions were inadequate in content as well as deficient in procedural enforceability. Champions of various minorities forced upon the conference an awareness of the unique nature of the problem which is presented by the collective aspirations of ethnically self-conscious minority groups, especially when such groups enjoy the support of co-national states.

In response to the urgent pleas of Jewish organizations,[42] Britain and the United States successfully urged the conference to supplement the human rights articles by inserting into the treaties with Rumania and Hungary a provision for utilizing unclaimed Jewish assets to benefit surviving members of their decimated Jewish communities.[43] By taking the lead in this matter, which was vitally important for the restoration of the economic basis of Jewish community life in Rumania and Hungary, the United Kingdom and the United States demonstrated an active concern for the interests of Jewish minorities. It should be noted, however, that this was a "one stroke" phenomenon, which did not imply willingness to engage in continuing supervision of the treatment of Jews or other groups.

The peacemakers at Paris were subjected to a barrage of demands for the erection of safeguards for the positive minority rights of various groups in the states affected by the impending political settlement.

Schemes for the legal establishment and institutional guarantee of linguistic, educational, cultural, and other rights relevant to the perpetuation of ethnic distinctiveness were proposed by Jewish organizations, for the benefit primarily of Jewish minorities in some or all of the defeated states.[44]

The most ardent and systematic advocacy of the international protection of the positive ethnic rights of minorities came from the Hungarian Government. Before the conference began, Hungary had presented to the great powers a suggestion for the creation of a new version of the League minority system, to be based upon appropriate articles in the peace treaties or upon special minority treaties between the five permanent members of the United Nations Security Council and the individual states of Southeastern Europe.[45]

At the Paris Conference, Hungary pushed this proposal whenever the opportunity arose. It first argued for the expansion of the human rights articles in the peace treaties into a detailed "statute of minorities"; [46] later, Hungary submitted an elaborate draft with the suggestion that it be used as a model for a series of special minority treaties.[47]

This document was a drastically revised version of the legal instruments which had served as the foundation of the League minority system; it purported to constitute a reaffirmation of the old minority treaties (which Hungary contended were still legally effective), and to incorporate changes and additions which League experience had proved to be essential. It clearly reflected the "minority point of view," going far beyond the previous treaties in providing for both the substantive rights and the procedural competence of minorities. In addition, it explicitly recognized the legitimacy of the demand of kin-states for a role in the operation of a minority system.

The Hungarian proposal assumed that an approximate ethnic balance would be created in Eastern and Central Europe through the revision of frontiers. It had at least one significant virtue; it rested upon the realistic premise that no minority system could be erected in that part of Europe except upon the basis of *reciprocity*. Hungary was willing to be bound by a minority treaty in exchange for similar undertakings by the states in which Magyar minorities existed.

Hungary was unique in its adoption of this attitude at the Paris Conference. A number of states proposed to subject their neighbors to international control in this regard, but only Hungary exhibited a willingness to accept reciprocal obligations.

Yugoslavia asked that the treaties with Italy and Hungary should provide for the granting of special rights to Yugoslav ethnic groups, including the right of education in their mother tongue, but it was passionately opposed to the incorporation in the Italian Treaty of provisions binding states which acquired new Italian minorities to ensure to those groups even basic human rights and freedoms on a nondiscriminatory basis.[48] As for itself, Yugoslavia wished to have a free hand in its dealings with national minorities.

Similarly, Italy favored the international guarantee of positive minority rights for Italians who were divorced from their "proper" national state,[49] but Italian sensibilities were offended by the suggestion that the position of national minorities in Italy required external safeguards. In 1945, Foreign Minister De Gasperi had suggested the possibility of reciprocal Italo-Yugoslav engagements for granting a special status to minorities,[50] but by the time of the Paris Conference this conception of mutuality had been discarded, and it was argued that the new democratic Italy could be trusted to apply the principles of liberalism and justice to its national minorities.[51] Only states which did not undoubtedly adhere, as did Italy, to these enlightened principles, should be required to accept formal restrictions.

Greece displayed the same attitude, suggesting that an obligation to grant cultural and administrative autonomy to Greek communities be imposed upon Italy, but objecting to being bound with respect to its treatment of Italians in the Dodecanese Islands.[52]

The various proposals for the international recognition and protection of the rights of national minorities did not induce the Paris Conference to give serious consideration to the possibility of establishing a new version of the League minority system.

For the most part, these suggestions seem to have been studiously ignored. As we have seen, the conference was prepared to recommend that members of national minorities in the defeated states and the areas to be ceded by them to neighboring states should be entitled to ordinary individual rights without discrimination, and it was willing to endorse the principle that human rights in the proposed Free Territory of Trieste, including, in this case, the exceptional rights of linguistic and educational freedom, should be upheld by an institutionalized international guarantee. It was not interested however, in suggestions that it should go farther, making a positive effort to solve the minority problem on the basis of a systematic arrangement for the international guarantee of special rights for national minorities.

During the conference, the foreign ministers of Italy and Austria negotiated a bilateral agreement on the status of the German-speaking minority of the South Tyrol. This convention, in which Italy accepted the principle that the Germanic minority was entitled to preserve its ethnic character as well as to enjoy equality of basic rights, was welcomed as a constructive act of statesmanship. On the recommendation of the conference, the peace treaty with Italy included a statement that the Allied and Associated Powers had taken note of the agreement, and its text was annexed to the treaty.[53]

No provision was made in the peace treaty for establishing an international guarantee of the minority rights stipulated in this convention. The peacemakers approved the conclusion of the bilateral agreement primarily because it seemed to presage an amicable settlement of the minority problem which had troubled Austro-Italian relations, without requiring any sort of international action; their approval did not derive from any conviction that the accord might be construed to provide a legal basis for international supervision of the treatment of the ethnic group concerned.

An understanding of the handling of the issue of minority rights at the Paris Conference can best be attained by examining the positions assumed by the great powers.

The attitude of the Soviet Union seemed to be determined by political motives which precluded consideration of the merits of the issue. It supported Czechoslovakia in the demand for transfer of Magyars, and in the contention that the Hungarian scheme for international protection of minorities was a device for impeding that method of solution and thus for preserving the basis of future irredentism. The USSR dissented from the expressions of approval of the Austro-Italian minority agreement on the ground that it made inadequate provision for minority rights,[54] thus exhibiting an attitude which was ostensibly pro-minority but may have been more significantly anti-Italian. The real depth of the Soviet Union's concern for the protection of minorities was revealed by its sympathy with the Eastern European states in their reluctance to make commitments regarding their treatment of minorities; it could not contemplate with equanimity the prospect that an international agency might assert the competence to intervene in the internal affairs of states within the Russian sphere of influence. On the whole, the USSR threw its weight into the scales against the international recognition or enforcement of special minority rights.

The point of view of the American and British governments was largely determined by their incapacity to understand the need or desire for special rights designed to maintain the ethnic integrity of national minorities. General Walter Bedell Smith, an American delegate to the conference, remarked: "It is difficult for a citizen of the United States to understand the desire to perpetuate racial minorities rather than absorb them." This sentiment was echoed by Lord Hood, of the United Kingdom, who declared: "Our aim should be to assimilate racial minorities in the countries where they live rather than to perpetuate them."[55]

On the whole, American and British concern for the rights of national minorities was satisfied by incorporation in the peace treaties of general human rights provisions. The great powers of the West lacked the ideological motivation for supporting the recognition and guarantee of the right of minorities to avoid assimilation.

The attitude of the United States and Britain was also colored by a sort of isolationism, a disposition to leave the solution of the complex nationality problems of Eastern and Central Europe to the states immediately concerned. They were willing to suggest general standards which should be observed, but not to undertake the responsibility of formulating solutions or of participating in their effectuation. Despite their expressed preference for a policy of assimilation, the United States and Britain were not opposed to the concept of minority rights. If Italy and Austria could agree to a plan whereby the German-speaking element in the South Tyrol should be permitted to perpetuate its distinguishing ethnic characteristics, that was all to the good. The important thing was that the two states should find a mutually acceptable solution — and one which did not require the supervisory and executory action of an international organization. In consequence of this Anglo-American attitude of benevolent passivity, the idea of the creation of a new system of internationally guaranteed minority rights foundered at Paris for lack of an influential champion.

SUMMARY

The Paris Peace Conference of 1946 did not attempt to formulate a systematic solution of the problem of national minorities in Europe. It faced that problem reluctantly, and dealt with it piecemeal.

The conference endeavored to find an ethnic line for the new Italo-Yugoslav frontier, but made no concerted effort to eliminate the problem of national minorities by the method of frontier revision. It gave indirect support to the concept of transfer, by recommending that Hungary be bound to negotiate with Czechoslovakia on that subject; it did not, however, agree that the method of transfer should be resorted to, except on the basis of particular bilateral agreements. It resolved that the defeated states should be legally obligated to respect the human rights of all their nationals without distinction, and that states acquiring new territory should accept similar obligations in regard to the populations so acquired; it did not seek to erect legal safeguards for the enjoyment of human rights on a nondiscriminatory basis by all national minorities in Europe, or in that region of Europe which was the focal point of the minority problem. The conference approved a plan for the international protection of the human rights of the inhabitants of the proposed Free Territory of Trieste, but it did not contemplate the application of that principle in any other case than this one of a wholly exceptional nature. It placed its seal of approval upon the Austro-Italian arrangement for special minority rights in the South Tyrol, but it did not specifically endorse the concept of positive minority rights.

Perhaps the most striking and significant feature of the proceedings at Paris was the de-internationalization of the minority problem. Most of the states which had co-national minorities in other states gave clear indications that they considered themselves the natural and legitimate guardians of their ethnic kinsmen. Even the one governmentally-sponsored scheme for the re-creation of an international system for dealing with the problem of national minorities, the plan submitted by Hungary, introduced the premise that the special relationship existing between a minority and its co-national state should be formally recognized.

No one arose to challenge the view that the treatment of a particular minority was an issue between host state and kin-state, rather than a matter of concern to the organized international community. On the contrary, the tendency to treat minority questions as bilateral problems was strongly encouraged by the conference, which urged Czechoslovakia and Hungary to settle between themselves the fate of the Magyars in the former country, and expressed profound satisfaction that Italy and Austria were able to handle their minority problem on a purely bilateral basis. It appeared that the international community was handing the troublesome problem of national minorities back to the states immediately concerned.

This declaration of international nonresponsibility for the solution of the minority problem was largely the work of the great powers. The Soviet Union occupied a position somewhat analogous to that of France in the years of the League minority system. Just as France had been impelled by its diplomatic interests in Eastern and Central Europe to oppose undue interference by the League Council in the affairs of the minority states, so the Soviet Union now exhibited marked hostility to the imposition of any measure of international control over the policies of governments in that area. The United Kingdom was not disposed to undertake again the onerous responsibility of acting as a mediator in disputes between the quarrelsome minorities and majorities of

Eastern and Central Europe. The United States maintained a "hands off" policy; it regarded European minority problems as matters to be solved by bilateral negotiation, and was prepared to accept solutions of virtually any type so long as they were mutually acceptable to the states concerned and were not flagrantly inhumane in their execution. The leaders of the international community refused the responsibility of taking the initiative in the development of a definitive international solution of the problem of national minorities.

CHAPTER 12: *THE UNITED NATIONS AND THE GENERAL PROBLEM OF MINORITIES*

When the United Nations came into official existence on 24 October 1945, it appeared as a revised version of the League of Nations, with an organizational apparatus which suggested that it was to carry on a range of activities which included, but was not limited to, those with which its predecessor had been concerned. There was one notable exception; nothing in the pattern of organization implied clearly that the United Nations would continue the efforts of the League to afford protection to national minorities.[1] The Preparatory Commission had proposed that the Commission on Human Rights should include minority protection among the objects of its work;[2] however, the record of the San Francisco Conference supported the supposition that the omission of specific provisions for international guardianship of minorities was a significant indicator of the intentions of the framers of the Charter.

In fact, the structural clue was somewhat misleading. It did not reflect a definitive decision to exclude minority protection from the work of the United Nations. The Charter was in many respects an "incomplete" document, a skeleton which stood ready to receive fleshy parts. The San Francisco Conference had exercised indisputable logic when it refrained from establishing a regime for minorities in advance of the operative elaboration of the human rights system.

Nevertheless, the deduction from the Charter's *lacuna* was essentially accurate. The history of the United Nations to date bears out the original impression; as compared with the League of Nations, the new world organization is clearly less concerned with the rights of national minorities, and less inclined to undertake the task of achieving an international solution of the minority problem. This is one of the rare instances when international organization, having put its hand to the plow, has looked back and decided — or almost decided — to turn back.

The United Nations has not been permitted to forget about the problem. Its records are by no means devoid of references to minority rights and the need for their protection. The Soviet bloc, assorted other member states, certain nongovernmental organizations, and numerous events on the international scene have persistently reminded the organization that the minority problem remains with us. And if the United Nations is unable to ignore the problem, neither is it willing to appear to reject all connection with it or to repudiate the necessity of dealing with it. It is a fact of life in this generation that there exists a universal passion for at least talking favorably about human rights; a government or an international organization which assumed a pose of indifference with regard to any matter connected with human rights would do so at its peril. In this atmosphere, the central international agency is morally constrained to avoid a flat refusal to admit the issue of minority protection to its agenda. United Nations interest in the problem is not merely a matter of moral posturing; it is also a derivative of the recognition, albeit a reluctant recognition, that the problem is significantly related to the major purposes which the organization was established to achieve.

THE SUB-COMMISSION ON PREVENTION OF DISCRIMINATION AND PRO-
    TECTION OF MINORITIES

Reverting to the organizational criterion, we can test the attitude of the United Nations by examining the record relating to the one agency for dealing with the minority problem which has appeared during the course of the structural elaboration of the United Nations system.

The Nuclear Commission on Human Rights, charged with the responsibility of recommending the structural pattern required by the Economic and Social Council for dealing with matters in this general field, did not propose the creation of special machinery for the minority problem, although it did suggest that future consideration of, that question might be appropriate.[3] However, on the initiative of the Soviet Union, the Economic and Social Council, at its Second Session (1946), developed plans which, after modification by the Commission on Human Rights, culminated in the establishment of the Sub-Commission on Prevention of Discrimination and Protection of Minorities,* on 28 March 1947.[4] This agency, theoretically composed of experts serving in their individual capacities rather than as instructed governmental representatives,[5] was established as a subordinate body of the Commission on Human Rights, for the following purposes:

> to examine what provisions should be adopted in the definition of the principles which are to be applied in the field of the prevention of discrimination on grounds of race, sex, language or religion, and in the field of the protection of minorities, and to make recommendations to the commission [on Human Rights] on urgent problems in these fields [as well as] to perform any other functions which may be entrusted to it by the Economic and Social Council or the Commission on Human Rights.[6]

Its terms of reference were revised in 1949, to put more explicit stress upon its function of undertaking *studies* and to remove the implication that it should concern itself with "urgent problems" in its fields of interest.[7]

The experiences of this Sub-Commission, the exclusive official agency of the United Nations for studying the problem of national minorities and formulating plans for implementing international concern with the problem, are highly instructive. Its members, who have exhibited the lively interest in the prestige

---

* Hereinafter referred to as the Sub-Commission.

and survival of their agency which is characteristic of all office-holders, national or international, have had the delicate task of steering between the Scylla of being ignored and the Charybdis of being abolished.

On the one hand, the work of the Sub-Commission has not been very seriously taken into account by the United Nations. It is clear that serious frustrations are inherent in the organizational niche which the Sub-Commission occupies. It cannot communicate directly with states, or even with the Secretary-General, but finds itself at the terminus of an involved set of channels which extends through the Commission on Human Rights, to the Economic and Social Council, and thence to the General Assembly. Moreover, the Sub-Commission's low status in the structural hierarchy has a symbolic as well as a technical significance; its position is a roughly accurate index of the interest of the organization in its subject matter.

Its parent body, the Commission on Human Rights, has given its work so little attention that the Sub-Commission was obliged at its Fifth Session, in 1952, to enlist the support of the Economic and Social Council in insisting that the Commission should consider the Fourth and Fifth Reports, as well as a part of the Third Report, of the Sub-Commission.[8] Members of the Sub-Commission have given frequent expression to the sense of dissatisfaction and frustration produced by the indifference of higher organs to their work, and they have felt themselves handicapped by the lack of interested guidance. Thus, Jonathan Daniels, the American member, opined at the Fifth Session that "Owing mainly to the consistent failure of the Commission on Human Rights to take any notice of or action on the reports of the Sub-Commission, the latter's work had in the past borne little relation to reality." [9]

When the Sub-Commission has not been ignored, it has frequently been rebuffed, especially by the Commission on Human Rights. Its requests for assistance in obtaining data necessary for studies have normally met with favorable consideration; beyond that, when the Sub-Commission has sought to undertake more ambitious activities or has submitted major substantive proposals, it has been generally unsuccessful. The quality of its work has been subjected to much criticism, some of it quite valid, by governmental representatives. It has become almost standard practice, however, for the Human Rights Commission to characterize the Sub-Commission's proposals as "premature," in so far as it considers them at all, rather than to express serious disagreement on the substantive merits of those proposals. This practice has led to the development of a querulous mood in the Sub-Commission; after one such incident, members of the body observed that "It seemed that the purpose had been to postpone the application of the Sub-Commission's work for fear that it might give the minorities hopes which it was not considered opportune to raise at that stage," and that "even if the Sub-Commission amended its proposals they might again be considered premature." [10]

The clearest indication of the low esteem in which the Sub-Commission is held in the United Nations is the fact that its right to meet and its very existence have been constantly in peril. The Economic and Social Council, which controls the calendar of meetings, failed to schedule a session of the Sub-Commission in 1948 — an action which "amounted to suppression," in the view of E. E. Ekstrand, then chairman of the group.[11] In 1950, the Council decided that the Sub-Commission should not hold a 1951 session, and reversed that decision only after the General Assembly made a formal request to that effect.[12] At its Thirteenth Session, in the fall of 1951, the Council approved a plan for the extensive revision of its organizational pattern, which included the discontinuation of the Sub-Commission after its Fourth Session. Formally speaking, the life of the agency was merely to be suspended until the end of 1954, but it was clear that the Council intended the definitive elimination of the Sub-Commission from its network of subordinate bodies.[13] In resentful reaction to this decision, the Sub-Commission entered a plea for reconsideration in its Fourth Report.[14] Again the General Assembly intervened, inviting the Economic and Social Council to continue the Sub-Commission indefinitely and in particular to authorize a session in 1952.[15] The Council gave in to this pressure,[16] and the Sub-Commission held its Fifth Session from 22 September to 10 October 1952. Nevertheless, it was still not assured of regular sessions; the parent body failed to arrange a meeting of the Sub-Commission in 1953, and proposed instead that it should convene, with a substantially revised roster of members, early in 1954.[17]

It would be invidious and inaccurate to assert that the Sub-Commission has been subjected to these vicissitudes simply because there is widespread sentiment among members of the United Nations for frustrating and discontinuing all efforts to achieve, by international means, the promotion of the rights of minorities. There are legitimate grounds for doubting that the Sub-Commission is, in theory or in practice, the ideal instrument for dealing with the question of what the United Nations can or should do on behalf of minority groups, and there have sometimes been good reasons for postponing or eliminating particular sessions of the Sub-Commission. The initial decision of the Economic and Social Council to avoid having the group meet in 1951 was apparently motivated primarily by budgetary considerations, a circumstance which may indicate that the protection of minorities has a low priority among United Nations projects, but which does not necessarily reflect a conspiracy against United Nations action in this field.[18] Representatives of the United States and France led the movement in the Council in 1951 to abolish the Sub-Commission, with Britain and India playing strong supporting roles.[19] Their arguments were to the effect that the Council's subordinate bodies in general, and the Sub-Commission on Prevention of Discrimination and Protection of Minorities in particular, had proved to be ineffective, and that the work of the Sub-Commission could be done more economically and efficiently by other means. Speaking for the United States, Mr. Kotschnig held that the prevention of discrimination and the protection of minorities were "too important" to be handled by an agency "working on the fringe of the Council's activities," and that prospects for action on these problems would be enhanced by moving them "nearer the fulcrum of the Council's activities." [20] In keeping with this view, the Council resolved not merely to discontinue the Sub-Commission but also to request the Secretary-General to advise on future methods whereby it might more efficaciously pursue "its efforts to abolish all forms of discrimination and to protect minorities." [21]

It is doubtful whether these expressions of interest in the

development of a more effective United Nations program on behalf of minorities should be taken at face value. In the light of the record of the Council, and of the policy viewpoints of the leading supporters of its abortive effort to eliminate the Sub-Commission, the protestations of deep concern for furthering the activities of the United Nations in this field do not ring true. The opponents of the Council's resolution invariably treated the move to end the Sub-Commission as a device to terminate the possibility of United Nations action for the protection of minorities. Haiti and the Soviet Union, which have consistently ranked as the foremost champions of the Sub-Commission, both made this point, and the Soviet Union, true to style, added the propagandistic contention that the Western Powers were trying to eliminate all barriers to ruthless domestic policies of discrimination and persecution.[22] The Soviet Union was telling an untruth; the Western Powers were, it is true, concerned to avoid outside interference in their affairs and to avoid responsibility for protecting minorities elsewhere, but the Soviet allegations about their domestic policies were made without any sense of responsibility to the facts. The supporters of the abolition of the Sub-Commission were telling somewhat more than the truth when they expressed a desire for a more positive approach to the international treatment of the problem of national minorities. The non-Communist opponents of that move were telling less than the truth, for they withheld the confession that they were actuated by a passion for writing a concern for human rights "into the record," a passion which made them indifferent to any serious consideration of ways and means and intolerant of any proposal, however well intentioned, which might be interpreted as a retreat from the most advanced human rights ideology.

It is notable that the Sub-Commission has had to look for salvation to the General Assembly — the great world forum which has so often presented the spectacle of the massing of votes by the Asian-Arab states, a large group of sympathetic Latin American states, and the Soviet bloc, in support of highly idealistic and sometimes highly irresponsible propositions which accord with doctrinaire anticolonialism and which are unacceptable to the more conservative and cautious group led by the United States, Britain, and Western European powers. When the Assembly voted in 1952 to keep the Sub-Commission in existence, only Denmark deserted the Western European–Commonwealth–North American bloc to support that decision, and only Nicaragua joined members of that bloc in opposition.[23] It is clear that the maintenance of the Sub-Commission is a part of the program of ideological symbolism to which the General Assembly lends itself as a result of widespread sympathy, genuine and feigned, for the anticolonialist position. This situation may guarantee the survival of the Sub-Commission, but it does not by any means guarantee that its work will be seriously taken into account. Many of its supporters are concerned with the Sub-Commission as a symbol, not as a working institution.

At its spring session in 1953, the Commission on Human Rights took a number of actions which seemed to betray a new and more positive appreciation of the Sub-Commission and its work. It eliminated the backlog of unexamined reports from the Sub-Commission, refrained from casting any doubts upon the indefinite survival of the agency, and recommended that the Economic and Social Council establish a pattern of regular annual sessions, of three weeks duration, for the Sub-Commission.[24] It is probably not a coincidence that this action occurred at a session of the Commission which was marked by evidence of the growing capacity of the anticolonial bloc to force acceptance of its ideological position.[25]

The Sub-Commission has been criticized on various grounds, but it would seem that its most serious offense has been to raise the inconvenient suggestion that political organs of the United Nations should adopt some of its proposals for bringing the minority problem into the sphere of active consideration. The Economic and Social Council and the Commission on Human Rights, in encouraging the Sub-Commission to study the problem and in sending back proposals marked "Premature — for further study," may have betrayed a disposition to keep the problem indefinitely bottled up in an obscure place, so as to avoid the embarrassing necessity of either repudiating or accepting the doctrine that minorities are entitled to special international protection. Indeed, the American delegate to the Economic and Social Council suggested as much when he observed that "it might be argued that its [the Sub-Commission's] existence had provided the Council with a ready excuse for not taking sufficiently effective measures. . ." [26] The existence of the Sub-Commission may equally be a symbol of ideological sympathy for human rights and a testimonial of political unwillingness to undertake the task of protecting minority rights.

In summary, the status of the Sub-Commission in the United Nations system points to the conclusion that the world organization is unwilling to repudiate the idea that the rights of national minorities are a fit subject for international action, but that it is also unwilling to come to grips with the implications of that idea.

HUMAN RIGHTS AND MINORITY RIGHTS

The United Nations has not ignored the fact that its predecessor, the League of Nations, made a systematic effort to protect the rights of national minorities, albeit not on a universal scale. This precedent has been frequently recalled, usually with reference to the fact that the effort was a failure. If the United Nations has refrained from undertaking a similar program, it has not been for lack of awareness of the history of organized international activities in this field. The new world organization has on numerous occasions faced the question of its general policy relating to national minorities, although it has avoided the formulation of a definite and explicit answer.

One possibility was that the treaties and declarations upon which the League minority system had rested might still be regarded as valid,[27] and that the United Nations should simply assume the role of guarantor and continue the old system without substantial change. This prospect aroused little enthusiasm, but in response to a request by the Sub-Commission at its First Session, the Economic and Social Council asked the Secretary-General to provide a legal opinion on the matter.

The resultant *Study of the Legal Validity of the Undertakings Concerning Minorities,* released on 7 April 1950,[28] combined detailed analysis of the legal situation, which in itself provided at best a rather indecisive answer to the question, with analysis of the prevailing political and philosophical attitudes toward the issue of special minority rights, which swung the balance decisively to the view that the League minority system was not merely suspended but was dead. It is possible to take issue with the opinion on strictly legal grounds,[29] but the Secretariat study was thoroughly realistic in its conclusion that no useful purpose was to be served by maintaining a position that was legally doubtful and politically unacceptable. As the authors of the study pointed out, the United Nations had displayed no inclination to resuscitate an inherited system for minority protection but had proceeded on the assumption that it was free to deal with the minority problem in whatever way it chose. Moreover, there was implicit in the document a lack of sympathy for the concept of positive minority rights, and an endorsement of the tendency of the United Nations to utilize new approaches to a solution of the problem.

There had never been a practical possibility that the United Nations would hitch itself to the League minority system. The consideration of the question of the continuing legal validity of that system was a means of clearing the ground for whatever action the United Nations might wish to take.

One of the major points enunciated in the *Study of the Legal Validity of the Undertakings Concerning Minorities* was that the preponderant element in the new approach to minority rights is the promotion of fundamental human rights for all human beings. "All the international decisions reached since 1944 have been inspired by a different philosophy" from that of the League, namely, the international protection of human rights, without regard for minority and majority groupings.[30] Concerning the provision of special minority rights, the authors observed: ". . . it is a system which has to a large extent been supplanted by another and which does not possess the standing that it had immediately after the First World War." [31]

However, it was not true that the United Nations had clearly and firmly rejected the view that national minorities needed and were entitled to a special regime of rights and safeguards, in favor of the complete identification of the minority problem with the general problem of human rights.

At its First Session, the General Assembly adopted an Egyptian draft resolution calling upon governments "to put an immediate end to religious and so-called racial persecution and discrimination," a proposal put forward with explicit reference to allegedly oppressive treatment of minorities in Central Europe.[32]

Commenting on this and another Assembly decision, the Department of Public Information stated that "to the United Nations the prevention of discrimination and the protection of minorities, constitutes a Charter obligation. . . ." [33] Simultaneously with the adoption of the Universal Declaration of Human Rights, the Assembly formally expressed the view that "the United Nations cannot remain indifferent to the fate of minorities," and called for studies to enable the organization "to take effective measures for the protection of racial, national, religious or linguistic minorities." [34] The creation of the Sub-Commission by the Economic and Social Council was a move taken in accordance with this point of view. In his *Annual Report* for the period from 1 July 1951 to 30 June 1952, the Secretary-General held that "The prevention of discrimination and the protection of minorities, which the General Assembly considers to be two of the most important branches of the work undertaken by the United Nations, continue to be major concerns of the Organization." [35]

These examples support the thesis that the United Nations has not committed itself decisively to the theoretical position that the minority problem has been wholly absorbed into the larger problem of human rights, losing its status as a distinct issue calling for separate treatment. In fact, the organization has repeatedly considered the possibility of according to national minorities "the recognition of certain special rights and the rendering of certain positive services" [36] designed to facilitate the maintenance of their distinctive qualities as groups.

THE GENOCIDE CONVENTION

The issue of special minority protection first arose in connection with the project of formulating the Convention on the Prevention and Punishment of the Crime of Genocide, launched by the Economic and Social Council on the initiative of the First General Assembly.[37]

The *Ad Hoc* Committee on Genocide, which began its work on 5 April 1948, had before it a Draft Convention provided by the Secretariat, defining the crime which was to be proscribed according to a three-fold classification: physical genocide — the destruction of groups by the actual destruction of individuals; biological genocide — the prevention of births within a group;

and *cultural genocide* — the "brutal destruction of the specific characteristics of a group" by various measures designed to undermine its cultural and linguistic traditions.[38] The reference to cultural genocide was obviously motivated by the sense of obligation to provide the *Ad Hoc* Committee with a comprehensive list of ideas; the Secretariat paper pointed out that only one of the experts who had been consulted (Professor Raphael Lemkin, the prime mover of the genocide project) believed that the concept of cultural genocide should be included, and it went to some pains to argue that forced assimilation and transfer of minorities should not fall within the definition unless they were carried out by flagrantly immoderate methods. The skepticism of the Secretariat regarding cultural genocide was made more explicit in a later note, in which the will of the General Assembly was interpreted as calling for the definition of genocide with reference "to the actual destruction of a human group and not to restrictions, ill-treatment or oppression of that group." [39]

Despite strong opposition by the United States and France, the *Ad Hoc* Committee voted overwhelmingly to retain the concept of cultural genocide in the draft convention.[40]

The debate was continued and the decision reversed, when the General Assembly held its Third Session in the fall of 1948. The agenda item relating to the Genocide Convention was referred to the Sixth (Legal) Committee, where the battle to retain the cultural genocide provision was waged by a group of states which included prominently the Soviet bloc and a number of Asian-Arab states, against a determined opposition which was conspicuously representative of European and European-derived peoples. One interesting deviation from the pattern suggested above was the position of India, whose objection to the inclusion of cultural genocide was clearly related to the fact that Pakistan, an ardent supporter of the provision, proclaimed that it could hardly wait to haul its neighbor before a tribunal as a violator of the cultural rights of its Moslem minority.[41] The Committee voted to delete the reference to cultural genocide,[42] and the General Assembly upheld that decision, despite efforts by Venezuela and the Soviet Union to overturn it by amendment.[43] Thus, the United Nations declined its first invitation to give official support to the concept of positive minority rights.

Despite this outcome, it may be argued with some cogency that the approval of the Convention by the General Assembly constituted a significant action on behalf of the rights of minorities. The first resolution of the General Assembly on the subject pointed out that "Genocide is a denial of the right of existence of entire human groups. . .," [44] and Article II of the Convention defines the crime in terms of "intent to destroy, in whole or in part, a national, ethnical, racial or religious group, as such." [45] The Convention reflected the bitter memory of Hitler's ruthless policies, especially his extermination of Jews; it may have been the product of an international bad conscience over the failure to take action to frustrate the genocidal projects of the Nazi Government, and of a determination to support the somewhat shaky foundations of the law of the International Military Tribunal at Nuremberg and to expand the scope of that law to cover peace-time crimes against humanity. Clearly, the Convention was designed to single out "groups," including such groups as national minorities, as potential victims of viciously inhumane policies who have particular need for international protection. In this sense, the passage of the Genocide Convention was a strikingly ambitious effort to deal with the problem of national minorities, regardless of the fact that it related only to the prohibition of physical destruction. Who can doubt that the right to life in the literal sense is the most basic right of all?

Nevertheless, it is not clear that the United Nations, in adopting the Genocide Convention, regarded its action as a response to the need for dealing with the problem of national minorities. One of the points most persistently made by the successful opponents of the incorporation of cultural safeguards in the Convention was that their adversaries had chosen the wrong time and place for their campaign; they referred to the fact that a special Sub-Commission had been established to deal with the minority problem, and suggested that more appropriate occasions would arise for bringing forward proposals looking to the protection of minority rights. Thus, the United States insisted that the matter of cultural oppression "should appropriately be dealt with in connection with the protection of minorities," [46] a statement which indicated that the United States did *not* regard the Genocide Convention as being connected with that problem. Similarly, the commentary accompanying the Secretariat's draft convention undertook to maintain a distinction between the protection of minorities and the prohibition of genocide.[47] Further evidence is provided by the fact that the Sub-Commission was not called upon to participate in the development of the Genocide Convention, and that the item was referred to the Sixth (Legal) Committee at the Third General Assembly rather than to the Third (Social, Humanitarian, and Cultural) Committee, which normally handles matters related to the minority question. Indeed, in the light of the usual reception of such proposals in United Nations organs, it seems questionable whether the Convention would have been adopted if it had been presented to the Assembly as a measure for the protection of minorities, rather than as an expression of disapprobation for Hitler and respect for his victims and a contribution to the development of a more humane system of international law.

It is clear that members of the United Nations will vote to repudiate Hitlerism; it is not equally clear that they will vote to carry on the League's effort to protect minorities, even by other means. This observation does not detract from the undoubted significance of the Genocide Convention from the point of view of national minorities, but it should be taken as a warning against the misapprehension that the United Nations, in accepting the Convention, was expressing the will to face boldly and act positively with respect to the minority problem.

THE DECLARATION OF HUMAN RIGHTS

The General Assembly adopted the Genocide Convention on 9 December 1948; on the following day, it adopted the Universal Declaration of Human Rights. On the latter occasion as on the former, it was confronted with the question of accepting or rejecting the proposition that national minorities are entitled to special rights related to the aim of perpetuating their distinctive characteristics. On both occasions, its response was the same.

The project of developing an international Declaration of Human Rights, adumbrated at the San Francisco Conference, got under way during the summer of 1947. The Drafting Committee of the Commission on Human Rights, at its first session, received a Secretariat draft which included an article calling for the right of minorities to use their own languages and to maintain schools and other cultural institutions, which would be supported "out of an equitable proportion of any public funds available for the purpose." [48] The Secretariat draft was exceptional in this respect; suggested versions of the Human Rights Declaration submitted by Chile, Cuba, Panama, India, the United States, and the United Kingdom contained no such provisions. [49] In the Annexes to its First Report to the Commission on Human Rights, the Drafting Committee reproduced the Secretariat draft, with its minority rights article, a French suggestion similarly drawn but without the stipulation for possible governmental support of minority institutions, and the committee's own proposal for an article relating to positive minority rights, which followed the general lines of the French proposal. The committee suggested that the Sub-Commission should be asked for advice concerning the article on minority rights, about which it obviously felt some uncertainty. [50]

Meeting for the first time from 24 November to 6 December 1947, the Sub-Commission had before it the proposed minority rights articles mentioned above, in addition to similar proposals from nongovernmental sources. [51] It proceeded to produce a draft of its own, which was more carefully qualified than any previous formulation. The Sub-Commission's article insisted that minority groups eligible for linguistic and institutional rights should be "well defined" and "clearly distinguished" from other elements of the population and should "want to be accorded differential treatment," and it conferred rights only within the limits of compatibility with public order and security. [52] A proposal by A. P. Borisov, member from the Soviet Union, that minority rights be strengthened by providing that governments have an obligation to provide funds and arrangements for group autonomy was strenuously opposed and voted down in the Sub-Commission. [53]

At the Second Session of the Commission on Human Rights, the Working Group on the Declaration rejected an American proposal to abandon the project of an article on positive minority rights and a Byelorussian proposal along the lines of the Borisov plan to require effective governmental support of minority cultural development, and recommended the retention of both the

Drafting Committee's and the Sub-Commission's texts as alternative suggestions for a minority rights article.[54] The Commission followed this advice, incorporating the two texts under Article 31 of its draft declaration with the parenthetical note that it, having reached no decision on the matter, was reproducing these proposals for further consideration by governments.[55]

The number of alternative texts continued to grow in 1948. The second report submitted by the Drafting Committee to the Commission on Human Rights listed, in addition to the familiar versions of the article, a French proposal which surpassed the Sub-Commission draft in its circumscription of minority rights, by adding the proviso that linguistic and institutional privileges should be accorded only to the extent that such a policy was "in conformity with the degree of legislative unity in the State." The report also included a singularly brief formulation suggested by the United Kingdom to the effect that "Minorities shall be entitled to preserve their culture, religion and language," and an American text which purported to replace three articles of the draft declaration and which related to minority rights only in providing that "Everyone is entitled to . . . participate in the customs and the cultural life of the community and of groups in the community. . ." [56]

This was the high point of the drive to include provision for positive minority rights in the Declaration of Human Rights. It should be noted that the Commission had never gone farther than to include unagreed texts of minority rights articles in its Second Report. At its Third Session, from 24 May to 18 June 1948, it accepted a proposal, initiated by India, the United Kingdom, and China,[57] and strongly supported by the United States, to omit from the declaration any reference to the rights of minorities to use their native tongues and to maintain educational and cultural institutions.[58]

Thus, when the decisive stage in the formulation of the Declaration of Human Rights was reached in the fall of 1948, the General Assembly was confronted with a draft, embodied in the Third Report of the Commission on Human Rights,[59] from which all proposals for recognition of positive minority rights had been deleted. The issue was thoroughly debated in the Third Committee, which received proposals from the Soviet Union, Yugoslavia, and Denmark to remedy this omission,[60] but the Committee was willing only to recommend that the Assembly accept a suggestion from the representative of Haiti that those proposals be transmitted to the Commission on Human Rights and its Sub-Commission, for utilization in future studies looking toward the discovery of methods by which the United Nations might act effectively on behalf of minorities.[61]

At its plenary meeting on 10 December 1948, the General Assembly resisted a Soviet attempt to insert a minority rights article, adopted the Universal Declaration of Human Rights, and passed a resolution on the "Fate of Minorities," in which it undertook to refute any impression of indifference to the minority problem and accepted the Haitian proposal which the Third Committee had recommended.[62]

The Declaration of Human Rights was by no means insignificant from the standpoint of national minorities; as the opponents of a special minority article had insistently argued, its hortatory influence was directed to securing respect for the human rights of members of minorities as well as all other persons, and its strictures against discrimination were especially important for members of such groups. Nevertheless, the Assembly explicitly recognized that in refusing to include a provision on positive minority rights it had left in abeyance the solution of the problem of minorities.

THE COVENANTS ON HUMAN RIGHTS

After the adoption of the Declaration with its purely moral validity, the Commission on Human Rights gave priority to the development of a Covenant, under which states would accept legal obligations to respect an internationally defined list of rights and freedoms. At its Sixth Session, the General Assembly decided to break the projected multilateral convention into two independent parts, a Covenant on Civil and Political Rights and a Covenant on Economic, Social, and Cultural Rights.[63]

During the long and tortuous process of working out acceptable drafts of the Covenants, which has involved repeated consideration of the matter by the General Assembly, the Commission on Human Rights, and the Sub-Commission, inter alia, the documentation has come to include draft proposals by Yugoslavia and the USSR which undertake to facilitate the cultural survival and development of national minorities by granting linguistic and institutional rights.[64] In addition, the Sub-Commission adopted in 1950 — and reiterated in 1951 and 1952 — the following draft article:

> Persons belonging to ethnic, religious, or linguistic minorities shall not be denied the right, in community with the other members of their group, to enjoy their own culture, to profess and practice their own religion, or to use their own language.[65]

These three proposals were reproduced under the heading, "Additional Articles," in the Sixth, Seventh, and Eighth Reports of the Commission on Human Rights.[66]

It was not until 1953 that the Commission gave serious attention to the question of incorporating an article on minority rights in its own recommended versions of human rights treaties. At its Ninth Session, it took the surprising step of adopting such a provision, inserted as Article 25 of the Draft Covenant on Civil and Political Rights.[67] The significance of this action should be carefully and cautiously evaluated. The Commission acted on the basis of the draft proposed by the Sub-Commission, which was the least detailed and explicit of the proposals before it; it modified that draft by prefacing it with the words, "In those States in which ethnic, religious or linguistic minorities exist. . ." In view of the fact that this amendment was proposed by the representative of Chile,[68] it appears that its approval by the Commission constituted a deliberate recognition of the contention that minorities as such do not exist in the Western Hemisphere. This interpretation is supported by the following passage from the Ninth Report:

> The majority of the members argued that the term "minorities" should be understood to cover well-defined and long-established minorities; and that the rights of persons belonging to minorities should not be interpreted as entitling any. group settled in the territory of a State, particularly under the terms of its immigration laws, to form within that State separate communities which might impair its national unity or its security.[69]

The Commission's approval of the concept of positive minority rights appears to have been qualified in such a manner as to permit states to hold the provisions of Article 25 inapplicable, if they deny that ethnically differentiated groups in their population constitute minorities in the classical European sense, or if they look with disfavor and apprehension upon the efforts of such groups to perpetuate their distinctive qualities.

In any event, the drafts formulated by the Commission on Human Rights are subject to revision by the General Assembly. For reasons not relevant to the purposes of this analysis, the issue of the ultimate adoption by the United Nations of the Covenants on Human Rights is very much in doubt. If this project is carried to completion, the Covenant on Civil and Political Rights may contain an article on minority rights, but that article will not reflect a general recognition by members of the organization that national minorities are entitled to the enjoyment of special rights which it is the duty of international organization to uphold in the face of nonrecognition by their own governments.

The general coolness of the United Nations toward proposals for special minority rights is illustrated by the reception given to the Sub-Commission's recommendation for "Interim Measures" — a proposal adopted in 1949, on the initiative of Jonathan Daniels, which calls upon the General Assembly to put its moral weight behind the proposition that minority groups should be afforded opportunities and facilities for preserving their cultural heritage.[70] Despite insistent reiteration by the Sub-Commission at each of its subsequent sessions, this recommendation has been held back by the Commission on Human Rights for alleged prematurity.

At its Ninth Session, the Commission returned to the Sub-Commission for further study both its formal Definition of Minorities and its standing request for Interim Measures, while it adopted not only the minority rights article mentioned above, but also proposals sponsored by the Sub-Commission that the General Assembly be asked to pass a resolution condemning discrimination and recommending that governments provide protection for minorities whose requirements are not met by the principle of nondiscrimination, and that the Economic and Social Council be requested to support the principle that "special attention should be paid to the protection of any minority" that might be created by the revision of boundaries or the establishment of new states.[71]

This combination of actions by the Commission is most illuminating. It is now prepared to support minority rights to the extent of endorsing admonitions of a relatively vague and inexplicit nature, addressed to any states which may feel that they are the kind of states for which the concept of minority rights makes sense. What is most significant is that the Commission is *not* prepared to suggest that *all* members of the United Nations, regardless of their attitudes toward national minorities, should be pressed to recognize minority rights, even by so innocuous a device as a resolution of the General Assembly. Implicit in the Commission's position is an attitude of firm respect for the unilateral right of states to decide whether they have population groups which they wish to define as minorities eligible for special status. The intended impact of the minority rights article adopted at the Ninth Session cannot be accurately measured without taking into account this general attitude, expressed by the Commission at the same session..

Finally, the idea of formulating a special multilateral convention under United Nations auspices, devoted exclusively to the establishment of positive minority rights, has received unfavorable consideration. This possibility, suggested by Sweden at the Third General Assembly,[72] was raised by M. R. Masani, the Indian expert, at the Third Session of the Sub-Commission.[73] An elaborate draft convention, compiled by three members, was presented to the Sub-Commission in 1951, but that body was unwilling to give serious consideration to the proposal that it proceed at that time to promote the rights of minorities by such means.[74] Although the concept was again mentioned before the Sub-Commission in 1952, by a spokesman for the International League for the Rights of Man,[75] there seems to be little prospect that a general convention on minority rights will be produced by the United Nations.

FUNDAMENTALS OF THE UNITED NATIONS APPROACH

In examining the record of the United Nations with respect to the general problem of minority rights, we have found that the world organization has, in the first place, sought to promote respect for the human rights of all individuals without regard for their membership in minorities or majorities, through its adoption of the Declaration of Human Rights and its efforts to complete Covenants on Human Rights. Secondly, it has addressed to states a general admonition not to persecute minority groups, in Resolution 103 (I) of the General Assembly, and has ushered into legal existence the Convention on Genocide with its prohibition of the most drastic varieties of antiminority policy. In the third place, it has given formal recognition to the concept that national minorities present a special problem for solution by international means, in the General Assembly Resolution on the "Fate of Minorities," adopted in conjunction with the Declaration of Human Rights, and in the act of creating a special Sub-Commission to deal with the problem. Finally, the United Nations has definitively rejected the utilization of the Genocide Convention and the Declaration of Human Rights as instruments for the establishment of positive minority rights, and has thus far refrained from establishing such rights by any other device, even though the Commission on Human Rights has held open the possibility that the Covenant on Civil and Political Rights may be used for that purpose.

In the light of this analysis, it would seem to be a valid conclusion that there is little prospect that the United Nations will continue, in any form, the experiment launched by the League of Nations in the international definition and protection of special rights, of a positive nature, for national minorities. The final rejection has not occurred; if it does occur, it may be masked as an acceptance. The favorite tactic in the United Nations has been neither to accept nor to reject proposals for minority rights, but to "postpone" them. The classic example of this tactic occurred in 1948, when the United States led a group of states in deleting the cultural genocide clauses from the draft Genocide Convention, on the ground that the cultural rights of minorities should be safeguarded in the human rights documents, and simultaneously fought to eliminate reference to those rights in the draft Declaration of Human Rights, on the ground that they were out of place there. In general, this attitude has prevailed: wherever the issue is presented, it is out of place; whenever it is presented, it is premature.

Aside from tactical maneuvers to avoid the necessity of bluntly rejecting the concept of minority rights, it is clear that many members of the United Nations do reject that concept, and there is no substantial evidence that their attitude will not continue to be dominant in the United Nations. The reason for the refusal to admit rejection of the concept is clear enough; it is a matter of international public relations in an era of intense ideological competition. The reasons for the actual rejection are more complex.

The heart of the matter, at least in theoretical terms, is the question of national attitudes toward *assimilation*. In Eastern and Central Europe, the classic *locus* of the problem of national minorities, the assertion that the right not to be assimilated is a basic human right would occasion no surprise. Consequently, it is not surprising that the representatives of the peoples living in that area, or those who wish to appear as genuine representatives of those peoples, should champion the positive rights of minorities. The movement to establish those rights has been consistently led by the Soviet Union, its European satellites, and Yugoslavia. It has been joined sporadically by Denmark and Sweden, and by various members of the anticolonial bloc who have evidently been swayed by the feeling that forced assimilation is related to the assertions of cultural superiority with which colonial peoples are painfully familiar. Minority rights proposals have gained the votes of many statesmen who have been actuated mainly by vague sentiments of good will, but it has been left primarily to Eastern Europeans to state clearly that the case rests upon the conviction that minorities are justified in rejecting assimilation. In the debates concerning the Declaration of Human Rights, a spokesman for Yugoslavia argued that minorities must be protected against the danger of "losing their national character," and insisted that the individual could not enjoy human rights in any meaningful sense unless adequate recognition was given to the ethnic collectivity of which he was an integral part;[76] a Byelorussian representative held "that the right to his native culture was a basic right of every human being." [77] The Soviet Union has been an indefatigable producer of draft formulations of minority rights and of speeches extolling the virtues of Soviet nationality policy, representing the minority rights movement in the United Nations as an effort to universalize the benefits enjoyed by Soviet minorities, and scolding its opponents for claiming to worry about the security risks involved in such an innocuous matter as allowing minorities to speak their own language and maintain their own schools.[78]

On the other hand, the assimilationist position has strong and varied bases of support in the United Nations. Many governments are not simply unwilling to grant positive minority rights, but are also fundamentally unable to understand the desire for them or to convince themselves that anyone could seriously regard them as basic human rights. Countries of immigration, accustomed to receiving their minorities as individual persons who have voluntarily severed their ties with their old ethnic units and moved to become part of a new society, disapprove of anything which might encourage immigrants to enter with the intention of maintaining their separateness. States whose minorities have persistently opposed segregation are bewildered by the concept that differential treatment might be regarded as a boon rather than a badge of second-class citizenship. Vigorously nationalistic peoples are offended by the suggestion that there is anything immoral about policies designed to promote national solidarity. Security-conscious states are alert to the dangers posed by undigested groups whose loyalties might permit them to be exploited by foreign powers. These considerations, in varying combinations, account for the fact that whenever the issue must be squarely faced, the United States takes the lead and most Latin American, Western European, and British Commonwealth states join in opposing the concept of special minority rights. It is worthy of note that when assimilation becomes the focal question, the anticolonial bloc is split; proud possessors of a new national independence are not likely to welcome restrictions which would "hamper a reasonable policy of assimilation which no State aiming at national unity could be expected to renounce."[79] Mrs. Roosevelt assumed the universal validity of the American tradition — and betrayed a bad memory — when she stood as Chairman in the Commission on Human Rights and "recalled that previous debates on the question had brought out that the aim of States was to assimilate and absorb large foreign groups, and to make them part of the nation." [80]

The question of assimilation has played a curiously indecisive role in the debates of the Sub-Commission. In this body, if anywhere in the United Nations organization, we might expect to find a frank exploration of the philosophical ground that lies between assimilationists and anti-assimilationists. It cannot be argued that this is the "wrong place" for such a discussion, and the Sub-Commission's members are at least relatively free to discuss matters as independent thinkers rather than as governmental messenger boys. Yet, one searches in vain for a consistent correspondence between the views of its members concerning assimilation and their attitudes toward granting positive rights to minorities. It would appear that these experts believe that they have a mandate to espouse the cause of minority rights, even if they disbelieve in the assumptions upon which that cause rests. The resolutions emanating from the Sub-Commission are much more favorable to minority rights than the tone of the debates which the resolutions should presumably reflect.

The ambiguity in the positions and words of several members has been startling. Jonathan Daniels, the American member during the first five sessions, has been an outstanding advocate of measures designed to promote the cultural rights of minorities, and yet he displayed a consistent and typically American skepticism toward the principle of special minority status at least until 1 October 1952, when he took the position that it was urgently important for the Sub-Commission to "protect the rights of certain minority groups which desired to maintain their own customs, language and culture." The theoretical position of A. Meneses Pallares, member from Ecuador, is summarized in his remark that the goal of the United Nations should be "to find means to ensure the rapid assimilation of minority groups";[82] nevertheless, he has participated actively, and with apparent approval, in the preparation and passage of proposals which rest upon precisely the opposite theoretical basis. Miss Elizabeth Monroe of the United Kingdom was, during her period of membership, the self-appointed theoretician of the group. She gave clear evidence that she understood the difference between the unwilling minority which craves only nondiscriminatory treatment and the insistently self-conscious minority which demands differential treatment, and she urged that groups of the latter type should be granted the rights needed for cultural self-preservation; yet, when confronted with a draft convention for special minority rights, she opposed it on the ground that "it was not the function of the Sub-Commission to formulate minority rights separate and distinct from human rights," and expressed doubts that it was desirable to single out national minorities for protection.[83]

In terms of formally adopted positions, the Sub-Commission has definitely been the official organ of the United Nations most favorably disposed toward the establishment of positive minority rights. But even in this agency, the general tendency of the United Nations to approve the theory and practice of assimilation has been strongly manifested.

There has been a general tendency in United Nations debates for speakers to state blandly that the minority problem does not exist in their own countries, or that it has been satisfactorily solved by enlightened domestic policies, but then to concede that there may be need for international action on behalf of minorities in benighted foreign lands. Beyond this, assimilationists have, in their most tolerant moods, been prepared to admit that their policy views are not universally applicable, and that positive minority rights might be desirable in some parts of the world. Thus, during the debate on the insertion of minority rights articles in the Declaration of Human Rights, Mrs. Roosevelt expressed the view that a program for promoting universal human rights offered the best solution for the minority problem, but conceded that in Europe the problem might require different treatment.[84] The British Government took the position that neither the policy of identical treatment nor the policy of differential treatment of minorities was universally acceptable, and that consequently each country should be left free to adopt either solution.[85] In the Sub-Commission's discussion of a general convention on minority rights, Miss Monroe, among others, denied the possibility of a uniform solution for the whole world;[86] at about the same time, she endorsed the assertion that while the United Nations should avoid creating minority consciousness, the Sub-Commission had a clear duty "to provide an international recourse for minorities who genuinely need it." [87]

Despite Miss Monroe's bow to the needs of minorities, the clear implication of this line of thought is that policy should be determined not by the needs of minorities but by the preferences of states, who should be left free by international organization to deal with their minority groups in whatever way they might choose. Thus, the concessions of assimilationists are essentially meaningless; it is to be international policy to establish a standard of human rights to be granted to all persons on an equal basis, to refrain from recognizing any right of minorities to expect from their governments a pattern of differential treatment favorable to the perpetuation of their culture, and implicitly to endorse domestic policies of assimilation. This is the general policy of the United Nations.

There are other factors to be considered in explaining the general rejection of the concept of special minority rights in the United Nations. It does not simply reflect an inhumane lack of sympathy with the desires of minorities, or an obtuse failure to appreciate the values of cultural diversity, or an exaggerated devotion to the sovereign right of states to determine their own domestic policies. It is pre-eminently a political attitude, with ramifications which connect it with major political issues far beyond the range of the question of assimilation.

The minority question has not escaped involvement in the conflict between the United States and the Soviet Union and their respective coalitions. It has frequently been brought before the United Nations not for solution but for exploitation.

There is good reason to doubt the sincerity of the persistent advocacy of minority rights by the USSR. It would appear that Soviet policy has been far less generous to minorities than its theoretical expositions would suggest or many prewar Western commentators seemed to believe. The Soviet demands for United Nations action on behalf of minorities have regularly been vitiated by rigid insistence on the doctrine that minority affairs fall within the realm of domestic jurisdiction so as absolutely to preclude all international efforts to protect minorities or supervise their treatment. Finally, Soviet representatives have seldom put forward a proposal for minority rights or nondiscrimination without treating it as the prelude to a polemical attack upon the United

States for its shortcomings, real and alleged, in this field. The issue of special minority rights has been used as an anti-American political weapon, without regard for the fact that minorities in the United States are almost exclusively concerned with gaining equality of treatment rather than rights designed to aid in resisting assimilation.

As for the United States, it began its participation in the United Nations with a genuine inability to understand the concept of positive minority rights, except in a most academic fashion. It is possible that American statesmen have been discouraged from developing a sympathetic attitude toward that concept by the fact that the Soviet Union and its cohorts were its most vehement sponsors; American policy may reflect calculated pro-assimilationism less than suspicious anti-Communism. Moreover, the United States, like many other countries, hesitates to support the international recognition of special minority rights for fear of its own vulnerability to propagandistic criticism from governments whose real motives may be less respectable than that of upholding minority rights.

In 1952, significant changes occurred in the utilization of the minority issue as a weapon in the Soviet-American struggle. It appears that the USSR suddenly realized that the "prevention of discrimination" end of the club was superior to the "protection of minorities" end, as an anti-American instrument, inasmuch as American minorities could be heard complaining about discrimination but not demanding cultural autonomy. Consequently, the Soviet Union and Poland urged at the Fourteenth Session of the Economic and Social Council that the Sub-Commission should be instructed to emphasize the problem of discrimination in its future work. The American representative rose to the occasion and launched a counteroffensive; recalling that "instances of the liquidation of whole minority groups were found in certain parts of the world at the current time," he intimated that the Soviet bloc was trying to divert world attention from the minority problem and declared that the United States regarded the protection of minorities as a matter of perhaps greater importance than the prevention of discrimination.[88]

It was not immediately clear whether the United States had gained the offensive. At the next session of the Sub-Commission,

Jonathan Daniels embraced the idea of minority protection with unwonted warmth and was met with veiled allegations that he was changing the subject because the issue of discrimination was embarrassing to the United States.[89] The American intention became clear, however, in February 1953, when Henry Cabot Lodge, Jr., used the forum of the General Assembly's First Committee to denounce Soviet persecution of Christians, Moslems, and Jews,[90] and the Senate followed up the attack by giving unanimous approval to a resolution denouncing "the vicious and inhuman campaigns conducted by the Soviet Government and its puppet governments . . . against minority groups," including religious and ethnic groups, and urging the President to protest these outrages in the United Nations, in order that the organization might "take such action in opposition to them as may be suitable under its Charter." [91]

Thus, the United States undertook to seize the minority issue as a political weapon to be used against the Soviet Union. However, American policy had insured that it would be a relatively poor weapon. The United States, having refrained from ratifying the Convention on Genocide, had put itself in no position to raise that issue; having led the fight to prevent international legislation on the protection of minority rights, it had helped to prevent the United Nations from acquiring uncontested competence to deal with its complaints. Soon thereafter, when the United States withdrew its support from the project of producing Covenants on Human Rights for ratification,[92] it further reduced the possibility of effective United Nations response to its allegations. Moreover, much of the publicly available evidence used by American critics of Soviet treatment of minorities was most closely relevant to the charge of Russification — a charge which the United States, as a prominent supporter of the assimilationist solution of minority problems, was peculiarly unfitted to raise in the United Nations.[93]

The question of minority rights has also become entangled in the complex issues of the program for political emancipation which the anticolonial bloc has made its major concern in the United Nations.

The Asian-Arab states, with the support of many Latin American states and the Soviet bloc, have waged a persistent campaign to maximize the obligations of the powers which administer non-self-governing territories subject to the provisions of Chapter XI of the Charter, and to accelerate progress toward independence by peoples who live under the United Nations system of trusteeship. This pressure has been resisted by the representatives of the old system of European colonialism, who are confident that they are sound judges as to the rate of progress that can be safely attempted and actually achieved, and who resent efforts to force upon them the enlargement of international commitments which they have voluntarily accepted.

The most interesting response to anticolonial pressures has been made by Belgium, whose Permanent Representative to the United Nations, Fernand Van Langenhove, began in 1951 to develop the idea that the obligations of Chapter XI should be deemed to apply not only to colonial powers with respect to their overseas possessions, but also to other states with respect to primitive peoples or subdued nations living within their metropolitan or contiguous territory.[94] This position was further developed in May 1952, in a communication submitted to the United Nations by the Belgian Government, which listed relatively primitive indigenous groups in many countries, including most of the members of the anticolonial bloc, as peoples who had been unjustly deprived of international supervision by an artificially restrictive interpretation of Chapter XI of the Charter.[95] The Belgian tactic was very much like that of the states bound by the League minority system, who had expressed their resentment and hostility toward the system by asking that it be universalized; Belgium was playing the game, "if you can't beat them, make them join you." It seems unlikely that Belgium was as much interested in the fate of the Adibasi of India or the Dyaks of Indonesia as in the possibility of embarrassing the anticolonial powers.

Beginning with the Fifth Session of the General Assembly in the fall of 1950, the anticolonial bloc has conducted a drive to strengthen its program of political emancipation by writing into the Covenants on Human Rights provisions establishing a legal right of self-determination for all peoples.[96] The intricate relationships between the minority question and this campaign are worthy of particular notice. Logically, the connection between the two matters is obvious; if there is a universal right of self-determination, it would appear that minorities are eligible to solve the problem of their own status by opting for secession in order to assume political independence or join the states of their ethnic brethren. In practice, however, the relationship between minority rights and national self-determination has been treated not as a problem of logic but as a matter of political tactics.

The Soviet Union, a self-styled friend of the anticolonial movement, has invariably treated minority rights and national self-determination as intimately related concepts. As early as 4 May 1948, Soviet spokesmen were attempting to tie together the minority issue and anticolonialism.[97] Thenceforward, many of the draft proposals emanating from Soviet sources combined demands for national self-determination and minority rights.[98] Indeed, it was a Soviet proposal joining the two issues which served to move the Fifth General Assembly into its position of supporting the self-determination campaign, and spokesmen for the Soviet bloc injected into the debate the explicit point that the two issues were interrelated.[99] In the light of the USSR's ideological history and political purposes, this conduct is understandable; Bolshevik nationality theory has always made this connection,[100] and Soviet policy in the United Nations has indicated that the USSR looks upon both self-determination and minority rights as valuable propaganda counters for use against the Western powers. The Soviet Union realized that it was unable to put its minority rights legislation through the United Nations because of the lack of solid support from the anticolonial bloc; it may have believed that, by tying minority rights to the kite of national self-determination, it could gain unanimous anticolonial support and thereby secure United Nations endorsement of *both* its favorite ideological weapons.

In contrast to Soviet policy, the Asian and Arab friends of dependent peoples have tried insistently to keep the two issues of minority rights and self-determination divorced from each other. They have regarded the campaign for recognition of the right of self-determination as merely a new phase of their effort to expand the commitments accepted by states which control non-self-governing territories under Chapter XI. When the

Polish delegate asserted in the Commission on Human Rights, on 17 April 1952, that: "The right to self-determination could not be fully ensured without guaranteeing the right of national minorities to use their native tongue and to have their own cultural and educational institutions," [101] the Lebanese and Indian representatives responded that minority rights constituted an entirely separate issue, irrelevant to the problem of self-determination. The position of the anticolonial states had previously been made perfectly clear; according to Mr. Azkoul of Lebanon, "the pivot of the whole problem was not the position of minorities, but that of countries that had lost their independence as a result of aggression. *The main issue was that of Non-Self-Governing Territories. . . .*" [102] It might be suggested that the Asian and Arab states are themselves reluctant to permit international interference with their own treatment of minorities. In all probability, however, they are decisively motivated by the recognition of the general unpopularity of the minority rights movement in the United Nations and the consequent fear that if self-determination is tied to minority rights, the latter will pull the former down to defeat.

This apprehension has been noted and exploited by Belgium. Just as Belgium has tried to halt the campaign to expand obligations relating to non-self-governing territories by burdening it with the logic of universalization, so it has attempted to defeat the closely related national self-determination movement by associating it with minority rights. At the Eighth Session of the Commission on Human Rights, something close to a personal feud developed between Joseph Nisot of Belgium and Mrs. Mehta of India. Nisot posed as a staunch friend of self-determination for any and all peoples, including national minorities; when he pressed from Mrs. Mehta the admission that her Government was concerned with the principle of self-determination solely as an instrument for promoting the emancipation of colonial peoples, he retorted triumphantly that anyone who favored self-determination for a selected clientele only, and not for all peoples, was not a genuine believer in the noble ideal.[103] Two motives stood out in the Belgian tactic: to embarrass the USSR, by showing that the principle of national self-determination was relevant to the captive peoples in the Soviet empire as well as to colonial peoples,[104] and, more importantly, to use the minority rights issue to thwart the ambitions of the anticolonial bloc. The United Kingdom appears to have been blind to the possibilities inherent in the Belgian line at first, but later saw the light and joined forces with Belgium.[105] Their espousal of the rights of minorities was obviously only an expedient device for discomfiting their anticolonial attackers.

Finally, the United States insisted upon divorcing the two issues. Speaking before the Commission on Human Rights on 17 April 1952, Mrs. Roosevelt argued for the deletion of the paragraph concerning minority rights from the Soviet draft resolution on national self-determination. Her objection was pointed toward the effort to achieve by indirection the approval of provisions for minority rights which had consistently been rejected when presented in a straightforward manner; the United States was still standing for the right of states to pursue a policy of assimilation.[106]

Thus, the Soviet bloc tied the issues of minority rights and self-determination together, hoping that the popularity of the latter would carry the former through. The anticolonial bloc divorced the two, fearing that the unpopularity of minority rights would doom national self-determination. Belgium linked the two, hoping for what the anticolonials feared, while the United States separated the two, fearing that for which the Soviets hoped. Certainly, the minority problem entered into the discussion on self-determination, but it was never considered on its own merits or for its own sake.

If the United Nations had wished, in its early years, to establish a general system for dealing with the problem of national minorities, it would have been confronted by formidable practical difficulties. It could not have imposed obligations to respect minority rights upon states which wished to pursue policies of assimilation unhampered by international interference, without having in its possession some unusual means of compelling acceptance. The League of Nations had been able to use, for this end, the political dependence of the succession states and the desires for membership of certain other minor states; it is not clear that such instruments were available to the United Nations. A United Nations effort to impose minority obligations upon a selected group of states would have encountered stiff political resistance. If the organization had undertaken to establish a universal system of minority protection, it would have had to rely, most precariously, upon the prospect that states would subject themselves to it voluntarily — and the very states whose minority policy would most require international supervision would have been the least likely to accept it. Even if minority rights were written into the conventions relating to genocide and human rights, their legal validity would depend upon ratification by states.

These practical difficulties are essentially irrelevant, however, since the United Nations has displayed a definite disinclination to attempt the formulation, in general terms, of an international solution to the problem of national minorities. It is possible that a future session of the General Assembly will adopt a Covenant on Civil and Political Rights which includes an article on minority rights, but it is doubtful that such an event would constitute a genuine reversal of the trend which has developed since 1946. In so far as that trend can be said to have established a United Nations policy regarding minorities, it is the policy of subsuming the minority question under the problem of universal respect for human rights, while giving implicit endorsement to the right of states to follow a policy of assimilation. The United Nations has not formally accepted the thesis that this is in itself a potentially adequate solution of the minority problem, but it has not yet been willing or able to move beyond it.

CHAPTER 13: *THE UNITED NATIONS AND SPECIFIC MINORITY PROBLEMS*

The problem of national minorities does not always appear as a *general* problem, calling for a general solution on the basis of a general philosophy. Indeed, it may be true that it is *never* a general problem in this sense, and that the United

Nations has been on firm ground in refusing to treat it as such. At any rate, the issue of minority rights frequently arises as a highly *specific* problem — as one aspect of sometimes very complicated international disputes or situations. When this occurs, statesmen and officials of international organizations are challenged to forego the luxury of either ignoring the problem or considering it in the abstract; it becomes a concrete issue, requiring specific treatment.

The record of the United Nations in dealing with such situations reveals three definite trends:

(1) Willingness to consider the international guarantee of minority rights in exceptional cases;

(2) Inclination to accept and even to encourage the transfer of populations as a solution of minority problems; and

(3) Preference for bilateral solutions of particular minority questions, negotiated between the interested states without reference to the concept of international responsibility for the fate of minorities.

The present chapter will be devoted to an analysis of cases illustrative of these trends.

INTERNATIONAL GUARANTEE OF MINORITY RIGHTS

Despite the prevalent skepticism concerning the desirability or feasibility of a universal system of minority protection, members of the United Nations have not hesitated to consider the international protection of particular minorities in cases involving one or more of these three factors: the existence of an especially urgent *need* for intervention on behalf of minorities; the availability of an unusual *opportunity* for the imposition of legal obligations upon a minority-possessing state; and the existence of an exceptional degree of international *sympathy* for the claims and aspirations of a minority group.

The Palestine Case. When the problem of the future political status of Palestine was brought before the United Nations in April 1947, it was evident that these three factors were present in an unusual combination. The animosity which marked the relations between Jews and Arabs in the Palestine area made it clear that no peaceful political settlement could be achieved without the imposition of some degree of international regulation of intergroup relations. The fact that the United Nations assumed quasi-legislative competence in determining the outlines of the new international status of Palestine suggested that the organization had unusual resources for persuading any regimes that might be established to accept international supervision of their policy toward minorities. Vivid memories of the recent sufferings of Jews and feelings of solidarity within the Moslem world made it obvious that there would be strong political support for measures designed to safeguard both groups against oppression. Given these circumstances, it was reasonable to expect even an organization which was cool toward the idea of the international protection of minority rights to assume a positive attitude toward that concept in this particular instance.

The General Assembly undertook to achieve a Palestine settlement in its Resolution 181 (II), adopted on 29 November 1947, which strongly reflected the unanimous view of the United Nations Special Committee on Palestine that a solution must involve full safeguards for positive minority rights as well as for basic human rights.[1] The "Plan of Partition with Economic Union," embodied in the resolution, envisaged the formation of separate Jewish and Arab states in Palestine and required that each, before assuming independence, should make a Declaration to the United Nations incorporating, *inter alia*, an elaborate list of linguistic, religious, educational, and cultural rights for minority groups. These provisions for minority rights, which would also be included in the constitutions of the proposed states, would be under the guarantee of the United Nations. It was provided that no modification of the Declaration could be made without the assent of the General Assembly, that any member state could initiate consideration and recommendation by the Assembly in case of actual or threatened infractions, and that either party to a dispute relating to the application or interpretation of the Declaration could invoke the jurisdiction of the International Court of Justice. In addition, the plan called for the establishment of the City of Jerusalem as a *corpus separatum* to be administered by the Trusteeship Council under a Statute which should contain extensive provisions relating to the cultural and religious autonomy of the Jewish and Arab communities.

This ambitious scheme, which involved putting the United Nations very actively into the business of protecting positive minority rights in the Palestine area, came to naught as a result of the refusal of the Arab states of that region to accept the Assembly's recommendation.[2] The State of Israel came into existence on 15 May 1948, and its Foreign Secretary immediately notified the Secretary-General of Israel's willingness to co-operate in the implementation of the resolution on partition, including the signing of the proposed Declaration.[3] By this time, however, the problem confronting the United Nations was that of stopping the war between Arabs and Jews, rather than giving effect to the Assembly's plan. The hostilities produced a mass exodus of Arabs from the territory held by the Israeli forces, thus completing the transformation of the situation with which the scheme of partition with United Nations guarantee of minority rights had been intended to deal. The future of Palestine was to be determined by the fortunes of war rather than by preconceived plans of international organization; in this situation, the project of international protection of Palestinian minorities had no immediate relevance.

Count Folke Bernadotte, who served as United Nations Mediator for Palestine, reported to the Assembly, on 18 September 1948, that he had continued to hold out to the warring parties the suggestion of a settlement including the mutual acceptance of minority obligations to be guaranteed by the United Nations, and he intimated that it might still be possible to envisage a revised version of partition with a Conciliation Commission supervising the observance of reciprocal minority guarantees.[4] He had little faith, however, in the adequacy of Arab assurances of respect for Jewish minority rights in the event of the re-establishment of Arab control over all of Palestine,[5] and he indicated some skepticism as to the practicability of an international regime of minority rights even if the war ended in the political division of the area, by suggesting that the proposed Conciliation Commission might "lend its good offices, on the invitation of the parties, to any efforts toward exchanges of populations with a view to eliminating troublesome minority problems. . . ." [6]

For all practical purposes, Bernadotte's report contained the last reference to the possibility of the establishment of a scheme of international protection of minorities as a contribution by the United Nations to the pacification of Palestine. Subsequent resolutions by the Assembly referred to the possibility of setting up an international regime for Jerusalem which would be based upon the principle of respect for the religious and cultural traditions of both Arab and Jewish communities,[7] but the idea of imposing minority commitments upon sovereign states in the Palestine area was not revived.

The bulk of the Arab minority which the General Assembly had envisaged as a part of the Jewish State was concentrated on the territory of the Arab states bordering Israel, as the result of flight during hostilities.[8] The question of the immediate relief and ultimate disposition of these refugees assumed great importance for the states and international agencies concerned with the Palestinian situation.

In paragraph 11 of its resolution of 11 December 1948,[9] the General Assembly took the position "that the refugees wishing to return to their homes and live at peace with their neighbours should be permitted to do so at the earliest possible date. . . ." It indicated awareness of the prospect that many of them would not opt for return by instructing the Conciliation Commission to facilitate resettlement and rehabilitation as well as repatriation of the refugees. This clear adoption of the principle that the displaced Arabs had a right of readmission to areas which had fallen under the authority of Israel, in opposition to the Israeli contention that their final destiny should be settled by the general peace treaties to be negotiated between the Arab states and Israel, was the high-water mark of United Nations support for the Arab demands.

When the application of Israel for membership in the United Nations came before the *Ad Hoc* Political Committee of the General Assembly, during the second part of its Third Session, spokesmen for the Arab states were vehement in their insistence that Israel should be admitted only on the condition, *inter alia*, that it accept the principle stated above. It is a curious fact that the debates revealed very little interest in the possibility that the applicant state might be required to accept international obligations concerning its treatment of Arabs, either those who had remained in their homes during the exodus or those who might return to Israel if the principle of voluntary repatriation were implemented. Charles Malik of Lebanon mentioned the unfulfilled plan of the General Assembly for requiring Declarations concerning minority rights from new states in the area, and argued that Israel should not be admitted without a pledge "to implement the principle of repatriation and to respect the fundamental rights implied in the Assembly's decisions," [10] but he clearly shared the preoccupation of his Arab colleagues with the demand that Israel remove all barriers to repatriation of Arab refugees. It was left to the representative of Cuba to raise in explicit terms the question of Israel's acceptance of legal obligations to respect minority rights.[11] Mr. Eban's reply that the new state intended to provide constitutional safeguards for minority rights, even though it recognized no international legal obligation to do so in view of the fact that its offer to sign the Declaration had become obsolete during the course of the general abandonment of the partition resolution, satisfied the Cuban questioner and evoked no response from Arab delegates.[12] The Israeli spokesman refused to commit his government to an outright acceptance of the principle of unlimited voluntary repatriation, but promised that Israel would participate in a conciliatory manner in negotiations looking toward a reasonable and humane settlement of the refugee problem.[13]

The Assembly voted on 11 May 1949 to accept Israel as a member of the world organization. In so doing, it recalled its resolutions of 29 November 1947 and 11 December 1948, and formally took note of the declarations and explanations concerning the implementation of those resolutions which had been made by the representative of Israel before the *Ad Hoc* Political Committee.[14] These references, however, did *not* constitute a declaration that Israel had assumed definite obligations to permit unlimited repatriation or to guarantee minority rights to its present or future Arab population. The best evidence that Israel had made no such commitments was provided by the speeches of Arab delegates in the plenary meeting at which the resolution was voted; they regarded the admission of Israel as a repudiation of their demand for capitulation on the repatriation issue by the applicant state, and they asserted with bitterness that Israel "had given no definite assurances." [15] Neither friend nor foe of Israel,

nor the Israeli Foreign Minister himself, said anything to support
the inference that the new member was bound by unusual obligations as a result of the terms of the Assembly's resolution of admission. It would not have been surprising if an effort to impose
minority obligations upon Israel, in line with the Assembly's
policy expressed in the partition resolution, had failed; what is
striking is that the effort was not made.

The subsequent 'history of the Palestine case in the United
Nations reveals a gradual weakening of the Assembly's support
for the doctrine that all Arab refugees are entitled freely to choose
to return to their former homes. The world organization has
undertaken to provide relief and opportunities for the rehabilitation of the refugees; it has endorsed repatriation *and* resettlement, with a shift of emphasis to the latter principle, albeit with
a continuing willingness to appease the Arabs by "recalling"
paragraph 11 of Resolution 194 (III); it has increasingly shifted
the responsibility for working out an ultimate solution to the
states immediately concerned.[16]

This development in the attitude of the General Assembly
is intimately related to the assumption that the need for minority
protection is declining under present circumstances, and that the
actual return of substantial numbers of Arabs to Israel would
reverse that trend without improving the political prospects for
adoption of a system of international guarantees for minority
rights in the Palestine area. While the flight of the Arabs from
Israel had not been contemplated or planned by the United Nations, it was nevertheless a partial implementation of the concept
of solving the Jewish-Arab problem in the Middle East by population exchanges — an idea which had received considerable international support in the past and which was not unattractive to
many contemporary students of the problem.[17] There were
reports of Israeli plans to complete the disentanglement of populations by negotiating agreements for the exchange of the
remnant of its Arab minority for the Jews who lived precariously
in Arab states; Thomas J. Hamilton reported from Lake Success
that: "Such an exchange has long been under discussion by delegates here, who believe that it offers the best hope for the establishment of friendly or at least correct relations between Israel
and the surrounding Arab countries."[18] Although these plans

did not materialize, large numbers of Middle Eastern Jews did migrate to Israel, taking advantage of its permissive attitude toward Jewish immigration and its active interest in facilitating the removal of Jewish minorities threatened by the hostility of Arab populations.[19]

Sentiment in the United Nations was more favorable to the completion than to the reversal of this process. Lip-service had to be paid to the doctrine, espoused by Arab governments, that Arab refugees had a right of repatriation; in fact, it was clear that the United Nations would count itself fortunate to avoid the necessity of dealing with a situation in which the existence of large, dissatisfied minorities and hostile, apprehensive majorities on both sides would inexorably require the organization to undertake the protection of minorities in the interest of international peace. Events not initiated by the United Nations had diminished the scope of the minority problem in the Palestine region, to the extent that the organization was able to abandon without challenge its earlier offer to provide minority guarantees; for the future, it was not inclined to encourage a trend of events which would require it to reconsider its retirement from this field of activity.

The Italian Colonies Case. The problem of the disposition of the former Italian Colonies in North Africa was brought before the General Assembly in September 1948, as a result of the failure of the United States, Britain, France, and the USSR to agree upon a solution. In accordance with Annex VI of the Italian Peace Treaty, the great powers were bound in advance to accept whatever solution the General Assembly might recommend. Hence, there was no obstacle in this case to the imposition by the United Nations of legal obligations for the respect of minority rights upon the state or states to which the territories detached from the Italian Empire might be assigned. There was at least a *prima facie* case that external guarantees of minority rights might be desirable, in view of the fact that the colonies contained substantial religious and ethnic minorities, including Jews and Italian settlers.[20] In addition, influential blocs of United Nations members were actively concerned with the rights and interests of particular minority groups in the territories. Thus, as in the case of Palestine, the three essential factors were present to establish the expectation that the United Nations might display a positive interest in minority rights.

The most significant aspect of the Italian Colonies case for the purposes of this analysis is the indication that the attitudes of members of the United Nations toward the international treatment of the minority problem vary according to the strength of their regard for particular minorities. In general, it is the interventionist disposition of kin-states which makes the minority problem a matter of international concern; in the League era, the policy of kin-states was a major factor in the operation of the system for protection of minorities; this case reveals clearly that the possibility of the expression of formal interest in the fate of minorities by the United Nations depends heavily upon the specific sympathies of influential states.

In the debates of the First Committee of the General Assembly and its subcommittees on the problem of the Italian Colonies, in 1949, representatives of European and American peoples displayed a lively interest in safeguarding the rights of minorities. This behavior, which contrasted so sharply with the normal attitude of those governments toward the issue of minority rights in general, was clearly motivated by a special regard for the interests of Italians who live among the non-European peoples of North Africa. The Italian Foreign Minister, Count Sforza, who participated as the representative of an interested but nonmember state, took the public position that there was no possible conflict between the interests of the Italian settlers and the peoples of the colonies, and painted such a glowing picture of the friendly and helpful relationships which the Italians had established with the natives that it was impossible for him to suggest that his compatriots would be endangered if the government of those areas passed from European hands. He deviated from this position only to the extent of indicating that his government wished to negotiate a treaty with an independent Tripolitania, for the safeguarding of Italian interests.[21] This euphemistic statement was probably less expressive of the actual sentiments of the Italian Government than a newspaper dispatch from Rome, dated 11 March 1951, in which Arnaldo Cortesi reported: "Second only to Trieste in importance as far as the Italians are concerned is the problem of safeguarding Italian minorities in the former Italian colonies of Eritrea and Libya." [22]

With or without the prompting of Italian officials, many Western statesmen worked for a United Nations decision favorable to the rights of minorities, some of them with a frank avowal that they had the Italians in mind as chief beneficiaries.[23] The United States displayed an exceptional willingness to have the United Nations single out minorities for special protection in this case, supporting a proposal to require that Libyan minorities be represented on an advisory council,[24] and taking the initiative in developing a plan for the cession of the eastern provinces of Eritrea to Ethiopia, with the requirement that the Government of Ethiopia bind itself to respect the rights of minorities.[25] Similarly, a number of Latin American states discarded their habitual bias against minorities and in favor of assimilation and entered actively into the project of "doing something for Italy" — in this instance, by supporting the underwriting of a special position for minorities in Libya and Eritrea.[26]

An interesting and significant inconsistency was observable in the position of the Arab states. When the issue of providing special representation for minorities in Libya was being considered, Mr. Al-Jamali of Iraq insisted that minorities should not be singled out for special privileges but treated as "an integral part of the population"; he was joined by Fawzi Bey of Egypt, who expressed opposition to the very concept of an "international minority." [27] Seven members of the Arab bloc voted against this proposition when it came before the First Committee.[28] The concept of minority rights was distasteful to the Arab spokesmen when it was applied to a prospectively independent Arab state; on the other hand, when the possibility arose that Eritrea, with its large Moslem population, might be federated with Ethiopia, the same Mr. Al-Jamali who had disavowed belief in the propriety of singling out minorities joined with the representatives of Brazil, India, Liberia, and the United States in drafting a resolution which would require the adoption of a Federal Constitution containing an elaborate set of linguistic and cultural rights for minorities.[29]

With respect to Libya, the Fourth General Assembly voted to appoint a United Nations Commissioner who would have the function of guiding that territory toward becoming an independent state, not later than 1 January 1952, and provided that he should be advised by a Council of ten members, including one representative of the minority groups.[30]

The Commissioner, Adrian Pelt, reported to the Fifth Session of the Assembly that the Libyan Preparatory Committee, convened to prepare for the calling of a National Assembly, had voted to exclude representatives of national minorities from that body; Mr. Pelt approved that decision, but expressed concern about the problems posed by the existence of minority groups, particularly the Italian community, and indicated that he had suggested the possibility of negotiations, under his auspices, between the minority groups and the National Assembly.[31] The General Assembly recommended "That a National Assembly duly representative of the inhabitants of Libya" be convened to implement the decision to make Libya an independent state, but made no explicit reference to the status of minorities.[32] Some problems of Italo-Libyan relations, including matters relating to the status of Italian nationals in Libya, were treated in a separate Assembly resolution,[33] but no formal stipulations were laid down for a solution of the problem of the rights of those minorities whose members would become Libyan nationals upon the establishment of an independent regime.

Libya assumed independence on 24 December 1951. The final reports of the United Nations Commissioner called the attention of the Sixth General Assembly to the serious problems with which the new state was faced, including the political problem of resolving the antagonisms between different groups within its population,[34] but the Assembly, in welcoming Libya into the family of nations, did not address itself to the problem of minorities.[35]

Minority groups in Libya had been apprehensive about their fate after the establishment of independence; in 1951, the Jewish Community had proposed that the United Nations take measures to safeguard the rights of Italians, Maltese, and Greeks, as well as Jews.[36] Even though the Libyan Constitution, according to Mr. Pelt, guaranteed the basic liberties of minorities,[37] Jewish spokesmen subsequently pointed out that the Jewish community of Libya had failed to receive constitutional guarantees essential to the maintenance of its traditional institutions; as a consequence of this and of a pervading sense of insecurity, the large majority of Libyan Jews emigrated to Israel before 1953.[38]

The Fourth General Assembly approved a temporary Italian trusteeship over the former colony of Italian Somaliland, with the prospect of independence for the territory after ten years.[39] The debate concerning the disposition of Somaliland had revealed little specific interest in the minority problem, quite possibly because it was recognized that the return of Italy as Administering Authority would automatically exclude the necessity of protecting the most favored minority, the Italian settlers. However, the Trusteeship Agreement approved by the Assembly followed the requirements of the decision by the Fourth General Assembly in incorporating a Declaration of Constitutional Principles which excluded discriminatory policy regarding human rights and guaranteed that "due regard" would be paid to the traditional institutions of the peoples of the territory.[40]

The former Italian colony whose minority problem excited the most active interest in United Nations discussions was Eritrea. The reason was not far to seek: the leading proposal for settlement was the partial or complete union of Eritrea with Ethiopia; Arab states were hostile to the imposition of minority obligations upon an independent Moslem state of Libya, but they had no such desire to shield Ethiopian sovereignty; pro-Italian states felt no anxiety regarding the fate of Italians in Somaliland under the regime decided upon by the Assembly, but their motivations for protecting Italians operated at least as strongly in regard to the projected Eritrean solution as in regard to Libya. Hence, the case of Eritrea was the only one marked by a convergence of the pressures operating to safeguard the interests of Moslem and of Italian minorities.

At the Third General Assembly, the First Committee had approved — and the Assembly had rejected — a resolution calling for the cession of Eritrea, except for the Western Province, to Ethiopia, under conditions which included "the provision of adequate guarantees for the protection of minorities." [41] At the Fourth General Assembly, similar proposals were considered, but the decision was to postpone a final solution of the Eritrean question, pending investigation by a United Nations Commission which would be instructed to consult representatives of all groups in Eritrea and to formulate proposals which would take into account the views and interests of minorities.[42]

In the *Report of the United Nations Commission for Eritrea to the General Assembly at its Fifth Session*,[43] there was general agreement that there should be safeguards for the position of Italian and other minorities if Eritrea were to be federated with Ethiopia; only the Norwegian representative argued that the United Nations should rely exclusively upon Ethiopian assurances regarding the treatment of minorities, without attaching any formal conditions to the authorization for union. The Italian Government had officially expressed its interest in protecting the Italo-Eritrean population,[44] whereupon the representatives of Burma and South Africa agreed that the General Assembly should suggest that arrangements concerning the status of the Italian minority should be negotiated by Italy and Ethiopia. Despite the Commission's recognition of the necessity of definite action regarding the minority problem, it did not follow up the French suggestion that constitutional safeguards for minorities should be "accompanied by an adequate system of guarantees ensuring their effective implementation."[45]

The Assembly voted, on 2 December 1950, that all of Eritrea should be federated with Ethiopia under the sovereignty of the Ethiopian Crown, subject to the requirement that the Federal Act and the Eritrean Constitution should stipulate that all inhabitants of Eritrea, except persons possessing foreign nationality, should become nationals of the Federation, and that human rights should be ensured to all residents of Eritrea on a nondiscriminatory basis.[46] Before the vote, the Foreign Minister of Ethiopia pledged his government to respect the rights of Moslem and Italian minorities.[47]

The Commissioner for Eritrea, appointed by the United Nations under the provisions of this resolution, reported in 1952 that the Constitution adopted by the Eritrean Assembly included specific linguistic and cultural rights for minorities in addition to assurances of equal enjoyment of general human rights.[48] In accepting this report and confirming the completion of all measures for effectuating the Eritrean settlement, the Assembly took formal notice of the fulfillment of the conditions regarding the rights of the Eritrean population which it had stated at its Fifth Session.[49]

The legal status of the Eritrean minority problem following the political settlement sponsored by the General Assembly is somewhat ambiguous. Allegations of violations of the protective clauses incorporated in the Federal Act and the Eritrean Constitution might be held to be matters within the competence of the General Assembly, on the grounds that those clauses were adopted as a result of instructions from the Assembly and that the United Nations received verbal assurances from the Ethiopian Government. Because of the sympathies for Arab and Italian minorities in Eritrea which prevail among members of the United Nations, the Assembly might choose to assert its jurisdiction in such cases on a political basis, without strict regard for the validity of its legal grounds. On the other hand, the General Assembly did not exhibit a clear intention to establish international jurisdiction over the treatment of minorities in Eritrea; it apparently required only that the Eritrean Constitution provide for non-discrimination, not for the positive minority rights which were in fact embodied in that document. It contented itself with requiring that safeguards for minorities be written into the Federal Act adopted by Ethiopia and, upon the approval of the United Nations Commissioner, by Eritrea, and into the Eritrean Constitution. It is perhaps significant that the Assembly did not demand that those written safeguards or the verbal assurances of the Ethiopian representative should be embodied in a formal international document. If disputes should arise concerning the violation of minority rights in the Eritrean sector of the Federation, political pressures for United Nations intervention might be counterbalanced by pressures reflecting the widespread concern in the organization for avoiding precedents supporting infringement of the domestic jurisdiction of member states. Despite the ambiguity of the legal position and the uncertainty of the prospective balance of political forces, it must be said that the United Nations displayed a rare willingness in the Eritrean case to involve itself in minority problems.

Two other cases give evidence of the fact that leading members of the United Nations which have adopted a general attitude of opposition to the international safeguarding of minority rights are willing to make exceptions in particular situations. The settlement of the thorny problem of Trieste which was agreed upon at the Paris Peace Conference of 1946 [50] involved the establishment of a Free Territory which would be administered by a Governor appointed by and responsible to the Security Council. In accordance with the Permanent Statute incorporated in Annex VI of the Italian Peace Treaty, the Governor would have been responsible for dealing with the explosive ethnic situation resulting from the mixture of Italian and Yugoslav populations, on the basis of upholding equal enjoyment of human rights by all and the official recognition of both the Italian and Slovene languages. Even though the Security Council formally accepted its mandate for administration of the Free Territory on 10 January 1947,[51] subsequent political developments prevented the implementation of this agreement, and the United Nations did not assume its projected role in the Trieste Territory.

A similarly abortive international decision regarding a minority problem was reached by the great powers in the course of their negotiations for formulation of an Austrian Treaty, re-establishing the normality of the international position of Austria. Because of their eagerness for a settlement, the Western powers agreed with extreme reluctance, in 1949, to accept the demands of Yugoslavia, supported by the USSR, for the incorporation into the draft treaty of provisions establishing linguistic and cultural rights for the Croatian and Slovene minorities in Austria. The draft article on minority rights would clearly have placed this aspect of Austrian domestic policy within the realm of international jurisdiction, although it did not provide that the United Nations should play the role of guarantor.[52] This agreement became obsolete when the Soviet Union lost interest in pressing Yugoslav claims as a delayed result of Tito's rebellion against the Kremlin; thereafter, the prospect of a minority rights article in the eventual Austrian Treaty vanished, and the Austrian and Yugoslav Governments reached a bilateral understanding concerning the issue.[53]

The disappearance of the political necessity for accepting the incorporation of minority provisions in an Austrian Treaty was received by the United States Government with obvious relief; in a popular commentary on the treaty negotiations, it avoided reference to the minority problem except to say that the USSR had been insincere in championing Yugoslav demands and to note that "The rights of the Slovene minority were protected under the new Austrian Constitution." [54] The reference to constitutional safeguards made it clear that the United States did not consider it essential to establish international guarantees for minorities in Austria.

POPULATION TRANSFER

The wartime trend toward the general acceptance of the principle of transfer of populations as a solution for difficult minority problems has continued during the early years of United Nations activity, and has to some extent been fostered by the world organization. For the most part, transfer activities since World War II have been initiated and carried out independently of the United Nations and with, at most, its tacit approval. In so far as it is true that the United Nations is merely the sum of its parts, the aggregate of its member states, the organization can be said to have shared in the creation of an international atmosphere in which the idea of the physical elimination of minorities by removal to a kin-state has become the virtually automatic response to the recognition of a troubled majority-minority situation. The United Nations itself, as an organization, has seldom been involved; despite the general agreement among advocates of the transfer device that its proper operation, in principle, requires international supervision and assistance, postwar transfers have been carried out without the consent, consultation, or participation of the organization.

Since the close of hostilities in 1945, the phenomenon of human uprootedness which was a major characteristic of the war years has continued to play a prominent role in international life. The majority of the persons who have participated in the massive population movements have been members of national minorities, en route to states where their ethnic characteristics will make them members of the national majority. By 1952, Israel, which had begun independent existence with a population of 665,000 Jews, included 1,425,000 Jews within its population,[55] and thousands of Jews in other countries were awaiting the opportunity to migrate. Communal troubles and the resulting climate of insecurity following the partition of the subcontinent of India produced the spontaneous shifting of approximately twelve million Hindus and Moslems across the frontiers of Pakistan and India.[56] In 1950–51, Turkey reluctantly opened its frontiers to 150,000 persons of Turkish origin who were expelled by Bulgaria after invocation of the terms of the 1925 exchange agreement concluded between the two countries.[57] Far Eastern countries virtually eliminated their Japanese minorities by forcing their return to Japan between 1945 and 1947.[58] The American press published persistent reports of large scale movements of ethnic groups within the area constituted by the Soviet Union and its European satellites.[59] These shifts combined with the process of completing the population transfers initiated in the period of the Potsdam Conference to create a picture of minority movement unprecedented in an era of nominal peace.

In principle, the problem of minority transferees, who had a definite destination, was differentiated from the problem of refugees, who simply found themselves, voluntarily or compulsorily, outside the state of their previous residence. In practice, the distinction was not always so clear-cut, as was illustrated by the case of the Arab refugees from Israel. To the greatest extent permitted by circumstances, the United Nations confined its relief and resettlement activities to cases involving refugees rather than transferees, although Turkey did invoke the advice and assistance of United Nations agencies in dealing with its problem of resettling minority transferees from Bulgaria.[60]

The Balkan Case. Although approval of the concept of transfer, especially in relation to particular minority problems, has frequently been voiced in United Nations debates, the organization has given its formal endorsement to that concept in only one case — the case involving the relations of Greece with its Balkan neighbors.[61]

On 19 December 1946, the Security Council approved the establishment of a Commission of Investigation to ascertain the facts concerning a Greek complaint that Albania, Bulgaria, and Yugoslavia were supporting guerrilla activities against the Greek Government.[62]

This Commission reported on 27 May 1947 that the situation

in the Balkans was complicated by the existence of minority problems. Greece's neighbors were assertively interested in the fate of related minority groups in Greece, and they purported to base their hostility upon the mistreatment of those minorities. Greece, on the other hand, alleged that the other states were stimulating disloyalty among the minority groups and utilizing them for purposes of subversion. The investigators found some truth in the allegations of both sides, and concluded that the Security Council should "recommend to the governments concerned that they study the practicability of concluding agreements for the voluntary transfer of minorities." It was proposed that, in the meantime, facilities should be provided by the governments and by a United Nations Commission or Commissioner to assist members of minorities in voluntary emigration.[63]

The Greek problem was shifted to the agenda of the General Assembly at its Second Session, as a result of the impasse which was created in the Security Council by Soviet use of the veto power. The First Committee was confronted with three draft proposals relating to the minority aspects of the case: an American proposal to adopt the suggestion of the Security Council's Commission of Investigation that the governments negotiate an agreement for voluntary transfer; a Soviet draft calling upon Greece to guarantee the removal of discrimination and the provision of positive minority rights; and a Swedish proposal requesting the four Balkan governments concerned "to study the practicability of concluding agreements for guaranteeing the minorities a non-discriminatory treatment . . . and for the voluntary transfer of minorities." [64]

In the debates of the First Committee regarding the Greek problem, the minority issue was hardly discussed at all. It was *exploited* by governmental representatives hostile to Greece; allegations of Greek abuse of minorities were wielded as a political weapon by Communist opponents of the West in this early skirmish of the cold war, but the Committee evinced little disposition to treat this complex minority problem in terms of its own substance as one element in the political disturbance of the Balkans.[65] In view of this Communist exploitation of the issue, it would appear that the American support for the concept of transfer was motivated not so much by a desire to solve the minority problem as such, as by the hope of striking a propaganda weapon from the hands of the Communist adversaries. The American position did not reflect sympathy for either minorities or kin-states; it reflected a desire to remove minorities from Greece so that they could no longer play the disloyal game of internal disruption, and so that their kin-states could no longer use their plight as a pretext for activities directed against Greece or as the basis for propaganda tirades in international forums.

The Assembly adopted a resolution establishing the United Nations Special Committee on the Balkans, and instructing it, *inter alia*, to assist the four governments in carrying out the suggestion that they explore the possibility of reaching agreements for the voluntary transfer of minorities.[66] For all practical purposes, this marked the end of United Nations consideration of the minority problem in the Balkans. The Special Committee noted in its first report that it was extraordinarily difficult to engage in serious study of the minority problem without the coöperation of the interested states,[67] and it later suspended that project because of its inability to elicit the coöperation of Albania, Bulgaria, and Yugoslavia, the states whose agreement would be essential to the operation of any transfer scheme.[68]

The United Nations had reacted to the evidence that a minority problem existed by endorsing a solution by transfer; yet, it is difficult to judge whether this reaction reflected an almost automatic acceptance of the view that troubles of this sort can and should be solved by transfer or a calculated attempt to undermine a propaganda position of the Soviet bloc.

BILATERAL VERSUS INTERNATIONAL SOLUTIONS

There has been a great deal of debate, both inside and outside the United Nations, concerning the question of international competence and responsibility for formulating solutions to the problems posed by the existence of national minorities. The debate has been conducted within both legal and political terms of reference; it has revolved around the legal question of United Nations jurisdiction and the political question of the expediency of United Nations intervention with respect to minority issues.

The Indian-South African Case. The classic example of this debate is offered by the perennial problem of the treatment of Indians in South Africa. This case has been kept before the United Nations since 1946 because of the interest of India, and, to a lesser extent, of Pakistan, in the situation of some 285,260 South African nationals of Indian origin [69] who are subject to an increasingly stringent policy of segregation and racial discrimination in their country. It involves a demand not for special minority rights, but for the granting of first-class citizenship, on the basis of full equality, for the Indian minority.

The case was brought before the General Assembly at its First Session by India, and has figured in the debates of each subsequent session except the Fourth. The action of the Assembly can be traced through a series of five resolutions, extending from 8 December 1946 to 5 December 1952, in addition to a recommendation adopted on the latter date concerning the related issue of South Africa's policy of *Apartheid*.[70]

As to the substance of the dispute, these resolutions reveal an increasingly firm and vigorous attitude of disapproval of South African treatment of the Indian minority, a trend symbolized by the shift from a noncommital attitude in the resolution of 1949, to pointed reference in the 1950 recommendation to the Assembly's Resolution 103 (I) of 19 November 1946, concerning racial persecution and discrimination, and to the Declaration of Human Rights. They reveal a tendency for the Assembly to expand the area of South African policy with which it is concerned to include the treatment meted out to all non-European groups in the population of the Union, as evidenced by unfavorable references to the Group Areas Act and the policy of *Apartheid* in the resolutions passed at the Fifth and Sixth Sessions, and the separate resolution condemning *Apartheid* adopted at the Seventh Session.

As to the question of procedural methods for settling the matter, the series of resolutions shows a persistent adherence by the Assembly to the concept that the dispute should be terminated by negotiations among the directly interested states, but also a growing willingness to suggest the utilization of mediatorial agencies, to provide for United Nations assistance in the creation of such agencies, and finally to inject directly into the dispute a United Nations Good Offices Commission.[71] The Assembly has brought the United Nations more and more deeply into the dispute by these tactics, as also by assuming an increasingly mandatory attitude toward South Africa, evidenced by reiterations of its previous resolutions with the implication that South Africa has been at fault in refusing to give effect to them, and especially by expression, in the resolutions voted at its Sixth and Seventh Sessions, of disapproval of the failure of the Government of the Union to postpone or suspend the enforcement of the Group Areas Act in accordance with the request of the Fifth General Assembly.

Definite and determined initiative and leadership in this case has been provided by India. When India first brought the matter to the attention of the General Assembly,[72] it reviewed the history of the problem, cited evidence that South Africa had long admitted the legitimacy of Indian concern and diplomatic intervention regarding the status of the Asian minority, and asserted that the United Nations had competence in the matter because a situation likely to impair friendly relations between member states had arisen from violation of bilateral agreements concluded between India and South Africa in 1927 and 1932 at Capetown.

During the consideration of the Indian complaint at the Second Session of the General Assembly, the Indian representative undertook to broaden the legal and political foundations of the case. Mrs. Pandit added to the bilateral plank the assertion that South Africa had disregarded its human rights obligations under the Charter, thereby creating a problem which was legally under the jurisdiction of the Assembly and politically a matter of grave concern to the entire world.[73] This introduction of a new jurisdictional argument may have been conceived as insurance against the effect of the South African plea that the bilateral case was legally invalid, on the ground that the Capetown Agreements were not genuinely "instruments giving rise to treaty obligations," and politically unacceptable, on the ground that the precedent set by India's action opened up the danger of "exploitation of domestic issues by foreign States as a political weapon." [74] However, it was a significant presage of the future development of India's case; in subsequent years, India neglected and tacitly abandoned the claim that United Nations jurisdiction rested upon the bilateral treaty basis.[75]

The reason for this change was not primarily technical, but was political in the largest sense. India was interested in minimizing the bilateral aspects of the case and transforming it into an international case. The bilateral aspect was useful in the beginning; India started with the assertions that it had a special legal competence to invoke United Nations action and a special moral-political claim, as a kin-state, to display interest in the fate of persons who were admittedly nationals of the Union but were ethnically related to its own people. An Indian delegate stated in 1946 that "the Government of India had always considered it a duty to look after the interests of Indians in South Africa." [76] But the Indian Government was interested in its special position *only* as a device for bringing the United Nations into the picture. Once this had been done, India began to suggest that it was acting merely as any good member of the organization should act, guarding any oppressed group against infringement of the human rights provisions of the Charter by any member state.[77] India persistently undertook to broaden the dispute substantively, by bringing in reference to South Africa's general racial policy affecting Bantus and colored people as well as Asians,[78] hoping thereby to demonstrate that *all* members of the United Nations interested in preserving the Charter, and particularly the non-European members engaged in the anticolonial movement, had a direct concern in the case.

India's doctrinal efforts to push the case from bilateralism into multilateralism were accompanied by evidence that it preferred United Nations settlement of the problem to United Nations encouragement of negotiations between the parties.[79] India's first choice appeared to be an international condemnation of South African policy, which would leave India with nothing to do except to receive assurances from the penitent sinner that it would sin no more against the people of Indian origin. Facing the hard fact that the Assembly would consider no attempt at a solution which did not involve negotiations between the parties (the Assembly persisted in the view that the case was primarily a bilateral dispute, not a situation in which all member states were almost equally involved), India was willing to negotiate – but only if the United Nations would equip it with a dispatch case full of internationally adopted moral condemnations of South Africa to carry to the conference table.[80] What India most wanted to avoid was the necessity of sitting down with South Africa to discuss the case on a purely bilateral basis, without even the spiritual presence of the international community.

This attitude was dictated, it would appear, by the fear that Indian diplomats would be powerless to extract concessions from the South African Government unless they had at their disposal the weapon of United Nations moral support for their case, and by the more concrete consideration that India required the assistance of General Assembly directives to steer the conversation toward the question of human rights under the Charter, as a defense against South African insistence upon discussing the scheme of the Capetown Agreements for transporting the Indian minority to India.[81] India wished the United Nations to impose a solution on Indian terms, or at the very least to buttress the Indian position in bilateral negotiations.

South Africa began with a flat assertion of domestic jurisdiction. The Capetown Agreements did not constitute valid international engagements, and the United Nations Charter did not define human rights; hence, there were no grounds for United Nations consideration of the case. The Union Government was confident that its legal arguments conclusively proved the case for United Nations abstinence under Article 2, paragraph 7, of the Charter, and it proposed that the matter be submitted to the International Court of Justice for an advisory opinion.[82] South African representatives have repeatedly entered long and able arguments on this point into the records of the United Nations, but have never persuaded the General Assembly either to accept their contention or to submit the issue to adjudication.

In principle, South Africa regards General Assembly resolutions concerning its treatment of the Indian minority as absolutely invalid. Such measures are legally unjustified, since the members of the United Nations have not drafted or accepted a convention empowering the organization to protect minorities, and they are politically intolerable, according to the South African view.[83]

However, there is evidence that the fundamental objection is to the nature and content of the resolutions which have been passed. South Africa prefers no United Nations action at all; but it will accept and act upon a simple recommendation for negotiation by the parties, unencumbered by references which imply that the Union is a guilty and morally inferior party which must approach the conference table with a black mark upon its record of respect for international commitments.[84]

This attitude reveals a curious inconsistency in the South African position regarding jurisdiction. Domestic jurisdiction is asserted as a bar to United Nations intervention, but *not* as a bar to Indian intervention. It is true that spokesmen for the Union have frequently embarrassed India by pointing to the anomaly of India's claim to guardianship over persons whom it wants South Africa to treat as citizens in a full and unqualified sense,[85] and have sought to gain support by warning against setting the dangerous precedent of allowing kin-states to meddle in the domestic affairs of others for ulterior political purposes,[86] but in the final analysis, South Africa has admitted that there is some validity in the claim of a kin-state to protect ethnically related minorities,[87] and it has clearly recognized India's right to express an interest in its treatment of the Indian minority (although not in its general policy of *Apartheid*). This recognition is evidenced by repeated assurances that South Africa stands ready and willing to negotiate the minority question with India outside the United Nations and without reference to any General Assembly resolution.[88]

The paradox of a plea of domestic jurisdiction which precludes collective intervention but permits unilateral intervention, in the sense of diplomatic protest and bargaining, is explainable in terms of South Africa's political purpose. South Africa has never forgotten its original conception of the Indian minority as a group of temporary residents, destined for ultimate removal. Its earlier acceptance of Indian intervention was determined by the necessity of reaching agreement with India for the reception of the Indian minority. The failure of transfer schemes led South Africa to confer nationality upon its Indian population in 1944; at this point, it regarded the Indians as a permanent part of its population and considered that India's right to be consulted had been terminated.[89] When India brought the South African case before the United Nations and displayed a steadfast determination to press the issue at successive annual meetings of the General Assembly, South Africa reverted to the project of expelling the Indian population.[90]

It is not clear whether the South African Government now seriously entertains the idea of the mass expulsion of its Asians to India; at any rate, however, it recognizes that it holds a trump card for use in bilateral negotiations. If South Africa can contrive to negotiate with India without an agenda fixed by the United Nations and without the political handicap of international condemnation, it is in a strong position to insist that India prove its interest in the welfare of the minority by agreeing to cooperate in a transfer arrangement, which would dispose of the problem, or else disavow its interest in the minority, recognize the unrestricted sovereignty of South Africa over its nationals of Indian origin, and withdraw from the case, which would also dispose of the problem. South Africa's confidence in its capacity for diplomatic victory in bilateral negotiations arranged on its own terms would seem to account for the peculiar lack of logic which it has displayed with respect to the technical issue of jurisdiction.

The positions taken by other members of the United Nations on the issue of jurisdiction have similarly reflected political purposes more than concern for strict logic. Some states have simply been pro-Indian or pro–South African; in general, the trend has been toward Indian victories in the Assembly, achieved by the progressively effective mobilization of the anticolonial bloc against the more conservative European-oriented states.[91]

Most significantly, however, the purpose of avoiding United Nations responsibility for a solution of the minority problem by shifting the issue to the parties has been evident. Members have demonstrated a striking capacity to begin with any jurisdictional position and end with the same conclusion.

On occasion, debates have been marked by a straightforward acceptance of the concept of bilateral jurisdiction and responsibility; thus, a British spokesman remarked in 1946 that "His Government had always treated the matter as one for settlement between the two nations concerned." [92] On the other hand, the

United States has accepted the view, however unenthusiastically, that the United Nations is competent to deal with the matter; yet, its representative stated in 1952 that "The United Nations should not attempt to impose any solution to a problem that must finally be solved by the parties themselves." [93] Finally, France, Australia, and the Netherlands have managed to combine the view that South African treatment of its Indian nationals is strictly a matter of domestic jurisdiction, outside the purview of the United Nations, with the position that India and Pakistan should engage in direct negotiations with South Africa concerning the matter.[94]

Formally speaking, the United Nations has asserted its competence to deal with the question of the Indian minority in South Africa; it has not submitted the issue of jurisdiction for a judicial ruling or stated its competence in so many words, but it has beaten down challenges and passed a series of resolutions which reflect the assumption of international jurisdiction. However, an examination of the substance of its resolutions reveals that the organization has asserted its jurisdiction only for the purpose of promoting a bilateral settlement. In this sense, India has been defeated, for it has pursued the opposite course of asserting the principle of bilateralism for the purpose of securing a settlement by the United Nations, or one substantively influenced by the United Nations even though it might be formally reached through bilateral negotiations. But South Africa has also been defeated, for it has wished to exclude the United Nations altogether and impose a settlement on its own terms through the process of bilateral negotiation. The United Nations has pleased neither party, and thus far has failed to secure progress toward a solution, by its policy of promoting bilateral settlement, as desired by South Africa, and expressing moral disapproval of South African policy, as desired by India. '

This case provides little evidence that the United Nations is disposed to accept or assert responsibility for the protection of minorities. The organization has attempted to produce the settlement of a dispute between member states, not to protect a national minority within a member state; even its request that South Africa postpone implementation of the Group Areas Act was made for the purpose of preventing actions prejudicial to the success of bilateral negotiations,[95] not for the purpose of upholding the rights of the minority group with which the case was concerned. Confronted with a situation involving only the human rights of a minority, not positive minority rights, the United Nations has insistently pronounced it a matter for bilateral settlement, not a matter requiring solution by international organization.

This tendency, involving as it does the abandonment of the tentative internationalization of the minority problem which was effected by the League of Nations, has been characteristic of the United Nations. In so far as an international legal structure relating to the status of national minorities has been developed since World War II, this process has been carried out largely through the medium of bilateral treaties, made without reference to the United Nations.[96]

Allegations of mistreatment of national minorities by particular states have frequently appeared in United Nations debates. These charges, usually made by representatives of peoples ethnically related to the minorities concerned, have seldom reflected the purpose of persuading the United Nations to enter into the business of protecting minorities; more often, they have merely been parts of polemical exchanges between political opponents. By and large, such kin-state complaints have not been regarded as improper by relatively disinterested bystanders in the United Nations. The organization has been so intent upon rejecting the internationalization of the minority problem that it has shown no hesitation in recognizing the legitimacy of kin-state concern for related minorities in other states. The United Nations has been acutely aware of the danger of political complications that might arise if it should stimulate minority consciousness and undertake to intervene in the affairs of member states. It has shown little awareness of the danger to international peace which motivated the League of Nations to internationalize the minority problem: the danger of friction between host state and kin-state which arises when the problem is viewed in bilateral terms. The organization has virtually ignored this sound principle, injected by General Romulo of the Philippines into a discussion of the necessity for settlement of the Indian–South African case by bilateral rather than United Nations action: "Intervention by one State in the affairs of another was a real danger; intervention by the collective body of the United Nations for the sake of freedom and in accordance with the principles of the Charter was appropriate international action." [97]

The United Nations will, in extraordinary cases, reluctantly face the possibility of its necessary involvement in minority problems. Its reluctance is so great, however, that it cannot force a frown at the prospect that unpleasant minority situations might be eliminated by the physical transfer of populations. In the last analysis, the United Nations will insist, whenever it is remotely possible, that minority problems be solved in such a way as to permit it to escape the responsibility of participation.

CHAPTER 14: *CONCLUSION*

National minorities have not been eliminated in the years since 1919. Despite the tragic destruction of European Jewry, the virtual elimination of German minorities in Eastern and Central Europe, and the vast uprooting of Europeans of all descriptions in the last twenty years, the stubborn fact remains that the peoples of Europe are to a considerable extent intermingled. Nor is this by any means an exclusively European phenomenon; throughout the world, ethnic homogeneity is the exception rather than the rule. If the size of the minority problem has been reduced by the "repatriation" of Germans, it has been increased by the partition of the subcontinent of India. If many Jewish minorities have dissolved through extinction and emigration to Israel, the Overseas Chinese remain scattered throughout Southeast Asia. Minority problems differ in form and intensity in various parts of the world, but the fact is universal that men of different races, languages, religions, and national cultures are faced with the problem of living together in peace and amity.

The subjective and ideological bases of the minority problem remain intact. The self-consciousness and national aspirations of minority ethnic groups have not disappeared. There continue to be groups within states which cling tenaciously to the ideal of preserving their corporate identity. In some cases, the aspirations of national minorities extend beyond the cultural to the political realm, and involve demands for political autonomy, independence, or union with co-national states. As for national majorities, they exhibit little inclination to adjust their political thinking to the realities of the ethnographic situation. By and large, they continue to adhere to the concept of the national state, and consequently to regard national minorities as alien elements which impede the proper functioning of the state as the political instrument of the nation. Kin-states display no greater capacity to accommodate themselves to the political situation than do minority states to accept ethnographic realities; states continue to claim a legitimate interest in the affairs of related minorities, and in some cases to work, by one means or another, for territorial changes which might enable them to become national states in the full sense, giving political unity to national entities.

In short, the world is confronted not only with national minorities but also with the *problem* of national minorities. Indeed, the statement that such minorities exist is virtually equivalent to the statement that the problem exists; for, within the frame of reference set up by the ideology of nationalism, national states and national minorities are incompatible. The admixture of populations, the subjective fact of national consciousness, and the ideal of the national state combine to perpetuate a problem which has the greatest significance not only for constitutional but also for international relations.

Among the possible assumptions about the nature of the minority problem, with respect to the question of the policy level where its solution is to be sought, three are of paramount importance: (1) It is a domestic matter, to be treated unilaterally by the state possessing minorities. (2) It is a problem affecting the interests of the co-national state of a given minority group, as well as those of the host state, and is therefore to be solved on the basis of bilateral negotiation. (3) It is an international problem, susceptible of solution only on the level of the organized international community.

Minority states tend to uphold the first of these assumptions.

In the absence of special motivating factors, most states are moved to invoke the principle of internal sovereignty as an obstacle to outside interference with their treatment of any group of nationals.

It is clear, however, that there is no real possibility of confining the minority problem within the limits of domestic jurisdiction. Minorities tend to look to their co-national states for protective intervention, and those states generally assert an interest in the treatment of their ethnic kinsmen which effectively, if not legally, transforms the matter into a problem of interstate relations. The principle of bilateralism is never wholly absent from the attitudes of kin-states; even when they support the internationalization of the problem, they insist that recognition be given to their special interest in the fate of co-national minorities.

The end of the First World War was marked by the partial and somewhat tentative internationalization of the problem. The position of national minorities in certain states was held to be a matter of direct concern to the organized international community. Under the auspices of the League of Nations, a mechanism was created for systematic international control over the minority policy of a number of Eastern and Central European states. This step seemed to foreshadow the development of a trend toward removal of the problem from the spheres of domestic jurisdiction and of bilateral competence.

However, this trend did not materialize. Efforts to universalize the competence of the international agency concerned with the minority problem met with failure. The leading members of the League were too sympathetic with the concept of sovereignty to accept with enthusiasm the task of repulsing governmental assertions of competence to deal unilaterally with internal minority problems, and they were too much imbued with the philosophy of nationalism to offer vigorous resistance to efforts of kin-states to treat the status of minority groups as an issue between themselves and the host states. There was no vital impetus behind the movement of the international community to assume the authority and the responsibility for dealing systematically with the minority problem; when unilateralism and bilateralism came into evidence, the tendency toward internationalization was frustrated.

The retreat from the internationalization of the minority problem has been particularly evident since the Second World War. To a considerable extent, this movement has been expressed in international neglect. A comparison of the role of the minority problem in the international discussion which followed the First World War with its place in conferences and debates since 1945 indicates clearly that the statesmen of the present generation have relegated it to a relatively minor place among world problems.

This neglect is attributable in part to the overwhelming burden of problems which are, in appearance at least, more urgently important than the issue of national minorities. Moreover, interest in the problem may have declined in consequence of the fact that the remnant of European Jewry, the most pitied minority, has at least a potential haven in Israel, and that German groups, the most feared minorities, have been herded into Germany. There has been little effective pressure or clamor for a general and definitive solution by the United Nations.

The rejection of responsibility by international agencies has taken the forms of acquiescence in assertions of concern for co-nationals by kin-states, and of positive refusal to formulate and carry out decisions concerning particular minority disputes. The effective internationalization of the problem would require a vigorous policy of diverting minority complaints from kin-states to international organization, and excluding kin-states from involvement in situations relating to minorities. Far from insisting that the treatment of a national group is an issue between the minority, the state in which it lives, and an agency of the international community, the *de facto* leaders of the postwar world have been expending their energy in hopefully directing host and kin-states to bilateral conference tables and in evading requests that they treat the minority problem as a matter of general international concern.

The dominant powers have to some extent used international conferences and meetings of United Nations organs for the promotion of measures relevant to a general solution of the problem. They have frequently preferred to "postpone" rather than frankly to refuse consideration of the issue. They have abstained from explicit renunciation of the principle of international control over treatment of minorities, choosing not to exclude the possibility that the United Nations might assert competence to deal with troublesome minority issues. As our analysis of United Nations activities in this field has indicated, the abdication of international agencies has not been absolute.

Nevertheless, the evidence supports the general conclusion that the great powers have discarded the assumption made by the League of Nations, that bilateralism in regard to minority issues must be supplanted by a determined assertion of international authority and responsibility. After the First World War, consideration of the dangers to peace which might stem from disputes between host and kin-states led to the experiment in internationalization; since the Second World War, consideration of the difficulties of developing an international solution have led to the virtual bilateralization of the problem.

The second major issue regarding the problem of national minorities is the question of the type of solution which should be applied to it, a question closely related to the issue of the *locus* of competence and responsibility for dealing with the problem.

The peacemakers of 1919 found themselves in the position of having encouraged the peoples of Eastern and Central Europe to develop national political aspirations, on the basis of the slogan of national self-determination, which they were not in all cases willing or able to honor in the postwar settlement. By way of compensation for the incomplete fulfillment of the implications of national self-determination, and insurance against the disturbance of international relations resulting from oppression and efforts to compel the assimilation of minorities, the great powers decided that national groups in certain countries of that region should be granted a special set of minority rights. Over the objections of most of the states which were required to accept that commitment, the principle was established that host states should be bound to bestow upon national minorities special rights which would enable their members not only to enjoy the status of genuinely equal citizenship, but also to maintain and foster the cultural aspects of their distinctive group life. While the formal imposition and international guarantee of this principle applied to only a limited number of states, it was implicit in this international decision that all national minorities, which were by definition groups whose political status was determined in violation of the legitimizing principle of national self-determination, should enjoy treatment conforming to the standard laid down in the legal instruments of the League minority system.

The experiment in the international guarantee of minority rights did not produce satisfactory results. When the League structure crumbled under the impact of Axis aggression, and the question of the solution of the minority problem again arose, it was evident that the concept of the international protection of minority rights had very largely fallen into disrepute.

Our analysis of thinking and planning during the Second World War has indicated that there was a strong tendency to abandon the assumption that national minorities and national states could be reconciled. The League minority system had been based upon the premise that the legitimate interests of minorities, of host states, of co-national states, and of the international community could be brought into an harmonious pattern. If majorities were tolerant and liberal, if minorities were loyal and reasonable in their demands, if kin-states were willing to accept the *status quo* and respect the internationalization of the minority problem, and if the international agency were zealous and impartial in the performance of its protective functions, then no serious difficulties need arise from the existence of national minorities in national states. In general, wartime thought reflected the conviction that this conceptual scheme was unrealistic, and that a new approach to solution of the problem should be tried.

The tendency to bilateralize the minority problem, carrying with it the implication that host and kin-states are free to choose whatever methods of solution they may find mutually acceptable, has had the effect of eliminating the necessity for the formulation of a general international approach. Nevertheless, there has emerged, if not a clear consensus, at least a general orientation of international opinion as to methods of dealing with the minority problem.

For various reasons, the concept of positive minority rights has not been given international endorsement, and it seems unlikely to receive definite support from the United Nations, despite the fact that it was incorporated in the Draft Covenant on Civil and Political Rights by the Commission on Human Rights in 1953. Given the fact of jealous Soviet control over Eastern and Central Europe, it is an obvious political impossibility to revive the League system of an internationally imposed regime of special minority rights applicable to that area. Given the extreme sensitivity of most non-European states to any implication of inferior status, it is unrealistic to contemplate the establishment of an international standard of minority policy applicable only to them. Given the universal concern for guarding the sphere of domestic jurisdiction, the cautious attitude of states concerning the provision of opportunities for hostile interference in their affairs, and the conviction of many states that their own majority-minority situations are *sui generis*, it is clear that no universally binding determination that minorities should enjoy positive rights can be adopted.

Aside from the political improbability that a new system based upon the provision of positive rights for minorities could be erected today, there is widespread doubt concerning the desirability of the recognition of such rights. The moral prestige of the movement for special minority rights has not been enhanced by the fact that, during the era of the League system, its major governmental champion, Germany, proved to be the most vicious persecutor of minorities, and the most vehemently demanding minorities tended to become the most subversive. Similarly, in recent years, the sponsorship of the principle of positive minority rights by the Soviet Union has understandably, if perhaps illogically, contributed to doubts concerning its validity.

In the final analysis, the obstacle to international recognition of the minority rights approach to a solution of the problem is ideological in nature. The general temper of contemporary states is assimilationist. The prominence of the United States in world affairs ensures that international thinking will strongly reflect the concept of the ethnic melting-pot; the voting strength of the Latin American bloc in the United Nations guarantees that decisions will be affected by the overwhelming sentiment of the Western Hemisphere that national minorities are meant to be absorbed, not perpetuated. The leadership of India among non-

European peoples is devoted to a campaign for the negative rights of minorities, for the abolition of racial discrimination, rather than for positive rights facilitating ethnic differentiation.

The ambiguity of the implications of nationalism is evident in this situation. The reluctance of national majorities to accord a special status to ethnic fragments in their midst is explicable in terms of the ideal of achieving nationally homogeneous political units in which states can serve as embodiments of nations. On the other hand, the principle of nationalism can be invoked in support of the view that minorities are entitled, if not to independence or union with co-national communities, at least to the right of ethnic survival. The ultimate difficulty of nationalism is that in the real world, characterized by ethnographic confusion, the realization of some of the aspirations which it stimulates and legitimizes cannot be reconciled with the fulfillment of others which are its equally legitimate derivatives. The practical result in the current world situation is that the aspirations of national majorities tend to be realized at the expense of those of national minorities.

In so far as definite trends have emerged in postwar treatment of the minority problem, they combine to indicate the development of a general attitude favorable to the elimination of national minorities.

There is, first of all, a trend toward international endorsement or acceptance of population transfer — the physical removal of minorities. The principle of transfer has not been pushed to its logical conclusion, which would involve an uprooting and unmixing process global in its scope and inestimably vast in its proportions, nor has it received unqualified international sanction. In general, this device has been regarded as deserving approval only if applied with careful regard for humanitarian considerations and on the basis of bilateral agreement between expelling and receiving states. Nevertheless, the idea of transfer has become a dominant element in current thinking about the minority problem. The establishment of the state of Israel may be construed as an indirect expression of this mentality; support for this act rested largely upon the conviction that many Jews could attain security and ethnic satisfaction only by removing themselves from the national states of other peoples, and that a national political receptacle should be provided for those Jews who might wish to abandon their minority position. The trend has progressed far enough that we may now expect to find reassertions of the demand for transfer and of international support for that demand whenever particular minority problems give rise to serious difficulties.

A second trend relevant to the general approval of the elimination of minorities is implicit in the postwar emphasis upon the concept of human rights. This concept is not intrinsically incompatible with the preservation of national minorities, in the sense of either their literal physical presence or their separate ethnic existence in national states. In stressing the right of members of minorities not to be persecuted or subjected to discrimination, it in fact establishes the essential basis for minority existence. If human rights are combined with positive minority rights, or are interpreted broadly enough to include such rights, the result is to foster the distinctive national-cultural integrity of minority groups. The possibility is not excluded that the General Assembly of the United Nations may put itself on record as formally recommending such a policy.

However, the general tendency of the postwar movement for the promotion of human rights has been to subsume the problem of national minorities under the broader problem of ensuring basic individual rights to all human beings, without reference to membership in ethnic groups. The leading assumption has been that members of national minorities do not need, are not entitled to, or cannot be granted rights of a special character. The doctrine of human rights has been put forward as a substitute for the concept of minority rights, with the strong implication that minorities whose members enjoy individual equality of treatment cannot legitimately demand facilities for the maintenance of their ethnic particularism. Thus, the human rights movement has been spiritually allied with the idea that the collective identity of national minorities may quite properly be broken down by a process of assimilation.

Transfer, human rights, and assimilation form a conceptual combination which undercuts the status of national minorities in national states. In operation, a solution resting upon this basis would permit or compel at least the most ethnically self-conscious members of minorities to join national states appropriate to their ethnic character, thus breaking the back of the minority problem; the remnant would enjoy equal individual rights, but would be deprived of collective status or special rights, and subjected to assimilation. Thus, in theory at least, the problem of national minorities would be eliminated.

This approach to the solution of the minority problem does not represent a consciously adopted general policy of the United Nations, which is skeptical of the validity of any universal formula for dealing with the problem, and insistent upon avoiding responsibility for developing solutions in this field. It does, however, reflect the prevailing attitude in contemporary international organization.

This attitude is neither unanimously nor rigidly nor consistently maintained. The contrary view, that minorities are entitled to remain in national states with facilities for perpetuating their ethnic distinctiveness, has champions in the United Nations and is capable on occasion of gaining the verbal and sometimes the voting support of delegates who are ideologically incapable of frank opposition to any proposition which smacks of human rights. The Soviet bloc is committed to the international adoption of the principle of positive minority rights, even though it adamantly rejects the principle that the sovereign right of Communist states to determine minority policy for themselves should be impaired by any external agency. Although the United States is opposed to the concept of minority rights, it has given indications of being prepared to relax that opposition sufficiently to grasp the opportunity of exploiting the fact that the status of national minorities under the Soviet system does not conform to the liberal promises of Soviet nationality theory.

These deviations, some of them purely tactical in character, do not alter the basic position: substantively, the international temper of the times is favorable to efforts to deal with the problem by the physical and spiritual elimination of national minorities, within the general framework of respect for fundamental human rights; procedurally, it is favorable to the abandonment of the brief experiment in internationalization and a return to treatment of the problem on the bilateral level.

The problem of national minorities is a matter of general

international concern, despite the insistence of minority-possessing states that it is a domestic matter, the persistence of kin-states in making it a matter of bilateral dispute, and the inclination of relatively disinterested states to prevent it from being added to the burden of international responsibility carried by members of the United Nations. The League of Nations failed to make good its attempted international solution of the problem. It is not probable that efforts at bilateral solution will be more successful, or that international organization can effect a permanent withdrawal from the effort to deal with the problem in systematic fashion.

Nevertheless, the effective international treatment of the problem is now precluded. Just as the rights of minorities can command no more respect than other rights in a world torn by ruthless manifestations of power, so the problem of national minorities has no greater chance of solution than other international problems in a world divided by profound political and spiritual conflict.

BIBLIOGRAPHICAL NOTE

The classic bibliographical work in the field of national minorities is Jacob Robinson, *Das Minoritätenproblem und seine Literatur* (Berlin: 1928). A convenient supplement including more recent listings, is provided in a Memorandum by the Secretary-General of the United Nations (Document E/CN.4/Sub.2/85), published under the title, *Definition and Classification of Minorities* (Lake Success, New York: United Nations, 1950).

The essential background for an understanding of the problem of national minorities is provided by the literature of nationalism. In this field, it is still rewarding to go back to Ernest Renan, *Qu'est-ce qu'une nation?* (Paris: 1882); the "Essay on Nationality," in Lord John E. E. D. Acton, *The History of Freedom and Other Essays* (London: 1909); and A. E. Zimmern, *Nationality and Government* (London: 1918). The student should consult the works of Carlton J. H. Hayes, *Essays on Nationalism* (New York: 1926); and *The Historical Evolution of Modern Nationalism* (New York: 1931); along with such later contributions as the report by a study group of the Royal Institute of International Affairs, *Nationalism* (London: Oxford University Press, 1939); Hans Kohn, *The Idea of Nationalism* (New York: Macmillan, 1945); and Edward H. Carr, *Nationalism and After* (London: Macmillan, 1945).

The general theory of nationalism is explicitly related to the problem of minorities by studies on national self-determination and multinationalism, or national federalism. The outstanding work in the former category is Alfred Cobban, *National Self-Determination* (Chicago: University of Chicago Press, revised edition, n.d.); on multinationalism, see Otto Bauer, *Die Nationalitätenfrage und die Sozialdemokratie*, vol. II of *Marx-Studien*, edited by Max Adler and Rudolf Hilferding (Vienna: 1924); and Oscar I. Janowsky, *Nationalities and National Minorities* (New York: Macmillan, 1945). Basic sources for the highly relevant Soviet theory of nationality are the writings of Joseph Stalin. Two somewhat different compilations of his works on this subject have been issued under his name: *Marxism and the National and Colonial Question*, Marxist Library, vol. XXXVIII (New York: International Publishers, 1935); and *Marxism and the National Question* (New York: International Publishers, 1942).

There is no dearth of material on the status of minorities in particular countries and regions. Representative samples of recent literature of this type include A. H. Hourani, *Minorities in the Arab World* (London: Oxford University Press, 1947); Victor Purcell, *The Chinese in Southeast Asia* (New York: Oxford University Press, 1951); Solomon M. Schwarz, *The Jews in the Soviet Union* (Syracuse: Syracuse University Press, 1951); Andrew Mellor, *India Since Par-*

tition (New York: Praeger, 1951); and Leo Marquard, *The Peoples and Policies of South Africa* (London: Oxford University Press, 1952). The avid reader of any good newspaper can soon accumulate a pile of clippings sufficient to document the fact that the problem of national minorities is still with us.

Having gained an understanding of the theoretical setting and objective basis of the minority problem, the student can turn to studies concerning its international aspects. The indispensable book in this category is C. A. Macartney, *National States and National Minorities* (London: Oxford University Press, 1934), which combines general analysis of the problem with a careful evaluation of the minority work of the League of Nations.

The basic primary sources on the League minority system include the following documents: *Protection of Linguistic, Racial and Religious Minorities by the League of Nations* (1927.I.B.2); Official Journal, Special Supplement no. 73, *Documents Relating to the Protection of Minorities by the League of Nations* (1929); *Protection of Linguistic, Racial or Religious Minorities by the League of Nations* (C.8.M.5.1931.I). The most useful secondary works, in addition to Macartney, are P. de Azcárate, *League of Nations and National Minorities* (Washington: Carnegie Endowment for International Peace, 1945); Jacob Robinson *et al., Were the Minorities Treaties a Failure?* (New York: Institute of Jewish Affairs, 1943); and Julius Stone, *International Guarantees of Minority Rights* (London: Oxford University Press, 1932). The exceptional system of minority protection in Upper Silesia is thoroughly treated by Stone in his *Regional Guarantees of Minority Rights* (New York: Macmillan, 1933); and in Georges Kaeckenbeeck, *The International Experiment of Upper Silesia* (London: Oxford University Press, 1942).

German exploitation of the minority problem for political purposes is ably described and documented in Ralph F. Bischoff, *Nazi Conquest Through German Culture* (Cambridge: Harvard University Press, 1942); and *National Socialism: Basic Principles, Their Application by the Nazi Party's Foreign Organization, and the Use of Germans Abroad for Nazi Aims*, Prepared in the Special Unit of the Division of European Affairs, Department of State, by Raymond E. Murphy *et al.* (Washington: Department of State Publication 1864, 1943). For an understanding of the role of the minority problem in the events leading to the Second World War, consult John W. Wheeler-Bennett, *Munich: Prologue to Tragedy* (New York: Duell, Sloan and Pearce, 1948); and Alan Bullock, *Hitler, A Study in Tyranny* (New York: Harper and Brothers, n.d.).

As a perusal of the notes to Chapters 4 to 8 of this study will suggest, proposals relating to a solution of the minority problem were published during the Second World War in a tremendous variety of books and articles. The most valuable collection of wartime expressions of this sort is included in Louise W. Holborn, *War and Peace*

Aims of the United Nations, 2 volumes (Boston: World Peace Foundation, 1943 and 1948).

The essential starting point for a study of the transfer of minority populations is Stephen P. Ladas, *The Exchange of Minorities — Bulgaria, Greece and Turkey* (New York: 1932). Major contributions in this field include two works by Joseph B. Schechtman, *European Population Transfers 1939–1945* (New York: Oxford University Press, 1946); and *Population Transfers in Asia* (New York: Hallsby Press, 1949); and a distinguished book by Eugene M. Kulischer, *Europe on the Move* (New York: Columbia University Press, 1948). A valuable specialized study by MacAlister Brown, "Expulsion of German Minorities from Eastern Europe: The Decision at Potsdam and its Background" (MS., Harvard University Library, 1953), has been available to the author.

Documentary collections constitute the major sources for analysis of the proceedings of the Paris Peace Conference. Chapter 11 is based primarily upon materials from *Paris Peace Conference, 1946, Selected Documents* (Washington: Department of State Publication 2868, Conference Series 103, 1946); and volumes I, II, and IV of the compilation, *Hungary and the Conference of Paris* (Budapest: Hungarian Ministry of Foreign Affairs, 1947).

The working equipment for dealing with any aspect of the direct origins of the United Nations is the fifteen-volume collection of *Documents of the United Nations Conference on International Organization, San Francisco, 1945* (New York: United Nations Information Organizations, 1945). Stimulating, albeit conflicting, interpretations of the human rights provisions of the Charter produced at San Francisco are to be found in Jacob Robinson, *Human Rights and Fundamental Freedoms in the Charter of the United Nations, A Commentary* (New York: Institute of Jewish Affairs, 1946); and H. Lauterpacht, *International Law and Human Rights* (London: Stevens, 1950).

Developments relevant to the minority problem in the United Nations can be adequately surveyed only by immersing oneself in the flood of official documents which flows from the New York headquarters of the organization. For this purpose, the documentation of the Commission on Human Rights and its Sub-Commission on Prevention of Discrimination and Protection of Minorities is most important. A somewhat more casual acquaintance with treatment of the minority problem can be maintained by referring to the several volumes of the *Yearbook on Human Rights* (United Nations, 1946f.), the monthly *United Nations Review*, and the quarterly summary of United Nations activities in the journal, *International Organization* (Boston: World Peace Foundation).

Finally, no discussion of sources available to scholars in the United States should end without grateful acknowledgment of the invaluable materials provided by the *New York Times*.

NOTES

Abbreviations and Usages Adopted in Citation of Documents

Documents and publications of the League of Nations are identified by the prefix, LN.

The collection of documents, *Paris Peace Conference, 1946, Selected Documents* (Department of State Publication 2868, Conference Series 103, 1946), is cited as PPC.

Documents not otherwise designated are those of the United Nations. The following abbreviations are used in citation of United Nations documents:

UN – United Nations

SC – Security Council

GA – General Assembly

Ecosoc – Economic and Social Council

CHR – Commission on Human Rights

Sub-Commission – Sub-Commission on Prevention of Discrimination and Protection of Minorities

UNSCOP – United Nations Special Committee on Palestine

UNSCOB – United Nations Special Committee on the Balkans

OR – Official Records

Res. – Resolution

Cttee. – Committee

CHAPTER 1: BACKGROUND OF THE LEAGUE MINORITY SYSTEM

1. H. W. V. Temperley, ed., *A History of the Peace Conference of Paris* (1921), V, 113–115.

2. Quoted in Clemenceau's letter to Paderewski, 24 June 1919. The text is reproduced in Oscar I. Janowsky, *Nationalities and National Minorities* (1945), pp. 179–184.

3. The Convention concerning the Exchange of Greek and Turkish Populations, signed at Lausanne, 30 January 1923, provided in Article 1 for transfer to Greece of persons of the Greek Orthodox religion, and to Turkey of Moslems residing in Greece. Text in LN, *Protection of Linguistic, Racial and Religious Minorities by the League of Nations* (1927.I.B.2), pp. 106–111.

4. Article 1 stipulated: "Les Polonais, sujets respectifs des hautes parties contractantes, obtiendront la conservation de leur nationalité, d'après les formes d'existence politique que chacun des gouvernements, auxquels ils appartiennent, jugera convenable de leur accorder." Quoted in C. A. Macartney, *National States and National Minorities* (1934), p. 160.

5. Julius Stone, *International Guarantees of Minority Rights* (1932), p. 3.

6. For instance, Rumania held that it was bound only in so far as the treatment of its own nationals was concerned; it denied that Jews were, or could be, Rumanians, and proceeded to oppress them at its pleasure. Macartney, p. 168.

7. Stone, p. 3.

8. See Janowsky, pp. 19–32.

9. Prince Bernhard von Bülow, *Imperial Germany* (1914), p. 291.

10. Janowsky, p. 24.

11. Macartney, p. 152.

12. Cf. Arnold J. Toynbee, *Nationality and the War* (1915), p. vii, and *The World After the Peace Conference* (1925), p. 63.

13. Alfred Cobban, *National Self-Determination* (revised edition, n.d.), p. 6.

14. See Ray S. Baker and William E. Dodd, eds., *The Public Papers of Woodrow Wilson, Authorized Edition: War and Peace: Presidential Messages, Addresses, and Public Papers (1917–1924),* I, 16, 180.

15. Cf. H. W. V. Temperley, "How the Hungarian Frontiers Were Drawn," *Foreign Affairs,* April 1928, pp. 439–440; Baker and Dodd, I, 462.

16. Cobban, p. 20.

17. Macartney, p. 179.

18. Janowsky, pp. 108–109.

19. La Documentation internationale, *La Paix de Versailles* (1932), X, *Commission des nouveaux états et des minorités,* p. 227. (Hereinafter cited as *La Paix de Versailles.*)

20. Text in LN Doc. 1927. I.B.2, pp. 102–105.

21. Macartney, p. 206.

22. *Ibid.,* p. 211. Cf. Joseph B. Schechtman, *European Population Transfers, 1939–1945* (1946), p. 6.

23. Czechoslovakia, with its duality of national structure, and Yugoslavia, which was originally known as the Kingdom of the Serbs, Croats, and Slovenes, might be cited as exceptions. However, there was a strong tendency in these states to stress the national character of the regimes, even though they were not strictly uninational. Their populations were regarded as being divided between constituent national groups and national minorities. Cf. Macartney, p. 209.

24. See Arthur von Balogh, *Der internationale Schutz der Minderheiten* (1928), pp. 20–22. A Memorandum submitted to the Peace Conference by the Committee of Jewish Delegations, on 10 May 1919, is reproduced in Jacob Robinson *et al., Were the Minorities Treaties a Failure?* (1943), pp. 319–325.

25. Herbert Kraus, *Das Recht der Minderheiten* (1927), pp. 41–42.

26. See note 2, above.

27. See *La Paix de Versailles,* X, 62.

28. Temperley, ed., *A History of the Peace Conference of Paris,* V, 130.

29. M. O. Hudson credits Wilson, along with Lord Robert Cecil and the unofficial representatives of American Jewry, with having overridden the tendency of the Conference to neglect the problem. See his chapter, "The Protection of Minorities and Natives in Transferred Territories," in Edward M. House and Charles Seymour, eds., *What Really Happened at Paris* (1921), p. 473.

30. Robinson *et al.,* pp. 8–9.

31. The coöperative attitude of Benes, the Czechoslovak representative, was the most notable exception to this generalization. Austria, Hungary, and Bulgaria were also well-disposed toward the scheme, since they were interested in the fate of their co-nationals who were being assigned to other states. Macartney, pp. 241–242, 253–254.

32. See Paderewski's Memorandum of 15 June 1919, in *La Paix de Versailles*, X, 129–134. Bratiaɳu led the protest of the small powers in the plenary session of 31 May 1919. Temperley, V, 129.

33. Macartney, p. 251.

34. *Ibid.*, pp. 252, 290.

CHAPTER 2: THE PROTECTION OF MINORITIES BY THE LEAGUE OF NATIONS

1. A convenient compilation of these instruments is provided in LN, *Protection of Linguistic, Racial and Religious Minorities by the League of Nations* (1927.I.B.2).

2. For the text of the Declaration by Iraq, which was not made until 1932, see LN Doc. A.17.1932.VII.

3. For excerpts relevant to the minority system, see Julius Stone, *Regional Guarantees of Minority Rights* (1933), Appendix I.

4. Information Section, LN Secretariat, *The League of Nations and the Protection of Minorities of Race, Language and Religion* (revised edition, 1927), p. 16.

5. *Ibid.*

6. L. P. Mair, *The Protection of Minorities* (1928), pp. 207–208.

7. William E. Rappard, "Minorities and the League," *International Conciliation*, September 1926, no. 222, p. 334.

8. Note Wilson's identification of the beneficiaries of the scheme, in Baker and Dodd, eds., *The Public Papers of Woodrow Wilson. . .*, I, 463, 543.

9. Polish Minority Treaty, arts. 3–6. For the text of this treaty, see the reference in note 1, above.

10. *Ibid.*, arts. 3–5.

11. *Ibid.*, arts. 2, 7, 8.

12. *Ibid.*, art. 12.

13. *Ibid.*, art. 2.

14. Robinson *et al.*, *Were the Minorities Treaties a Failure?* p. 39.

15. P. de Azcárate, *League of Nations and National Minorities* (1945), p. 82.

16. Polish Minority Treaty, arts. 7, 8, 9. The other treaties and declarations contained virtually identical provisions.

17. In addition to the essentially uniform provisions analyzed above, many of the instruments contained stipulations applicable exclusively to certain minority groups, or other distinctive features. See Robinson *et al.*, pp. 236–237.

18. *La Paix de Versailles*, X, 22.

19. Temperley, ed., *A History of the Peace Conference of Paris*, V, 137.

20. Polish Minority Treaty, arts. 9 and 10. Cf. André N. Mandelstam, *La Protection internationale des minorités, première partie, La Protection des minorités en droit international positif* (1931), p. 127, and Balogh, *Der internationale Schutz der Minderheiten*, pp. 50–51, 175.

21. See Polish Minority Treaty, art. 1.

22. Stone, *International Guarantees of Minority Rights*, p. 247.

23. LN, *Official Journal*, Special Supplement no. 73, *Documents Relating to the Protection of Minorities by the League of Nations* (1929), p. 61.

24. Cf. Clemenceau's letter to Paderewski, 24 June 1919, in Janowsky, *Nationalities and National Minorities*, pp. 179–184.

25. Polish Minority Treaty, art. 12.

26. Azcárate, pp. 14–15.

27. See Clemenceau's letter to Paderewski; statement by Berthelot, French representative on the Committee on New States and Minorities, *La Paix de Versailles*, X, 142; comment by M. O. Hudson, American representative on that committee, in House and Seymour, eds., *What Really Happened at Paris*, p. 222.

28. Stone, *International Guarantees of Minority Rights*, pp. 138–144.

29. *La Paix de Versailles*, X, 84, 104, 127.

30. LN, *Protection of Linguistic, Racial or Religious Minorities by the League of Nations* (C.8.M.5.1931.I.), pp. 78–79.

31. *Ibid.*, esp. pp. 7–12.

32. It was always possible for any member of the Council to seize that body of a minority case, regardless of the findings or action of a Committee of Three. In practice, however, it was left to the committee to determine whether the Council should deal with a particular case.

33. The Court rendered advisory opinions in three cases concerning the rights of the German minority in Poland, and in one case regarding the right of minorities in Albania to maintain private schools. See *Publications of the Permanent Court of International Justice*, Series B, nos. 6 and 7, and Series A/B, nos. 40 and 64.

34. The European Nationalities Congress, meeting at Geneva in 1926, demanded that the League procedure be made a bilateral process in which minorities as such should be allowed to participate. Kurt Trampler, *Staaten und Nationale Gemeinschaften* (1929), p. 130.

35. Kraus, *Das Recht der Minderheiten*, p. 222.

36. LN Doc. C.8.M.5.1931.I., p. 10.

37. See the Observations submitted by Czechoslovakia, Greece, Poland, Rumania, and Yugoslavia to the Adatci Committee, LN, *Official Journal*, Special Supplement no. 73, pp. 70–74.

38. The government of Czechoslovakia proposed, on 5 April 1923, that "petitions which are incompatible with the dignity of the State" should be considered nonreceivable. LN Doc. C.8.M.5.1931.I., p. 28.

39. LN, *Official Journal*, Special Supplement no. 73, pp. 15–16, 35, 62.

40. Stone, *International Guarantees of Minority Rights*, p. 25.

41. The Committee of Three did not seize the Council of minority cases; legally, it ceased to exist after finding that a case should be considered by the Council, and its members, acting as members of the Council rather than as agents of the defunct committee, proceeded individually or conjointly to seize the Council of the case. (*Ibid.*, pp. 108–109.) However, regardless of this fine legal point, the practical effect of the committee system was to spread the responsibility for initiating action, and thus to diminish the onerousness of the duty of Council members.

42. The foregoing analysis applies only to the "general" League system for protection of minorities. The unique procedure established for Upper Silesia under the Geneva Convention contrasted sharply with this system in several important respects. See Georges Kaeckenbeeck, *The International Experiment of Upper Silesia* (1942), and Stone, *Regional Guarantees c'' Minority Rights*.

43. Janowsky, p. 123; Rappard, "Minorities and the League," p. 340; Macartney, *National States and National Minorities*, p. 390; Robinson *et al.*, p. 261.

44. Balogh, pp. 262–263.

45. The informal, mediatorial work of the Minorities Committees was not recorded in public documents, and has therefore never been thoroughly analyzed and evaluated. However, Robinson and his collaborators examined 96 cases which were treated by the Committees and/or the Council, and arrived at the conclusion that justice for the minorities was obtained in 80 of those cases. Robinson *et al.*, p. 113.

46. Azcárate, p. 67.

47. LN, *Official Journal* (1934), Verbatim Record of the Fifteenth Ordinary Session of the Assembly, Fourth Plenary Meeting, p. 2.

CHAPTER 3: THE FAILURE OF THE LEAGUE MINORITY SYSTEM

1. Although they were not uncritical of the system, Czechoslovakia accepted the principle of international protection of minorities and cooperated willingly in its implementation, and Austria, Hungary, and Bulgaria, which were prominent kin-states as well as minority states, displayed a sympathetic attitude toward the project of safeguarding minorities. See Robinson *et al.*, *Were the Minorities Treaties a Failure?* pp. 151–154.

2. Analyses of the criticisms and demands expressed by minority states are found in Macartney, *National States and National Minorities*, pp. 371–372, and Robinson *et al.*, pp. 154f. See also Paderewski's Memorandum of 15 June 1919 to the Committee on New States and Minorities, *La Paix de Versailles*, X, 129f; Observations submitted by Poland to the Council, 16 Jan. 1923, LN, *Protection of Linguistic, Racial or Religious Minorities by the League of Nations* (C.8.M.5.1931.I), pp. 31–35; Observations submitted by Czechoslovakia, Greece, Poland, Rumania, and Yugoslavia to the Adatci Committee, LN, *Official Journal*, Special Supplement no. 73, pp. 70–74.

3. *La Paix de Versailles*, X, 130, 132.

4. *Ibid.*, pp. 69, 131; Mair, *The Protection of Minorities*, p. 66; Robinson *et al.*, p. 178.

5. Azcárate, *League of Nations and National Minorities*, pp. 62–63; Mair, p. 77.

6. The quotation is from the statement of Zaleski, the Polish representative, before the Council on 6 March 1929. LN, Doc. C.8.M.5.1931.I., p. 93. Italics mine.

7. Janowsky, *Nationalities and National Minorities*, p. 131.

8. See the letter from Seipel, the Austrian Chancellor, to the Secretary-General, dated 9 April 1929. LN, *Official Journal*, Special Supplement no. 73, p. 65.

9. Mello-Franco's statement that the creators of the system "did not dream of creating within certain States a group of inhabitants who would regard themselves as permanently foreign to the general organisation of the country," but intended rather to establish a regime "which might gradually prepare the way for conditions necessary for the establishment of a complete national unity," was followed by Chamberlain's observation that "The object of the Minority Treaties, and of the Council in discharging its duties under them, was . . . to secure for the minorities that measure of protection

and justice which would gradually prepare them to be merged in the national community to which they belonged." LN, *Official Journal* (1926), pp. 142, 144.

10. See Stresemann's statement of 6 March 1929. LN, Doc. C.8.M.5.1931.I., p. 89.

11. *Ibid.,* pp. 9, 240–242.

12. Stone, *International Guarantees of Minority Rights,* pp. 165–167.

13. For instance, Greece and Albania contended against each other before the Court in the proceedings preliminary to the rendering of the Advisory Opinion on Minority Schools in Albania. See *Publications of the Permanent Court of International Justice,* Series A/B, no. 64, p. 7.

14. The tendency to treat the status of national minorities under the League system as analogous to the status of aliens under international law was evinced by the Permanent Court in 1928, when it held that minorities in Albania were entitled to be treated in accordance with a kind of *minimum* standard rather than a strictly *equal* standard. (*Ibid.,* p. 20.)

The same tendency can be inferred from Azcárate's consideration of the question whether equal treatment should invariably be deemed adequate to satisfy the requirements of the minority instruments, which strongly suggests the controversy over minimum and national standards for the treatment of aliens. (Azcárate, pp. 22–23.)

In 1932, Rumania contested the receivability of a petition, on the ground that the resources of the municipal courts had not been exhausted by the petitioner. (Macartney, p. 319, note.) This was an attempt to transfer the concept of *denial of justice* from the international law relating to protection of aliens to the regime of minority protection.

15. Cobban, *National Self-Determination,* p. 37.

16. Macartney, p. 491.

17. Cf. Macartney, p. 414; Robinson *et al.,* pp. 209, 216; Edward Noel-Buxton, *National Minorities Today* (1931), p. 3; Eduard Benes, *Democracy Today and Tomorrow* (1939), p. 230.

18. Robinson *et al.,* p. 226; Macartney, pp. 407–408.

19. Robinson and his collaborators also credit Austria, Hungary, Latvia, and Lithuania with relatively liberal minority policies. *Were the Minorities Treaties a Failure?* p. 238.

20. For detailed accounts of the discriminatory and oppressive measures of which minorities in the various minority states were the victims, see Otto Junghann, *National Minorities in Europe* (1932), chap. iv, and Mair, *The Protection of Minorities,* chaps. vi–xii.

21. See the Covenant of the League of Nations, art. 4, para. 5, and art. 5, para. 1.

22. Azcárate, p. 63.

23. Janowsky, p. 8.

24. Macartney, p. 394.

25. Azcárate, pp. 32, 44, 50.

26. Robinson *et al.,* pp. 256–257.

27. *Ibid.,* p. 260.

28. Noel-Buxton, p. 5.

29. Cf. Trampler's contention, "dass nur durch das eigene Volkstum der Weg zur Menschheit und der Weg zu Gott führt." *Staaten und Nationale Gemeinschaften,* p. 136.

30. Cf. Erich Hula, "National Self-Determination Reconsidered," *Social Research*, February 1943, p. 17.

31. For a careful study of Nazi policy with respect to *Auslandsdeutsche*, see *National Socialism: Basic Principles, Their Application by the Nazi Party's Foreign Organization, and the Use of Germans Abroad for Nazi Aims*, Prepared in the Special Unit of the Division of European Affairs, Department of State, by Raymond E. Murphy *et al.* (1943), Department of State Publication 1864.

32. Henry C. Wolfe, *Human Dynamite*, Headline Books, no. 20, Foreign Policy Association (1939).

33. Azcárate, pp. 44, 50.

34. *Ibid.*, p. 121.

35. Briand declared before the Assembly, in 1928: "If any act of justice were proposed which would disturb world peace . . . I should be the first to call upon those promoting it to stop, to abandon it in the supreme interest of peace." LN, *Official Journal*, Verbatim Record of the Ninth Ordinary Session of the Assembly, Tenth Plenary Meeting, p. 9.

36. Mair, p. 209; Martin Agronsky, "Racism in Italy," *Foreign Affairs*, January 1939, p. 391.

37. From 1922 to 1933, the post of rapporteur was filled by representatives of Brazil, Colombia, and Japan. Macartney, p. 350, note.

38. LN Doc. C.8.M.5.1931.I., p. 13.

39. Macartney p. 375.

40. Robinson *et al.*, p. 75.

CHAPTER 4: THE WARTIME SETTING OF THE PROBLEM

1. Frederick L. Schuman, *Germany Since 1918* (1937), Appendix III, pp. 112–116.

2. Hula, "National Self-Determination Reconsidered," *Social Research*, February 1943, p. 10.

3. Alfred von Wegerer, "The Origins of this War: A German View," *Foreign Affairs*, July 1940, p. 713.

4. See the text of Hitler's speech before the Reichstag, on 6 October 1939, *International Conciliation*, November 1939, no. 354, pp. 495–524.

CHAPTER 5: SOLUTION BY INTERNATIONAL ORGANIZATION: THE INTERNATIONAL GUARANTEE OF MINORITY RIGHTS

1. See Benes, "The Organization of Post-War Europe," *Foreign Affairs*, January 1942, p. 237, and "Czechoslovakia Plans for Peace," *ibid.*, October 1944, pp. 35–36.

2. Note the contradictory statements by Hubert Ripka, Minister of State, in Louise W. Holborn, ed., *War and Peace Aims of the United Nations*, I (1943), 438, and II (1948), 1036.

3. See *International Conciliation*, April 1939, no. 349, p. 187; Department of State *Bulletin*, 24 Aug. 1940, pp. 132–134, and 7 Feb. 1942, p. 128.

4. Albert Guérard, *Europe Free and United* (1945), p. 71.

5. Dr. Josip Smodlaka, Minister of Foreign Affairs in the Partisan Provisional Government, in an interview with C. L. Sulzberger, reported in *New York Times*, 11 April 1944.

6. For instance, Sean Lester, Acting Secretary-General of the League,

stated: "There are good reasons for holding that the obligations regarding the treatment of minorities . . . are not obligations which are abrogated by war between the parties to the instruments which created them or by annexation of the territory in which they operate. . . ." LN, *Powers and Duties Attributed to the League of Nations by International Treaties* (C.3.M.3.1944.V.), p. 36.

7. In an unpublished research paper, dated 22 November 1944, the Post-War Planning Committee of the Department of State assumed that the basic instruments of the League minority system should be regarded as still valid, and took the position that "The United States should favor the revision of these treaties to adapt them to changed conditions."

8. *International Conciliation*, April 1944, no. 399, p. 292.

9. *Ibid.*, pp. 341–342.

10. *Ibid.*, April 1941, no. 369, p. 200.

11. *Ibid.*, January 1944, no. 396, p. 27. Italics mine.

12. *Ibid.*, December 1946, no. 426, p. 561.

13. *New York Times*, 25 Dec. 1939.

14. *Ibid.*, 25 Dec. 1941.

15. Holborn, I, 633.

16. The Commission to Study the Bases of a Just and Durable Peace, *A Message from the National Study Conference on the Churches and a Just and Durable Peace* (1942), p. 12.

17. *New York Times*, 7 Oct. 1943.

18. Salo W. Baron, "Reflections on the Future of the Jews of Europe," *Contemporary Jewish Record*, July–August 1940, p. 365.

19. Jacob Robinson, "Uprooted Jews in the Immediate Postwar World," Commission to Study the Organization of Peace, *The United Nations and the Organization of Peace, Third Report and Papers Presented to the Commission* (February 1943), p. 302.

20. *New York Times*, 25 Feb. 1945.

21. Speech in London, 8 November 1939, Holborn, I, 672.

22. *Report of the Thirty-Ninth Annual Conference of the Labour Party, Bournemouth, 1940*, pp. 172–174.

23. *Parliamentary Debates, Lords*, vol. 130, col. 1115. (8 March 1944).

24. See, for instance, suggestions in Abraham I. Katsh, ed., *The Jew in the Postwar World* (n.d.), pp. 52–53, and Alexander S. Kohanski, ed., *The American Jewish Conference: Its Organization and Proceedings of the First Session* (1944), pp. 184, 188–189.

25. American Jewish Committee, *Toward Peace and Equity* (1946), p. 9.

26. American Jewish Conference, *Nazi Germany's War Against the Jews* (1947), pp. ix, xi, xiv–xv.

27. Janowsky, "Towards a Solution of the Minorities Problem," chap. vii in Kingsley and Petegorsky, *Strategy for Democracy*, pp. 111–116.

28. Janowsky, "Jewish Rights in the Postwar World," *Survey Graphic*, September 1943, pp. 350, 365.

29. Janowsky, *Nationalities and National Minorities*, pp. 145–163.

30. Max Laserson, "Minorities Problem Viewed Realistically," *New Europe*, March 1944, p. 27. See also Laserson, *The Status of the Jews After the War* (1940), pp. 19–20.

31. Unpublished research paper, dated 22 November 1944, by the Post-War Planning Committee of the Department of State.

32. Kohanski, p. 203.

33. *New York Times*, 15 Aug. 1944.

34. Ruth Hershman, ed., *The American Jewish Conference: Proceedings of the Third Session* (1946), p. 241.

35. Research Institute on Peace and Post-War Problems of the American Jewish Committee, *Jewish Post-War Problems: A Study Course* (1942–43), Unit I, p. 22.

36. Hersh Lauterpacht, *An International Bill of the Rights of Man* (1945).

37. Hans Kelsen, "International Peace — By Court or Government?" *The American Journal of Sociology*, January 1941, pp. 571–572.

38. Julius Stone, *The Atlantic Charter* (1943), p. 134.

39. *Parliamentary Debates, Lords*, vol. 130, col. 1130.

40. *Ibid.*, cols. 1130–1131.

41. One draft constitution for a European federation incorporated the major part of the standard minority treaty text. See R. W. G. Mackay, *Peace Aims and the New Order* (1941), pp. 266–268.

42. Janowsky, *Nationalities and National Minorities*, pp. 158–163.

43. Cf. the pamphlet, *Underwriting Victory* (n.d.), published by the Harvard Council on Post-War Problems, p. 9, and Robert M. Hutchins *et al.*, *Preliminary Draft of a World Constitution* (1948), pp. 6, 13, 28.

44. See p. 64, above.

CHAPTER 6: SOLUTION BY INTERNATIONAL ORGANIZATION: AN INTERNATIONAL BILL OF HUMAN RIGHTS

1. Jacob Robinson, "Minorities in a Free World," *Free World*, May 1943, pp. 451–453.

2. Joseph Tenenbaum, *Peace for the Jews* (1945), p. 118.

3. Mordecai Grossman, "Palestine and the Future of the Jews — A Pragmatic Approach," *Contemporary Jewish Record*, April 1944, p. 133.

4. C. J. Hambro, *How to Win the Peace* (1942), pp. 178, 299.

5. Alfred Hirschberg, "Human Rights or Minority Rights," *Contemporary Jewish Record*, February 1945, pp. 44–46.

6. Morris D. Waldman, "A Bill of Rights for All Nations," *New York Times Magazine*, 19 Nov. 1944, p. 49.

7. *International Conciliation*, February 1944, no. 397, p. 161.

8. Cf. Claude G. Montefiore, "Assimilation: Good and Bad," *Contemporary Jewish Record*, April 1944, p. 217.

9. *Parliamentary Debates, Commons*, vol. 351, col. 295.

10. Message to Congress, Holborn, *War and Peace Aims of the United Nations*, I, 22.

11. Message to Congress, 6 Jan. 1941, House of Representatives Doc. no. 1, 77th Congress, 1st Session.

12. House of Representatives Doc. no. 358, 77th Congress, 1st Session; Department of State *Bulletin*, 3 Jan. 1942, p. 3.

13. See Benes' lecture at Aberdeen University, 10 Nov. 1941, Holborn, I, 420; his article, "The Organization of Post-War Europe," *Foreign Affairs*, January 1942, p. 241; his speech before the Canadian Parliament, 3 June 1943, *President Benes on War and Peace* (Czechoslovak Sources and Documents, no. 4, 1943), p. 149.

14. Benes, "The Organization of Post-War Europe," p. 239. Cf. Hubert Ripka, *Small and Great Nations* (1944), p. 18.

15. See the lecture by Benes at Manchester University, 5 Dec. 1942, Holborn, I, 446.

16. Department of State *Bulletin*, 5 June 1943, p. 482.

17. See sec. XXVII, *Eighth International Conference of American States, Lima, 1938: Final Act* (Lima, 1938).

18. Report by the Inter-American Juridical Committee on the Dumbarton Oaks Proposals, 8 Dec. 1944, *American Journal of International Law*, vol. 39, Supplement (1945), p. 61.

19. *New York Times*, 4 Feb. 1945.

20. Final Act of the Inter-American Conference on Problems of War and Peace, Resolution XL, *Report Submitted to the Governing Board of the Pan-American Union by the Director General*, Pan-American Union Congress and Conf. Series, no. 47.

21. *International Conciliation*, April 1945, no. 410, p. 327. Italics mine.

22. Holborn, II, 193. Italics mine.

23. *Dumbarton Oaks Documents on International Organization* (1944), Department of State Publication 2192, Conf. Series 56, chap. ix, sec. A, para. 1.

24. Holborn, I, 224.

25. *Parliamentary Debates, Commons*, vol. 400, cols. 771–772. (24 May 1944).

26. See the endorsements of the principle of nonintervention by Roosevelt, on 14 April 1940 (Holborn, I, 25), and by Secretary of State Hull, on 26 October 1940. Department of State *Bulletin*, 26 Oct. 1940, p. 334.

CHAPTER 7: SOLUTION BY MORAL TRANSFORMATION: ASSIMILATION AND CULTURAL PLURALISM

1. The tendency of Eastern and Central European states to insist that members of national minorities emigrate or submit to assimilation became clear in the late stages of the war. Cf. *Congress Weekly*, 20 July 1945, p. 3; Sidney Hertzberg, "The Month in History," *Commentary*, November 1945, p. 32.

2. Benes, "Postwar Czechoslovakia," *Foreign Affairs*, April 1946, p. 401.

3. Schechtman, *European Population Transfers, 1939–1945*, pp. 477–478.

4. Benes, "The Organization of Post-War Europe," *Foreign Affairs*, January 1942, p. 237. Italics mine.

5. Ripka, *Small and Great Nations*, p. 14.

6. Czechoslovak Ministry of Information, *Statement of Policy of Mr. Gottwald's Government* (1946), p. 11.

7. Holborn, ed., *War and Peace Aims of the United Nations*, II, 1042; Zechariah Shuster, "Must the Jews Quit Europe," *Commentary*, December 1945, p. 15.

8. Quoted in *New York Times Magazine*, 16 May 1948, p. 26.

9. See John Stuart Mill, *Considerations on Representative Government* (1861), p. 289.

10. George H. Blakeslee, "Hawaii: Racial Problem and Naval Base," *Foreign Affairs*, October 1938, p. 93.

11. Cf. Louis Wirth, "Morale and Minority Groups," *The American Journal of Sociology*, November 1941, p. 421.

12. Donald R. Young, "Democracy and Minority Groups," in R. M. MacIver, ed., *Civilization and Group Relationships* (1945), p. 158.

13. Research Institute on Peace and Post-War Problems of the American Jewish Committee, *Jewish Post-War Problems: A Study Course*, Unit VI, pp. 27–28.

14. *Parliamentary Debates, Lords*, vol. 130, cols. 1130–1131.

15. Tenenbaum, *Peace for the Jews*, pp. 120, 123.

16. Reinhold Niebuhr, "Jews After the War," (Part I), *The Nation*, 21 Feb. 1942, pp. 215–216.

17. Address of 22 May 1943, *President Benes on War and Peace*, p. 48.

18. See its statement to the Anglo-American Committee of Inquiry, *Congress Weekly*, 15 Feb. 1946, p. 14.

19. American Jewish Committee, *To the Counsellors of Peace* (1945), p. 20.

20. See Laserson, *The Status of the Jews After the War*, p. 8; Jacob Lestchinsky, "Jews in the U.S.S.R.," *Contemporary Jewish Record*, September-October and November-December 1940, pp. 510–526, 607–621.

21. *Congress Weekly*, 5 April 1946, p. 5.

22. David Ben Gurion spoke for a substantial section of world Jewry when he declared: "We are Jewish and we are determined to remain so.... We shall be as Jewish as an Englishman is English. We do not need any justification. . . ." The Jewish Agency for Palestine, *The Jewish Plan for Palestine: Memoranda and Statements Presented by the Jewish Agency for Palestine to the United Nations Special Committee on Palestine* (1947), p. 317.

23. Macartney, *National States and National Minorities*, p. 422.

24. Lord John E. E. D. Acton, *The History of Freedom and Other Essays* (1909). See the "Essay on Nationality," esp. pp. 290–298.

25. A. E. Zimmern, *Nationality and Government* (1918), p. 50.

26. Macartney, p. 450.

27. For examples of this line of thought, see E. H. Carr, *Conditions of Peace* (1942), p. 65; Stone, *The Atlantic Charter*, p. 15; V. A. Firsoff, "The Problem of East Central Europe," *Contemporary Review*, December 1945, p. 366.

28. Robert Gordis, "The Role of Judaism in the Postwar World," in Katsh, ed., *The Jew in the Postwar World*, p. 28.

29. See Guérard, *Europe Free and United*, p. 73; Carr, p. 65; Introduction by Hans Kohn in Walter Sulzbach, *National Consciousness* (1943), p. viii.

30. MacIver, "The Ordering of a Multigroup Society," in his *Civilization and Group Relationships*, p. 165.

31. Janowsky, *Nationalities and National Minorities*, pp. 145–150.

32. Holborn, II, 1108. This projected federation of nationalities was realized under the terms of a new constitution which became effective on 31 January 1946. See Embassy of the Federal People's Republic of Yugoslavia, *Constitution of the Federal People's Republic of Yugoslavia* (Washington, 1946).

33. Alexander S. Kohanski, "Problem of Minority Rights in East Central Europe," *New Europe*, July-August 1944, pp. 22–24; Julius Deutsch, "Central European Problem," *Free World*, June 1942, pp. 74–77; Stefan Osusky, "Liberty or Uniformity in Eastern Europe," *Contemporary Review*, November 1941, pp. 278–282.

34. Buber, Magnes, and Smilansky, *Palestine, A Bi-National State* (1946).

35. Otto Bauer, *Die Nationalitätenfrage und die Sozialdemokratie* (vol.

II of *Marx-Studien*, edited by Max Adler and Rudolf Hilferding, 1924).
See esp. sec. 22, "Das Personalitätsprinzip," pp. 353–366.

36. Cf. Firsoff, "The Problem of East Central Europe," pp. 366–367;
Hannah Arendt, "Concerning Minorities," *Contemporary Jewish Record*,
August 1944, pp. 366–368.

37. See Jacques Maritain, *A Christian Looks at the Jewish Question*
(1939); Joseph Sulkowski, "The Problem of National Minorities in its So-
ciological Aspects" (reprinted from *The Quarterly Bulletin of the Polish
Institute of Arts and Sciences in America*, October 1943), p. 31; A. H.
Hourani, *Minorities in the Arab World* (1947), p. 125.

38. Salo W. Baron, "The Spiritual Reconstruction of European Jewry,"
Commentary, November 1945, pp. 11–12.

CHAPTER 8: SOLUTION BY PHYSICAL ELIMINATION OF MINORITIES: FRONTIER REVISION, TRANSFER, AND ZIONISM

1. Otto Bauer, *Die Nationalitätenfrage und die Sozialdemokratie*, p. 171.

2. Note the second and third principles stated in the Atlantic Charter
(House of Representatives Doc. no. 358, 77th Congress, 1st Session). This
Anglo-American policy statement, which was incorporated by reference in
the Declaration by United Nations of 1 January 1942, was interpreted by
both Roosevelt and Churchill as an endorsement of the principle of self-
determination. See Department of State *Bulletin*, 28 Feb. 1942, p. 188, and
Randolph S. Churchill, ed., *The Sinews of Peace, Post-War Speeches by
Winston S. Churchill* (1948), p. 157.

3. Macartney, *National States and National Minorities*, p. 432.

4. Stephen P. Ladas, *The Exchange of Minorities — Bulgaria, Greece and
Turkey* (1932), p. 3.

5. See Eugene M. Kulischer, *Europe on the Move* (1948), chap. ix, pp.
255–273, and Table 20, pp. 302–304; Schechtman, *European Population
Transfers, 1939–1945.*

6. The text appears in *International Conciliation*, November 1939, no. 354,
pp. 495–524.

7. Program of the Nazi Party, adopted at Munich, 24 Feb. 1920, Schuman,
Germany Since 1918, Appendix III, pp. 112–116.

8. Schechtman, pp. 39–45, 255, 351–352; Kulischer, pp. 256, 259.

9. See Albert Viton, "Permanent Minorities: A World Problem," *An-
tioch Review*, Winter 1941, pp. 486–487; Jacob Robinson, "Minorities in a
Free World," *Free World*, May 1943, pp. 453–454; Edward Taborsky,
"Minority Problems in Central Europe," *The National Review*, September
1942, pp. 242–247.

10. Macartney, p. 449. This judgment is confirmed by Ladas, p. 721.

11. Sumner Welles, *The Time for Decision* (1944), pp. 20, 331–332;
Where Are We Heading? (1946), p. 127.

12. Welles, *The Time for Decision*, pp. 354–355.

13. *Ibid.*, p. 20.

14. Welles, *Where Are We Heading?* pp. 120, 125, 127, 129, 165, 327.

15. L. B. Namier, *Conflicts* (1942), p. 18.

16. See Benes, "The New Order in Europe," *The Nineteenth Century and
After*, September 1941, p. 154; "The Organization of Post-War Europe,"
Foreign Affairs, January 1942, p. 238; Address in London, 28 April 1942,

Holborn, ed., *War and Peace Aims of the United Nations,* I, 427; "Toward Peace in Central and Eastern Europe," *Annals of the American Academy of Political and Social Science,* vol. 232, March 1944, p. 166.

17. Benes, "Postwar Czechoslovakia," *Foreign Affairs,* April 1946, pp. 402–404.

18. Benes, "Czechoslovakia Plans for Peace," *Foreign Affairs,* October 1944, p. 36; "Postwar Czechoslovakia," p. 401.

19. Cf. statements by Hubert Ripka, Minister of State, and Jan Masaryk, Foreign Minister, in Czechoslovak Ministry of Foreign Affairs, *Czechoslovakia in Post-War Europe* (1942), pp. 61–62, and Holborn, II, 1036, 1042.

20. *Towards A New Poland: A Programme of the Polish Underground Movement* (pamphlet published in London, n.d.), p. 9.

21. Schechtman, p. 362.

22. See Robert E. Sherwood, *Roosevelt and Hopkins, An Intimate History* (1948), p. 710; Edward R. Stettinius, Jr., *Roosevelt and the Russians* (1949), pp. 38, 86, 184, 186, 211; MacAlister Brown, "Expulsion of German Minorities from Eastern Europe: The Decision at Potsdam and its Background" (MS., Harvard University Library, 1953), pp. 218, 223–225, 229, 270, 282.

23. *Parliamentary Debates, Commons,* vol. 406, col. 1484.

24. *Ibid.,* vol. 406, cols. 1574–1575; vol. 408, col. 1617. See also *Parliamentary Debates, Lords,* vol. 130, cols. 1097f., 1107f., 1128.

25. See Harley A. Notter, *Postwar Foreign Policy Preparation, 1939–1945* (1949), Department of State Publication 3580, General Foreign Policy Series 15, pp. 85–86, 564–565, 593–594.

26. "The United States Government should not favor any general transfer of minorities. . . . The objections to a general transfer of minorities do not necessarily apply to transfers of specially selected groups. However, the United States Government should admit such transfers only where it is convinced that they will improve relations between the countries concerned and contribute to greater stability in Europe. To achieve these ends, transfers should be carried out in orderly manner, over a period of time, with provisions for resettlement, and under international auspices." Unpublished research paper of the Post-War Planning Committee, dated 22 Nov. 1944.

27. Osusky, "Liberty or Uniformity in Eastern Europe," *Contemporary Review,* November 1941, p. 280.

28. Maritain, *A Christian Looks at the Jewish Question,* p. 73.

29. Ladas, p. 3.

30. See the Allied Declaration on German War Crimes, 13 January 1942, Holborn, I, 7–8.

31. Randolph S. Churchill, p. 250.

32. Cf. Kulischer, p. 319; Barbara Ward, *The West at Bay* (1948), pp. 240–243.

33. Welles, *Where Are We Heading?* p. 271. This statement can be reconciled with the advocacy of voluntary transfer. However, it seems thoroughly inconsistent with Welles' insistence on the necessity of a surgical operation to remove ethnic foreign bodies from the body politic of states; that thesis implies a compulsive procedure which violates the right of the individual here endorsed by Welles.

34. See the remarks by the Earl of Mansfield, 8 March 1944, *Parliamentary Debates, Lords,* vol. 130, col. 1101. Cf. Benes, "Postwar Czechoslovakia," p. 401.

35. Aurel Kolnai, "Danubia: A Survey of Plans of Solution," *Journal of Central European Affairs*, January 1944, p. 446.
36. Azcárate, *League of Nations and National Minorities*, p. 17.
37. *Ibid.* Cf. Niebuhr, "Jews After the War" (Part II), *The Nation*, 28 Feb. 1942, p. 254.
38. W. Friedmann, "Multi-National States," *Fortnightly*, May 1944, p. 287.
39. Vladimir Jabotinsky, *The War and the Jew* (1942), pp. 129–132.
40. Cf. "Statement by the World Jewish Congress to the Anglo-American Committee of Inquiry," *Congress Weekly*, 15 Feb. 1946, p. 14; Abram L. Sachar, *A History of the Jews* (1948 edition), pp. 426, 429.
41. Tenenbaum, *Peace for the Jews*, p. 11.
42. Cf. Jewish Agency for Palestine, *The Jewish Plan for Palestine . . .* , p. 113; Niebuhr, "Jews After the War" (Part II), p. 254.
43. "Statement by the World Jewish Congress to the Anglo-American Committee of Inquiry," p. 14.
44. Quotation from Rabbi Joseph H. Lookstein, *New York Times*, 5 Oct. 1948.
45. Max Beer, "Jewish Reconstruction," *New Europe*, November 1944, p. 25.
46. See statements by David Ben Gurion, Jewish Agency for Palestine, pp. 298, 323.

CHAPTER 9: THE POSTWAR AGENDA

1. See *Dumbarton Oaks Documents on International Organization* (1944), Department of State Publication 2192, Conf. Series 56.
2. Chap. I, para. 3; chap. IX, sec. A, para. 1.
3. See the preamble and articles 1 (para. 3), 13 (para. 1-b), 55, 62 (para. 2), 68, and 76. *Charter of the United Nations . . .* (1945), Department of State Publication 2353, Conf. Series 74.
4. H. Lauterpacht argues that the Charter does obligate member states to respect human rights. (*International Law and Human Rights* (1950); see esp. chap. ix, pp. 145–165.) For a conflicting interpretation, similar to the one advanced here, see Jacob Robinson, *Human Rights and Fundamental Freedoms in the Charter of the United Nations* (1946).
5. Anna C. Schneidermann, "Dumbarton Oaks Postscripts," *Congress Weekly*, 26 Jan. 1945, pp. 6–8; American Jewish Conference, *The Jewish Position at the United Nations Conference on International Organization* (1945), pp. 16–20, 46.
6. *Documents of the United Nations Conference on International Organization* (1945), VI, 498. (Document 976, I/1/40).
7. *Ibid.*, X, 327. (Document 157, II/3/5).

CHAPTER 10: THE POTSDAM CONFERENCE AND EUROPEAN MINORITY TRANSFERS

1. For decisions of the conference, see the *Protocol of the Proceedings*, dated 1 August 1945 (hereinafter cited as Potsdam Protocol), *A Decade of American Foreign Policy, Basic Documents, 1941–49*, Senate Doc. no. 123, 81st Congress, 1st Session (1950), pp. 34–48.
2. The Crimean (Yalta) Conference, 4–11 Feb. 1945, *Protocol of Proceedings, ibid.*, pp. 27–32. See Section VII, pp. 30–31.
3. Potsdam Protocol, Sections V and VIII.

4. James F. Byrnes, *Speaking Frankly* (1947), p. 30.

5. Ward, *The West at Bay*, p. 12.

6. This acquiescence by the United States and Britain implied acceptance of permanent Polish control over the area, and thus weakened their argument that the new Polish-German boundary should not be regarded as definitive. Cf. Carl J. Friedrich, "The Peace Settlement with Germany — Political and Military," *Annals of the American Academy of Political and Social Science*, vol. 257, May 1948, pp. 121-122.

7. Byrnes, p. 85.

8. Jan Masaryk made this assumption in 1946, when he observed that at Potsdam "the highest authorities accepted the idea of transfer." *The Central European Observer*, 11 Oct. 1946, p. 321.

9. Kulischer, *Europe on the Move*, pp. 282f.

10. See the following protests from victims and their sympathizers: letter from members of the "Parliamentary Delegation of Sudeten Labor," *The New Statesman and Nation*, 9 June 1945, p. 374; "Czechs and Germans," *ibid.*, 11 Aug. 1945, pp. 90-91; letter from H. N. Brailsford, *ibid.*, 20 Oct. 1945, pp. 262-263; article signed "Old Liberal," "The Case of the Sudeten Germans," *Contemporary Review*, August 1945, pp. 79-82.

11. See Czechoslovak Ministry of Information, *Statement of Policy of Mr. Gottwald's Government*, p. 30.

12. Kulischer, p. 289.

13. Quoted in Schechtman, "The Elimination of German Minorities in Southeastern Europe," *Journal of Central European Affairs*, July 1946, p. 164.

14. *Ibid.*, pp. 162-164.

15. Kulischer, p. 285.

16. Schechtman, "The Elimination of German Minorities in Southeastern Europe," pp. 154-162; Kulischer, p. 286, note.

17. Kulischer, p. 306.

18. *Ibid.*, pp. 286, 317.

19. *New York Times*, 10 April 1947.

20. Schechtman, "Resettlement of Transferred Volksdeutsche in Germany," *Journal of Central European Affairs*, October 1947, p. 280; Kulischer, pp. 316-317.

21. Kulischer, pp. 287-288.

22. Czechoslovakia followed the policy of securing Czech and Slovak immigrants in order to offset the labor shortage created by expulsion of Germans. *Ibid.*, p. 288. See Czechoslovak Ministry of Information, p. 27.

23. See statements by Czechoslovak leaders, Holborn, ed., *War and Peace Aims of the United Nations*, II, 1042, 1049; Czechoslovak Ministry of Information, pp. 55, 65.

24. Alfred Meissner, "The Transfer of Germans from Czechoslovakia," *Fortnightly*, April 1946, p. 251; Schechtman, "The Elimination of German Minorities in Southeastern Europe," p. 166; Hungarian Ministry of Foreign Affairs, *Hungary and the Conference of Paris* (1947), vol. II, Annex II, p. 150.

25. Hungarian Ministry of Foreign Affairs, II, 4-5.

26. Department of State *Bulletin*, 9 Dec. 1945, p. 937.

27. Hungarian Ministry of Foreign Affairs, II, 1-3, 10-12, 15-17. The quotation is from p. 16. Annex IV of this volume lists 184 notes from Hun-

gary to the Allied Control Council, relating to the treatment of Hungarians in Czechoslovakia.

28. *Ibid.*, pp. 25–26.

29. *Ibid.*, p. 26.

30. *Ibid.*, I (French edition), 40–50.

31. *Ibid.*, p. 109.

32. *Ibid.*, II, 5–7, 10–12.

33. *Ibid.*, pp. 15–17, 50–53, 131–138.

34. *Ibid.*, pp. 13–17.

35. See the text of a broadcast by Fierlinger, 2 July 1945, Holborn, II, 1046.

36. Hungarian Ministry of Foreign Affairs, II, 53–54.

37. *Ibid.*, pp. 69–74, 76–77. (Texts of the convention and of the appended protocol.) Ratifications were exchanged on 15 May 1946. *Ibid.*, pp. 83–84.

38. The two governments exchanged notes concerning the failure of implementation, 20 May and 4 June 1946. *Ibid.*, pp. 92–130.

39. *Ibid.*, pp. 88–90.

40. *Ibid.*, pp. 39–41, 44–47, 137.

CHAPTER 11: THE PARIS PEACE CONFERENCE AND THE MINORITY PROBLEM

1. See *Making the Peace Treaties, 1941–1947* (1947), Department of State Publication 2774, European Series 24; Philip E. Mosely, "Peace-Making, 1946," *International Organization*, February 1947, pp. 22–32.

2. *United States and Italy, 1936–1946* (1946), Department of State Publication 2669, European Series 17, p. 178.

3. *Making the Peace Treaties*, p. 23. Senator Vandenberg stated, on 16 July 1946, that the frontier proposed by the Soviet Union would put 500,000 Italians in Yugoslavia and no Slavs in Italy, whereas the line advocated by the three other powers would leave 118,000 Italians in Yugoslavia and 115,000 Slavs in Italy. *Congressional Record*, 79th Congress, 2nd Session, vol. 92, part 7, p. 9062.

4. *Making the Peace Treaties*, p. 27.

5. Observations on the Draft Peace Treaty, *Paris Peace Conference, 1946, Selected Documents* (1946) (hereinafter cited as PPC), Department of State Publication 2868, Conf. Series 103, pp. 177–178.

6. PPC, p. 602; *Making the Peace Treaties*, pp. 39, 48–49.

7. See the list of signatories to the Italian Peace Treaty, *Treaties of Peace with Italy, Bulgaria, Hungary, Roumania and Finland* (1947) (English versions), Department of State Publication 2743, European Series 21.

8. *New York Times*, 1 May 1946.

9. *Parliamentary Debates, Commons*, vol. 423, cols. 2018–2019.

10. PPC, p. 401.

11. *Ibid.*, pp. 367, 373–378.

12. *Ibid.*, pp. 1064, 1105; Hungarian Ministry of Foreign Affairs, *Hungary and the Conference of Paris*, IV, 95–100, 128–175.

13. Hungarian Ministry of Foreign Affairs, IV, 29, 113.

14. PPC, p. 606.

15. This Yugoslav amendment was adopted by the Political and Territorial Commission for Italy. PPC, p. 421. It was subsequently approved by the conference, and became art. 20 of the definitive Italian Treaty.

16. PPC, p. 1195. See the Hungarian Treaty, art. 1, para. 4 (e).

17. Hungarian Ministry of Foreign Affairs, IV, 15–16.

18. *Ibid.*, pp. 5, 25–34, 60–71, 113.

19. PPC, p. 1106.

20. *New York Times*, 21 Sept. 1946. Cf. Hungarian Ministry of Foreign Affairs, IV, 72–78, 117.

21. Hungarian Ministry of Foreign Affairs, IV, 3, 17–20, 35–47, 49–59.

22. *Ibid.*, pp. 23, 85, 101.

23. *Ibid.*, pp. 102–104; PPC, pp. 1114, 1195.

24. Hungarian Ministry of Foreign Affairs, IV, 105–110; PPC, pp. 1191–1195.

25. Hungarian Ministry of Foreign Affairs, IV, 101. Italics mine.

26. See art. 14 of the draft treaty for Italy, art. 3 of the draft for Rumania, art. 2 of the drafts for Bulgaria and Hungary, and art. 6 of the draft for Finland. PPC, pp. 86, 655, 840, 1017, 1222. The human rights provisions in the definitive treaties appear in the articles listed above, except in the case of the Italian Treaty, where they are incorporated in art. 15.

27. PPC, pp. 200–201, 706.

28. See the identical provisions on human rights in the four great power drafts of a permanent Statute for Trieste. *Ibid.*, pp. 1355, 1360, 1373, 1387.

29. *Ibid.*, pp. 734–735, 905–907, 1113–1114. For the proposals of Jewish organizations, see *New York Times*, 24 Feb. 1946 and 20 Aug. 1946; World Jewish Congress, *Statements Submitted to the Conference of Foreign Ministers of France, Union of Soviet Socialist Republics, United Kingdom and the United States of America by the World Jewish Congress, Board of Deputies of British Jews, American Jewish Conference*, Paris, 28 June 1946.

30. Treaty of Peace with Rumania, art. 3, para. 2; Treaty of Peace with Hungary, art. 2, para. 2.

31. The conference supported the application of the provision to Rumania and Hungary by a two-thirds majority, and to Bulgaria by merely a simple majority. See PPC, pp. 819, 1195.

32. *Ibid.*, p. 85; *Making the Peace Treaties*, p. 39.

33. See the Address by Senator Vandenberg on 16 July 1946, *Congressional Record*, 79th Congress, 2nd Session (Senate), vol. 92, part 7, p. 9065; PPC, p. 420.

34. PPC, pp. 420–421.

35. *Ibid.*, pp. 1113, 1195.

36. Statement to the Senate Foreign Relations Committee, 4 March 1947. Department of State *Bulletin*, 16 March 1947, p. 488.

37. See American Jewish Committee, *Toward Peace and Equity*, pp. 9, 148–149; World Jewish Congress, p. 2.

38. PPC, pp. 445, 598, 1280–1281.

39. *Ibid.*, pp. 430–431, 607. See the Treaty of Peace with Italy, art. 21, and Annex VI.

40. See, for instance, arts. 39 and 40 of the Treaty of Peace with Hungary.

41. See the testimony by Byrnes before the Senate Committee on Foreign Relations, 4 March 1947, *Hearings . . . on Peace Treaties with Italy, Rumania, Bulgaria, and Hungary*, 80th Congress, 1st Session, pp. 3–29.

42. World Jewish Congress, p. 2; *New York Times*, 3 Aug. 1946.

43. PPC, pp. 747–748, 831, 1130–1132, 1206–1207. See art. 25 of the Rumanian Treaty and art. 27 of the Hungarian Treaty.

44. World Jewish Congress, *op. cit.*; American Jewish Committee, *op. cit.*
45. Hungarian Ministry of Foreign Affairs, I, 56–62, 136–137.
46. PPC, pp. 1065–1066.
47. For the text of this draft, see Hungarian Ministry of Foreign Affairs, I, 143–171.
48. PPC, pp. 438, 603, 1110; *New York Times*, 31 Aug. 1946.
49. PPC, pp. 193–199.
50. Department of State *Bulletin*, 11 Nov. 1945, p. 763.
51. PPC, pp. 186–187, 200–201.
52. *Ibid.*, pp. 435–437.
53. See the Treaty of Peace with Italy, art. 10, para. 2, and Annex IV.
54. PPC, pp. 416–417.
55. Both quotations are from *New York Times*, 5 Sept. 1946.

CHAPTER 12: THE UNITED NATIONS AND THE GENERAL PROBLEM OF MINORITIES

1. See F. P. Walters, *A History of the League of Nations* (1952), I, 175, II, 813.
2. Report of the Preparatory Commission of the UN (1946), p. 36.
3. Report of the (Nuclear) CHR, 29 Apr.–20 May 1946, Doc. E/38, p. 228.
4. The origins of the Sub-Commission, beginning with a Soviet proposal for the establishment of separate bodies to deal with the prevention of discrimination and the protection of minorities, and culminating in the adoption of an American plan to combine the two agencies, may be traced through the following documents: E/SOC/DC/5; E/56/Rev.1; Ecosoc Res. 2/9, 21 June 1946; E/CN.4/6; E/259, chap. iv; Ecosoc Res. 46 (IV), 28 March 1947.
5. For a critical discussion of the extent to which members of the Sub-Commission are genuinely "independent experts," see Inis L. Claude, Jr., "The Nature and Status of the Sub-Commission on Prevention of Discrimination and Protection of Minorities," *International Organization*, May 1951, pp. 300–312.
6. Doc. E/259, p. 5.
7. Report of the Fifth Session of the CHR, 9 May–20 June 1949, Doc. E/1371, p. 9.
8. See Report of the Fifth Session of the Sub-Commission, 22 Sept.–10 Oct. 1952, Doc. E/CN.4/670; Ecosoc Res. 443 (XIV), 23 June 1952.
9. Doc. E/CN.4/Sub.2/SR.85.
10. Doc. E/CN.4/Sub.2/SR.66.
11. Doc. E/CN.4/Sub.2/SR.19.
12. Ecosoc Res. 336 (XI), 16 Aug. 1950; GA Res. 419 (V), 1 Dec. 1950; Report of Ecosoc, 16 Aug. 1950–21 Sept. 1951, OR–GA, Sixth Session, Supplement no. 3 (Doc. A/1884), p. 106.
13. See Doc. E/SR.557, and Ecosoc Res. 414-B-I (XIII), 18 Sept. 1951.
14. Doc. E/CN.4/641, pp. 48–51.
15. GA Res. 532-B (VI), 4 Feb. 1952.
16. Ecosoc Res. 443-B (XIV), 26 June 1952.
17. Report of the Ninth Session of the CHR, 7 April–30 May 1953, Doc. E/2447, pp. 78–79.

18. See the records of the debate in the Third Cttee., 278th Meeting, 6 Oct. 1950, OR–GA, Fifth Session.

19. Docs. E/AC.34/2; E/AC.24/L.36 and Corr. 1; E/AC.24/92 and 93; E/SR.555 and 557.

20. OR–Ecosoc, Thirteenth Session, 555th Meeting, 17 Sept. 1951, p. 708.

21. Ecosoc Res. 414–B (XIII), 18 Sept. 1951.

22. Doc. E/AC.24/SR.92.

23. OR–GA, Sixth Session, 373rd Plenary Meeting, 4 Feb. 1952.

24. Doc. E/2447, pp. 76–94.

25. Note the success of the anticolonial bloc with respect to the issue of implementing the right of national self-determination. *Ibid.*, pp. 53–55, 71–75.

26. OR–Ecosoc, Thirteenth Session, 555th Meeting, 17 Sept. 1951, p. 708.

27. See pp. 59–60, above.

28. Doc. E/CN.4/367. See also Add. 1 of this document, dated 27 March 1951.

29. In a *Memorandum Concerning the Validity of the Post-Versailles Treaties and Other Instruments of International Protection of Minorities*, submitted to the Secretary-General on 1 Dec. 1948, the World Jewish Congress upheld the thesis that the League minority system remained legally intact.

30. Doc. E/CN.4/367, p. 70.

31. *Ibid.*, p. 41.

32. GA Res. 103 (I), 19 Nov. 1946. For reference to Egypt's allegations of minority persecution and the ultimate deletion of these claims from the text of the resolution, see *New York Times*, 10 Nov. 1946 and 20 Nov. 1946.

33. UN, Department of Public Information, *For Fundamental Human Rights* (1948), p. 44.

34. GA Res. 217 (III), 10 Dec. 1948.

35. OR–GA, Seventh Session, Supplement no. 1, p. 87.

36. *Definition and Classification of Minorities* (Memorandum submitted by the Secretary-General), Doc. E/CN.4/Sub.2/85 (printed version, 1950), p. 2.

37. See GA Res. 96 (I), 11 Dec. 1946.

38. Doc. E/447.

39. Doc. E/AC.25/3, p. 6. In Rev. 1 of this document, the word "restrictions" was changed to "vexations."

40. See Docs. E/623; E/AC.25/SR.5, 10, and 14; E/794.

41. For Pakistan's assertions, see OR–GA, Third Session, Part I, Summary Records of the 63rd and 83rd Meetings of the Sixth Cttee., 30 Sept. and 25 Oct. 1948.

42. *Ibid.*, 83rd Meeting of the Sixth Cttee.

43. *Ibid.*, Verbatim Records of the 178th and 179th Plenary Meetings, 9 Dec. 1948.

44. GA Res. 96 (I).

45. GA Res. 260 (III), 9 Dec. 1948.

46. Cited in Doc. E/794, p. 7, note 9. Expressions of the American view are also found in Doc. E/623.

47. Doc. E/447, pp. 16–17.

48. Doc. E/CN.4/AC.1/3.

49. See Docs. E/CN.4/SC.1/3/Add.1, pp. 380–381; E/CN.4/AC.1/11, p. 51.

50. Doc. E/CN.4/21.

51. Docs. E/CN.4/Sub.2/7 and 16.

52. Report of the First Session of the Sub-Commission, 24 Nov.–6 Dec. 1947, Doc. E/CN.4/52, Draft Article 36, p. 9.

53. Doc. E/CN.4/Sub.2/SR.11.

54. Doc. E/CN.4/AC.2/SR.9.

55. Report of the Second Session of the CHR, 2–17 Dec. 1947, Doc. E/600.

56. Doc. E/CN.4/95.

57. Docs. E/CN.4/99 and 102.

58. Docs. E/CN.4/SR.73 and 74.

59. Doc. E/800.

60. Doc. E/CN.4/307/Rev.2.

61. Docs. A/C.3/SR.161, 162, and 163.

62. OR–GA, Third Session, 183rd Plenary Meeting, 10 Dec. 1948. See GA Res. 217 (III).

63. GA Res. 543 (VI), 5 Feb. 1952.

64. For Soviet drafts, see Docs. E/CN.4/273 and L.222, and A/1576. For Yugoslav drafts, see Docs. E/CN.4/435 and 573.

65. The Sub-Commission's article was based on a Drafting Committee proposal, contained in Doc. E/CN.4/Sub.2/112. It was adopted by the Sub-Commission on 23 Jan. 1950 (see Doc. E/CN.4/Sub.2/SR.57), and reiterated in the reports of its Fourth and Fifth Sessions, Docs. E/CN.4/641 and 670.

66. Docs. E/1681, 1992, and 2256.

67. Report of the Ninth Session of the CHR, 7 April–30 May 1953, Doc. E/2447, pp. 25–26, 135, 162–163.

68. Doc. E/CN.4/L.261.

69. Doc. E/2447, p. 26.

70. Report of the Second Session of the Sub-Commission, 13–27 June 1949, Doc. E/CN.4/351, pp. 13–14.

71. Doc. E/2447, pp. 207–213, 226–227, 229.

72. OR–GA, Third Session, Part I, Summary Record of the 83rd Meeting of the Sixth Cttee., 25 Oct. 1948.

73. Doc. E/CN.4/Sub.2/108.

74. Docs. E/CN.4/Sub.2/127; E/CN.4/Sub.2/SR.69 and 70.

75. Doc. E/CN.4/Sub.2/SR.87.

76. Doc. A/C.3/SR.161, p. 5.

77. Doc. A/C.3/SR.163, p. 5.

78. See, for instance, Doc. E/CN.4/AC.1/29.

79. See the speech by the representative of Egypt, OR–GA, Third Session, Part I, Summary Record of the 63rd Meeting of the Sixth Cttee., 30 Sept. 1948, p. 7.

80. Doc. E/CN.4/SR.73, p. 7.

81. Doc. E/CN.4/Sub.2/SR.96, p. 8. For an example of Daniels' earlier pro-assimilation position, see his remarks in Doc. E/CN.4/Sub.2/SR.15.

82. Doc. E/CN.4/Sub.2/SR.24, p. 6. See also the comments included in the Sub-Commission's First Report, Doc. E/CN.4/52, p. 14.

83. Doc. E/CN.4/Sub.2/SR.69, p. 6.

84. Doc. A/C.3/SR.161.

85. Doc. E/CN.4/SR.73.

86. Doc. E/CN.4/Sub.2/SR.70.

87. Doc. E/CN.4/Sub.2/137, p. 2.

88. OR–Ecosoc, Fourteenth Session, 621st Meeting, 26 June 1952.

89. Docs. E/CN.4/Sub.2/SR.104 and 106.

90. See *New York Times*, 26 Feb. 1953.

91. *Ibid.*, 28 Feb. 1953.

92. Doc. E/CN.4/SR.340.

93. Cf. Solomon M. Schwarz, *The Jews in the Soviet Union* (1951); Morris Fine, ed., *American Jewish Yearbook* (1953), pp. 331–336; and the editorial, "The Soviet's Minorities," *New York Times*, 30 June 1953.

94. Fernand Van Langenhove, "The Idea of the Sacred Trust of Civilization with Regard to the Less Developed Peoples" (June 1951), a pamphlet released by the Belgian Government Information Center, New York.

95. Doc. A/AC.58/1.

96. GA Res. 421–D (V), 4 Dec. 1950. For a summary history of the progress of the national self-determination movement in the United Nations, see Docs. E/CN.4/516, 649, and 676.

97. Doc. E/CN.4/AC.1/29.

98. See Docs. E/CN.4/185; E/CN.4/Sub.2/104; E/CN.4/L.21.

99. For the Soviet proposal, see Doc. A/1576; for the debate, see OR–GA, Fifth Session, 317th Plenary Meeting, 4 Dec. 1950.

100. Cf. Joseph Stalin, *Marxism and the National Question* (1942).

101. Doc. E/CN.4/SR.257, p. 5.

102. Doc. E/CN.4/SR.253, p. 9. For further evidence of the intention of the anticolonial bloc to avoid bringing minority rights into the picture, see OR–GA, Fifth Session, Summary Record of the 310th Meeting of the Third Cttee., 10 Nov. 1950.

103. Docs. E/CN.4/SR.253, 262–265.

104. See text of speech by Van Langenhove, UN Department of Public Information, Press Release PM/2434, 17 Nov. 1952.

105. Note the change in the British position, in Docs. E/CN.4/SR.257 and 264.

106. Doc. E/CN.4/SR.256.

CHAPTER 13: THE UNITED NATIONS AND SPECIFIC MINORITY PROBLEMS

1. See UNSCOP Report to the GA, 3 Sept. 1947, OR–GA, Second Session, Supplement no. 11, I, 45.

2. For a careful survey of the course of the Palestine case to mid-1949, see L. Larry Leonard, "The United Nations and Palestine," *International Conciliation*, October 1949, no. 545.

3. Doc. S/747.

4. Progress Report of the UN Mediator on Palestine (Doc. A/648), Part I, pp. 11, 33.

5. *Ibid.*, pp. 38, 45.

6. *Ibid.*, p. 33.

7. GA Resolutions 194 (III), 11 Dec. 1948 and 303 (IV), 9 Dec. 1949. See also the Statute for the City of Jerusalem, adopted by the Trusteeship Council, Doc. T/592.

8. Estimates of the number of Arab refugees have varied widely. In May 1949, an Israeli spokesman opposed an estimate of approximately 500,000 to

Arab claims of 1,000,000. (Doc. A/AC.24/SR.46.) Joseph B. Schechtman has cited estimates ranging from 600,000 to 750,000. (*Population Transfers in Asia* [1949], p. 123.) In his Annual Report to the Fourth GA, Secretary-General Lie used the figure of 940,000. (OR–GA, Fourth Session, Supplement no. 1, p. 102.) The population of Israel at the end of June 1952, included 175,000 non-Jews, most of them Moslem or Christian Arabs. (Morris Fine, ed., *American Jewish Yearbook* [1953], p. 424.)

9. GA Res. 194 (III).

10. Doc. A/AC.24/SR.45, p. 5.

11. Doc. A/AC.24/SR.48.

12. Doc. A/AC.24/SR.51.

13. Docs. A/AC.24/SR.45–51.

14. GA Res. 273 (III).

15. OR–GA, Third Session, Part II, 207th Plenary Meeting, 11 May 1949. The quotation is from the remarks of the delegate from Yemen, p. 320.

16. GA Resolutions 302 (IV), 8 Dec. 1949; 393 (V), 2 Dec. 1950; 394 (V), 14 Dec. 1950; 513 (VI), 26 Jan. 1952; 614 (VII), 6 Nov. 1952.

17. For a survey of past and present support of "The Case for Arab-Jewish Exchange of Population" by a sympathetic scholar, see Schechtman, *Population Transfers in Asia*, chap. iii, pp. 84–136.

18. *New York Times*, 23 July 1948.

19. For data concerning the movement of Jews from Arab countries to Israel, see Morris Fine, ed., *American Jewish Yearbook* (1952 and 1953). See also Abba Eban, "Israel: The Emergence of a Democracy," *Foreign Affairs*, April 1951, pp. 424–435.

20. See Report of the UN Commission for Eritrea, OR–GA, Fifth Session, Supplement no. 8 (Doc. A/1285), and Report of the UN Commissioner in Libya, *ibid.*, Supplement no. 15 (Doc. A/1340).

21. OR–GA, Fourth Session, 279th Meeting of the First Cttee., 1 Oct. 1949. For the text of Count Sforza's speech, see *New York Times*, 2 Oct. 1949.

22. *New York Times*, 12 March 1951.

23. Note, for instance, the statements by French and South African representatives in the First Committee at the Fourth Session of the General Assembly. Docs. A/C.1/SR.279 and 282.

24. Doc. A/1089, p. 10.

25. Docs. A/C.1/497; A/C.1/SC.17/L.19 and L.22.

26. Docs. A/C.1/SC.17/L.18, L.21, L.22, L.25.

27. David W. Wainhouse and Philip A. Mangano, "The Problem of the Former Italian Colonies at the Fourth Session of the General Assembly," Part I, Department of State *Bulletin*, 29 May 1950, p. 844, and Part II, *ibid.*, 5 June 1950, p. 889. See OR–GA, Fourth Session, 316th Meeting of the First Cttee., 8 Nov. 1949, p. 210.

28. Wainhouse and Mangano, Part II, Department of State *Bulletin*, 5 June 1950, p. 890 and note 45, p. 915.

29. Doc. A/C.1/SC.17/L.22.

30. GA Res. 289 (IV), 21 Nov. 1949.

31. See OR–GA, Fifth Session, 7th and 16th Meetings of the *Ad Hoc* Political Cttee., 9 and 18 Oct. 1950.

32. GA Res. 387 (V), 17 Nov. 1950.

33. GA Res. 388 (V), 15 Dec. 1950.

34. OR–GA, Sixth Session, Supplements no. 17 and 17A (Docs. A/1949 and A/1949/Add.1).

35. GA Res. 515 (VI), 1 Feb. 1952.

36. *New York Times*, 11 March 1951.

37. Adrian Pelt, "The United Kingdom of Libya – From Colony to Independent State," *United Nations Bulletin*, 15 Feb. 1952, p. 176.

38. Zechariah Shuster, "Survey of the European Scene," *Report of the 46th Annual Meeting of the American Jewish Committee* (1953), pp. 122–123.

39. GA Res. 289 (IV), 21 Nov. 1949.

40. See GA Res. 442 (V), 2 Dec. 1950, and the text of the Trusteeship Agreement, Doc. A/1294.

41. Doc. A/C.1/476.

42. GA Res. 289 (IV).

43. OR–GA, Fifth Session, Supplement no. 8.

44. Letter from Count Sforza to the Commission, 17 Apr. 1950, *ibid.*, p. 66.

45. Letter from Robert Schuman to the Commission, 15 Apr. 1950, *ibid.*, p. 70.

46. GA Res. 390–A (V).

47. OR–GA, Fifth Session, 315th Plenary Meeting, 2 Dec. 1950, pp. 534–535.

48. Final Report of the UN Commissioner in Eritrea, OR–GA, Seventh Session, Supplement no. 15.

49. GA Res. 617 (VII), 17 Dec. 1952.

50. See pp. 127, 134, 135–136, above.

51. OR–SC, 2nd Year, no. 3, 91st Meeting, 10 Jan. 1947.

52. Communiqué of the Sixth Session of the Council of Foreign Ministers (Paris, 23 May–20 June 1949), Department of State *Bulletin*, 4 July 1949, pp. 857–859. For a summary account of the article agreed upon, see *New York Times*, 25 Aug. 1949.

53. *New York Times*, 25 June 1952.

54. "The Austrian Treaty: A Case Study of Soviet Tactics," *Background*, Off. of Public Affairs, Department of State, May 1953, p. 7.

55. Data from Morris Fine, ed., *American Jewish Yearbook* (1952), p. 421, and (1953), p. 195.

56. This estimate is from Andrew Mellor, *India Since Partition* (1951), p. 45.

57. "Turkey: Frontier of Freedom," *Background*, Off. of Public Affairs, Department of State, June 1952.

58. Edwin O. Reischauer, *The United States and Japan* (1950), p. 241.

59. *New York Times*, 12 Sept. 1949; 15 Dec. 1949; 4 Aug. 1951; 13 Aug. 1951; 20 April 1952.

60. See *New York Times*, 15 April 1951, and *United Nations Bulletin*, 1 Sept. 1952, p. 242.

61. For a general analysis of this case, see Harry N. Howard, "Greece and the United Nations, 1946–49," Department of State *Bulletin*, 19 Sept. 1949, pp. 407–431, and "Greek Question in the Fourth General Assembly of the United Nations," *ibid.*, 27 Feb. 1950, pp. 307–322.

62. OR–SC, 1st Year, 2nd Series, 87th Meeting, 19 Dec. 1946.

63. Report by the Commission of Investigation Concerning Greek Frontier Incidents to the Security Council, Doc. S/360, I, 251.

64. Docs. A/C.1/191, 199, and 205.

65. See OR–GA, Second Session, Summary Records of the 60th–73rd Meetings of the First Cttee., 25 Sept.–13 Oct. 1947.

66. GA Res. 109 (II), 21 Oct. 1947.

67. OR–GA, Third Session, Supplement no. 8.

68. See the Supplementary Report of the UNSCOB for the period 17 June–10 Sept. 1948, Doc. A/644, para. 25.

69. This figure is taken from the official census of 7 May 1946. Union of South Africa, Union Office of Census and Statistics, *Official Yearbook of the Union. . .*, no. 24 (1948), p. 1078.

70. GA Resolutions 44 (I), 8 Dec. 1946; 265 (III), 14 May 1949; 395 (V), 2 Dec. 1950; 511 (VI), 12 Jan. 1952; 615 (VII), 5 Dec. 1952. The *Apartheid* Resolution is 616 (VII), 5 Dec. 1952.

71. See GA Resolutions 395 (V), 511 (VI), and 615 (VII).

72. See Docs. A/68, with Add.1 and Add.2; A/149.

73. OR–GA, First Session, Part II, Summary Record of the 1st Meeting of the Joint First and Sixth Cttees., 21 Nov. 1946.

74. *Ibid.*, p. 3.

75. See Docs. A/577 and 1289.

76. OR–GA, First Session, Part II, Summary Record of the 2nd Meeting of the Joint First and Sixth Cttees., 25 Nov. 1946, p. 9.

77. OR–GA, Third Session, Part II, Summary Record of the 263rd Meeting of the First Cttee., 9 May 1949.

78. See Doc. A/577, and the reactions of the South African delegate, OR–GA, Third Session, Part II, Summary Record of the 268th Meeting of the First Cttee., 11 May 1949.

79. Note India's position, OR–GA, Third Session, Part II, 212th Plenary Meeting, 14 May 1949.

80. Cf. the following draft resolutions, in the formulation of which India participated: Docs. A/C.1/244, Rev.1; A/C.1/461, Rev.1; A/AC.38/L.33; A/AC.53/L.20/Rev.1; A/AC.61/L.5/Rev. 1.

81. For information concerning the transfer provisions of the Capetown Agreements, see Doc. A/68, Add.1. At a preliminary meeting in Capetown in February 1950, called to draw up an agenda for the roundtable conference recommended by the Assembly in Res. 265 (III), India, Pakistan, and South Africa agreed to include the item, "reduction of the Indian Population in South Africa." See Doc. A/1289. Thereafter, India took great pains to avoid the risk of having to discuss this possible solution of the problem, instead of its preferred solution of utilizing United Nations pressure upon South Africa to induce modification of its racial policies.

82. See Doc. A/167; OR–GA, First Session, Part II, Summary Record of the 1st Meeting of the Joint First and Sixth Cttees., 21 Nov. 1946; Doc. A/205/Add.1.

83. OR–GA, Fifth Session, 45th Meeting of the *Ad Hoc* Political Cttee., 17 Nov. 1950, and 315th Plenary Meeting, 2 Dec. 1950.

84. OR–GA, Second Session, 119th Plenary Meeting, 20 Nov. 1947; Third Session, Part II, 212th Plenary Meeting, 14 May 1949.

85. Doc. A/167.

86. OR–GA, Fifth Session, 45th Meeting of the *Ad Hoc* Political Cttee., 17 Nov. 1950.

87. OR–GA, Third Session, Part II, 268th Meeting of the First Cttee., 11 May 1949.

88. See Docs. A/387 and 1787; OR–GA, Fifth Session, 315th Plenary Meeting, 2 Dec. 1950, and Seventh Session, 401st Plenary Meeting, 5 Dec. 1952.

89. Doc. A/167. It is India's contention that the Indians acquired South African citizenship in 1913. See OR–GA, First Session, Part II, 2nd Meeting of the Joint First and Sixth Cttees., 25 Nov. 1946.

90. For references to the possibility of transfer as a solution of the Indian minority problem in South Africa, see OR–GA, Second Session, 110th Meeting of the First Cttee., 15 Nov. 1947; Third Session, Part II, 263rd and 268th Meetings of the First Cttee., 9 and 11 May 1949; Seventh Session, 8th and 10th Meetings of the Ad Hoc Political Cttee., 3 and 5 Nov. 1952. See also Doc. A/1289.

91. GA Res. 395 (V) was strongly influenced by the provisions of a draft proposal submitted by Burma, India, Indonesia, and Iraq, Doc.A/AC.38/L.33. Res. 511 (VI) derived strictly from a draft prepared by the same group, with the addition of Iran, Doc. A/AC.53/L.20/Rev.1. Res. 615 (VII) constituted acceptance by the Assembly of a joint resolution sponsored by India and Pakistan along with thirteen other governments, all of them members of the Asian–Middle-Eastern–African group, Doc. A/AC.61/L.5/Rev.1.

92. OR–GA, First Session, Part II, 4th Meeting of the Joint First and Sixth Cttees., 27 Nov. 1946, p. 35.

93. OR–GA, Seventh Session, 10th Meeting of the Ad Hoc Political Cttee., 5 Nov. 1952, p. 48.

94. See OR–GA, Third Session, Part II, 266th Meeting of the First Cttee., 10 May 1949; Fifth Session, 42nd and 43rd Meetings of the Ad Hoc Political Cttee., 14 and 15 Nov. 1950.

95. GA Res. 395 (V), para. 3.

96. Minority agreements between India and Pakistan were signed on 19 April 1948 and 8 April 1950. See New York Times, 20 April 1948 and 9 April 1950. Texts of the latter treaty and the supplementary protocol of 16 August 1950 are published in UN, Yearbook on Human Rights for 1950, pp. 435–442.

Poland and Czechoslovakia exchanged guarantees of positive minority rights in a protocol to the Treaty of Friendship and Mutual Aid, signed 10 March 1947. See UN Treaty Series, vol. 25 (1949), no. 365.

Provisions relevant to the minority problem were included in the Convention on Cultural Cooperation, signed on 15 October 1947 by Hungary and Yugoslavia. Ibid., vol. 33 (1949), no. 515.

The Czechoslovakian-Hungarian dispute concerning the future of the Magyar minority in Czechoslovakia was resolved by the parties soon after they became fellow-members of the Soviet bloc. See New York Times, 29 July 1948; 26 Oct. 1948; 5 Dec. 1948; 16 Dec. 1948.

97. OR–GA, Fifth Session, 43rd Meeting of the Ad Hoc Political Cttee., 15 Nov. 1950, p. 263.

INDEX

Aaland Islands, 16
Acton, Lord, 86
Adatci, Baron, 23
Albania, 16, 192, 194
Al-Jamali, Fadil, 185
Allied Control Council for Germany, 115, 117
American Council for Judaism, 82
American Jewish Committee, 65, 84
American Jewish Conference, 63, 65
Anticolonialism, 150–151, 165–166, 171–175, 197, 200
Anti-Semitism, 84, 108–109, 134
Apartheid, policy of, 195, 199
Arab refugees in Palestine area, problem of, 179–183, 192
Asian-Arab bloc in United Nations, 150, 155, 171, 173–174
Assimilation, 92, 99, 155; advocacy of, 66, 78–86, 97, 112, 130, 141–142; American "melting-pot" idea, 58, 81–83, 209; conflict concerning, in League system, 31–36; conflict concerning, in United Nations, 165–171, 175–176, 209, 211–212; forcible promotion of, 9–10, 40, 47, 207; rejection of, 63, 73, 107–109
Atlantic Charter, 74
Attlee, Clement, 62, 115
Australia, 130–132, 135, 201
Austria, 7, 16, 25, 44, 117, 127–129, 140–143, 190–191
Axis Powers (World War II), 53, 58, 63, 95, 133–135, 208
Azkoul, Karim, 174

Balfour, Lord Arthur J., 48
Balogh, Arthur von, 29
Baron, Salo W., 62
Bauer, Otto, 89
Beck, Colonel Josef, 30
Belgium, 35, 89, 172, 174–175
Benes, Eduard, 56, 74, 80–81, 84, 96–97
Bernadotte, Count Folke, 179

Bilateralism: in minority issues, 3, 54, 138, 204–207, 213; bilateral minority treaties, 16, 30, 140, 190; bilateral transfer arrangements, 100, 120, 132; in League minority procedure, 22–23, 25–26, 38–39, 45; promotion by great powers, 122, 124, 142–144; promotion by United Nations, 194–203. See also Internationalization of minority problem
Borisov, A. P., 158
Bratianu, Ionel, 15
Brazil, 185
British Labour Party, 62
Bulgaria: exchange of populations, 12, 94, 101, 192, 194; in League system, 16, 25, 44, 47; post-World War II peace treaty, 125, 134, 136
Bülow, Prince Bernhard von, 9
Burma, 188
Byelorussia, 130, 158, 165
Byrnes, James F., 116, 135, 137

Canada, 89
Capetown Agreements, 196, 198
Cecil, Lord Robert (Viscount of Chelwood), 28, 62
Chamberlain, Sir Austen, 36
Chile, 158, 161
China, 76, 159
Churchill, Winston, 73, 77, 97–98, 102, 114, 127
Citizenship, relevance to minority problem, 17
"Clean hands" doctrine, 33. See also Loyalty of minorities to the state
Clemenceau, Georges, 14
Collective rights of minorities, 54, 113, 212; advocacy of, 25, 34, 63, 65, 68, 84; ambiguity of League system on, 19–20, 37
Collective security, 50
Commission to Study the Organization of Peace, 61
Concert of Europe, 8